The Wood Sanding Book

The Wood Sanding Book

SANDOR NAGYSZALANCZY

A Guide to Abrasives, Machines, and Methods

The Taunton Press

Cover photo: SANDOR NAGYSZALANCZY

© 1997 by Sandor Nagyszalanczy
Printed in the United States of America
10 9 8 7 6 5 4 3 2 1

A FINE WOODWORKING Book

FINE WOODWORKING® is a trademark of The Taunton Press, Inc.,
registered in the U.S. Patent and Trademark Office.

The Taunton Press, Inc., 63 South Main Street, Box 5506,
Newtown, CT 06470-5506
e-mail: tp@taunton.com

Library of Congress Cataloging-in-Publication Data

Nagyszalanczy, Sandor.
    The wood sanding book : a guide to abrasives, machines and
methods / Sandor Nagyszalanczy.
    p.   cm.
    Includes index.
    ISBN 1-56158-175-5
    1. Sanding machines.   I. Title
TT186.N337 1997   97-12591
684'.08 — dc21   CIP

About Your Safety

Working wood is inherently dangerous. Using hand or power tools improperly or
ignoring standard safety practices can lead to permanent injury or even death. Don't try
to perform operations you learn about here (or elsewhere) unless you're certain they are
safe for you. If something about an operation doesn't feel right, don't do it. Look for
another way. We want you to enjoy the craft, so please keep safety foremost in your mind
whenever you're in the shop.

To my good friend and colleague Chris Minick,
whose technical assistance has so enriched my knowledge of woodworking.
His tireless explorations of wood sanding and finishing products and techniques
have bestowed a cornucopia of gifts on woodworkers around the world.

Acknowledgments

I'd like to thank the following individuals for their technical support concerning abrasives and tools:

  Jon Behrle at Woodcraft
  Michael Bless at Products 2000 Inc.
  Katy Campbell and Tammy Nystuen, at 3M public relations
  Chris Carlson at S-B Powertools
  Mark Coblentz at Hartville True Value Hardware
  Phyllis Crystal at Uneeda Enterprises, Inc.
  Robert Davis at Blue Ridge Products
  Michael Frazier and Carter Williams at DeWalt
  Donna Green, Warren Weber, and Wayne Wenzlaff at Performax
  Todd Langston at Porter-Cable
  Jean Miskimon at Eisner & Associates
  Mike McQuinn at Ryobi
  Mike Nelson at Airware America
  Lyle Rawlins, marketing manager at Pacific Abrasive Supply Co.
  Mark Sheifer and Renata Mastrofrancesco at Delta
  Peter Spuller at Klingspor
  Chen Sun, president of Sunhill Machinery

These people deserve loads of credit for their assistance concerning methods for using abrasives:

  Steven Blenk, for help with power sanding turnings
  Larry Cavalier, R. W. Hansen, and Dub Parker (and of course, Chris Minick) at 3M

For general assistance and friendly support:

  David Enis, Jim Casebolt, and Roger Heitzman

For assistance with drum-sander testing:

  Gerald Bowden

Finally, I'd like to thank Ann Gibb and BouDou (the gritty kitty) for their tireless support and assistance with photography.

Contents

Introduction   1

1   The Anatomy of Coated Abrasives   4
Grits   5
Sizes and Grades   16
Backing Materials   22
Bonds and Coatings   26
Products Made from Coated Abrasives   32
Other Abrasive Products   35

2   Shaping, Leveling, and Smoothing Bare Wood   40
Abrasive Shaping   40
Leveling a Surface   44
Sanding Wood Smooth   50

3   Sanding to a Great Finish   62
Surface Evaluation and Repair   62
Dewhiskering   65
Cleaning the Surface   69
Scuff Sanding between Coats   70
Rubbing Out a Finish   74
Removing an Old Finish   87

4   Tips for Handling Sandpaper   88
Preparing Abrasive Paper for Use   88
Prolonging Paper Life   96
Curing Sanding Problems   103

5 Hand Sanding — 113

Sanding Flat Surfaces — 114
Cleaning Up Curves — 117
Sanding Moldings — 123
Sanding Details and Small Parts — 126
Sanding Round Parts and Turnings — 130

6 Power Sanding — 136

Steps to Efficient Power Sanding — 137
Working Safely — 146
Personal Protection against Dust — 148
Power-Tool Dust Collection — 151

7 Portable Power Sanders — 156

Portable Belt Sanders — 157
Orbital Sanders — 162
Random-Orbit Sanders — 166
Straight-Line Sanders — 168
Rotary Sanding Tools — 170
Discs, Wheels, Drums, Spindles, and Rolls — 173

8 Stationary Sanding Machines 184

Edge Sanders 185
Benchtop Narrow-Belt Sanders 190
Disc Sanders 192
Combination Belt/Disc Sanders 195
Drum Sanders 197
Oscillating Spindle Sanders 198
Thicknessing Sanders 201
Arbor-Mounted Sanding Wheels 206

Sources of Supply 209
Index 211

Introduction

Every woodworker knows how to smooth wood, right? All it takes is a piece of sandpaper and a little elbow grease. You can certainly get adequate results with basic sanding techniques, but if you haven't yet explored the full range of modern abrasive materials, machines and methods, you've only begun to scratch the surface (pun intended).

It's hard to believe that a mere hundred years ago crude materials, such as sharkskin or ordinary sand glued to a paper backing, were the only kind of abrasive commonly available to woodworkers. Today, a quick flip through the pages of any woodworking or hardware supply catalog will reveal dozens of types of sandpaper and innovative abrasive products and machines that perform many woodworking operations besides merely smoothing a surface. Woodworkers now routinely use abrasives to shape wood parts, thickness boards to precise dimension, trim waste, remove an old finish or polish a new one, clean up rough turnings, refine moldings, and more.

Modern abrasive technologies have an ever-increasing impact on the way both beginners and professionals are working with wood. Innovative sanding machines make jobs that were once difficult or troublesome to accomplish, such as planing highly figured woods or smoothing complex parts, much easier, faster, and more accurate. Also, new industrial abrasive products make many traditional sanding tasks less tedious. For instance, production sandpapers with anti-loading (stearated) coatings have a lubricity that keeps them from gumming up when smoothing resinous woods or when touch sanding between coats of a lacquer finish.

With the emergence of the American do-it-yourself market, power-tool companies have directed their attention to the needs of amateur and hobbyist woodworkers, developing many new abrasive tools specifically for them. Tools such as detail sanders and combination belt/disc sanders are easy to use and affordable. Many industrial abrasive machines designed for production woodworking have served as models for affordable, scaled-down tools designed for smaller woodshops. Machines once found only in large cabinet shops or furniture factories, such as oscillating spindle sanders, are now commonplace in one-person shops. Inexpensive versions of other industrial tools, such as pneumatic sanders, are now more available thanks to larger production volume and low-cost manufacturing abroad. We're also seeing more and more abrasive tools in the woodshop that were originally developed in other trades. For example, random-orbit sanders were originally designed for auto-body repair work, yet most woodworkers I know use them for removing waste quickly.

These abundant new developments in woodworking abrasives stem from the fact that abrasives perform many jobs traditionally done by bladed tools, but do them more easily and more safely. Safety is an important consideration for any woodworker, but especially for the beginner or novice: A careless slip when cleaning up a door frame with a belt sander has less grim consequences than the same slip made while trimming with a portable power plane!

The new abrasive materials and machines offer the promise of faster and better ways of working wood, but they also come with their share of challenges and problems. If you don't understand the tool and use it improperly, any abrasive device can quickly turn woodworking from a delight into a disaster: Even a belt sander can remove wood so fast that it can ruin a painstakingly built project in the wink of an eye. On a more insidious level, most abrasive machines are dust-spewing demons that can fill a shop with lung-choking clouds of fine particles. These can cause respiratory discomfort and long-term health problems.

Hence, while it's important to embrace (or at least be open to) new abrasives products and technologies, enthusiasm is best balanced with good judgment. Just as when you buy any new tool or try a new joinery technique, it pays to be well informed ahead of the purchase or practice. That way, you're most likely to choose the right equipment for your needs, get the most out of it, and spend the least amount of time overcoming pitfalls. With these issues in mind, I've written this book to aid woodworkers in search of truth and wisdom about sandpaper and abrasives. This book has four aims:

- To give extensive, up-to-date information about modern abrasive materials, from simple sandpaper sheets to discs, drums, belts, sleeves, and special wheels. I'll delve into all the aspects of abrasives important to the woodworker, including how grits are graded (coarse to extra fine) and what abrasive minerals, surface coatings, and backing materials and treatments are best for what particular jobs. This information is intended to help better prepare you to select the right product for the right job—and avoid buying costly products you don't need.

• To teach techniques for doing basic sanding jobs, such as shaping, leveling, and smoothing surfaces, polishing finishes, and removing waste, in ways that require the least effort and ensure the best results. I'll cover all manner of techniques for both hand sanding and power sanding, pointing out methods and tricks to make sanding easier, more accurate, and safer.

• To display and discuss the abrasive devices, tools, and machines currently in use, from simple sanding blocks to complex stationary machines. Included are the full range of portable power sanders, from old standbys, such as belt sanders, to recent introductions, such as detail and profile sanders. Detailed descriptions of what jobs each tool does best will help you make well-informed purchases (a "Sources of Supply" appendix at the end of the book provides listings of abrasive-tool manufacturers and suppliers). And a wealth of suggestions for using power sanders should help you get the most out of all your abrasive tools, both new and old.

• To help readers avoid or overcome common problems associated with sandpaper and sanding, such as cross-grain scratches, paper loading, and veneer sand-through. I'll also address the important issue of how to defend yourself against dust, including personal protection by means of masks and respirators and dust-collection strategies for your shop.

The information presented in this book will benefit any woodworker who is looking to make the most of modern abrasive products and sanding methods. If you're a professional or serious amateur already making extensive use of abrasives in your shop, you're sure to discover loads of techniques and tips to improve the quality of your work and to boost your productivity. If you're a beginner who uses sandpaper only for smoothing surfaces (and an old orbital sander is the only piece of power-sanding equipment you own), get ready to explore the many facets of a bold new world of abrasive woodworking!

1

The Anatomy of Coated Abrasives

We've come a long way since the days when smoothing or polishing a piece of wood meant you first had to make your own sandpaper by gluing crushed glass or beach sand to a sheet of parchment paper. It's ironic that we still refer to the many coated-abrasive products we use in the shop as "sandpaper," because they rarely contain sand, and, often, not even paper.

Regardless of what they're made of, modern coated abrasives (which, for tradition and familiarity's sake I'll refer to generically as "sandpaper" throughout this book) have played a big part in changing—and improving—the way that we work wood. While you can grab just any old piece of sandpaper and do a pretty good job of smoothing wood with it, modern industrial-coatings technology has given contemporary woodworkers a collection of very precise abrasive materials and methods by which to shape, thickness, level, dewhisker, smooth, and polish items made from wood. If we understand these materials and the techniques for using them, we stand to do all our woodworking sanding tasks more easily and effectively.

Lots of factors conspire to create the working properties of sandpaper and hence affect how well the product will perform a given task. These factors include all the various elements that make up sandpaper: the type of abrasive mineral; the size and grading of particles and their distribution on the backing; the type of backing material and its weight; the adhesive used to bond the particles to the backing; additional coatings applied atop the abrasive; and backing treatments used for mounting the product, such as hook and loop. This chapter explores all these elements in detail; the sidebar on pp. 6-7 explains the process by which the elements come together in the manufacturing process.

Besides demonstrating the complexity of a product as seemingly simple as sandpaper, the information in this chapter is meant to be a primer on coated abrasives, to help you understand the multitude of sanding products on the market and make more informed choices when purchasing sandpaper through a catalog or at a hardware store. Choosing an abrasive that has the characteristics that best suit your needs will improve the quality of your work, as well as save you time and money.

Grits

When I was a fledgling woodworker in the late 1960s, the choice of sandpaper I had at the local hardware store was very limited: I could buy cheap flint paper (which, with my limited budget, I often did). Most hardware stores also carried better-quality garnet sandpapers and perhaps a couple of other kinds, including aluminum-oxide and silicon-carbide papers.

These days, a casual look through the pages of an abrasive supply catalog reveals sanding products that employ traditional natural minerals (e.g., garnet) as well as a variety of different of synthetic abrasive materials. While it's good to have more choices, it can also be very confusing—if you don't know what to base your choices on.

Abrasive minerals have different degrees of hardness, sharpness, and toughness, so they vary in their suitability for specific woodworking tasks. For example, a very hard abrasive grit might be best for rubbing out a very hard finish (such as a catalyzed polyester) while a grit with a high degree of toughness will reduce

How Coated Abrasives Are Made

The idea of using ground-up rocks to smooth and polish a surface isn't new; the Egyptians and other early civilizations used loose abrasive grains (sand) to shape and polish many of their craft works. It's only in the last 200 years that woodworkers have cultivated the art of gluing sand or ground glass to a parchment backing to make their own sandpaper (some preferred a natural alternative—sharkskin, whose abrasive scales did a moderately good job of smoothing wood, though it has directional grain that allows it to cut only in one direction).

Modern coated-abrasive material is still made by gluing tiny rocks to a backing, though its manufacture is now a complex science and exacting technology rather than a folk art. In the gravity coating process commonly used to produce sandpaper (see the drawing on the facing page), a long ribbon of backing material (paper, cloth, or film) first receives the make-coat adhesive, which initially bonds the grit to the backing. The pregraded and presized mineral grains are then evenly distributed by a vibrating belt and spread onto the backing from a gravity-fed hopper. Heat is applied to dry the make coat. In the next step, the grit-covered backing is coated again with the size-coat adhesive, which further anchors each grain to the backing, and is then dried. The sandpaper may then receive an anti-loading coating atop the previous size coat, as well as coatings or treatments (PSA, hook-and-loop, anti-static coatings) on the reverse side of the backing. Bond adhesives and coatings are discussed on pp. 28-30.

Sandpaper may also be produced by electrostatic coating. The electrostatic process is just like the gravity coating process, with an important exception: The make-coat-covered backing material runs upside-down through an electrically charged field, where it receives a negative charge. The abrasive mineral grains, carried on a separate belt below the backing, move through the charged field and are given a positive charge. The attraction of unlike electrical charges pulls the grains up into the backing, where they embed in the sticky adhesive. The advantage of this process over grit gluing by gravity is that the bulkiest portion of each abrasive grain usually sticks into the glue, ensuring that the grain is well anchored. Thus electrostatically made sandpapers cut with a

the number of paper changes in your sanding schedule, which is important if you're a production woodworker.

The pages that follow describe the properties of all the types of grits currently available (and useful) to small-shop woodworkers. (There are many more types of grits available to industry, but there's no point in discussing products we smaller-shop woodworkers have little access to.) Once you've decided which type of grits are best for your needs, the sidebar on pp. 8-9 will help you decipher the coded information on the back of most abrasive products before you take a trip to your local supplier.

THE MANUFACTURING PROCESS

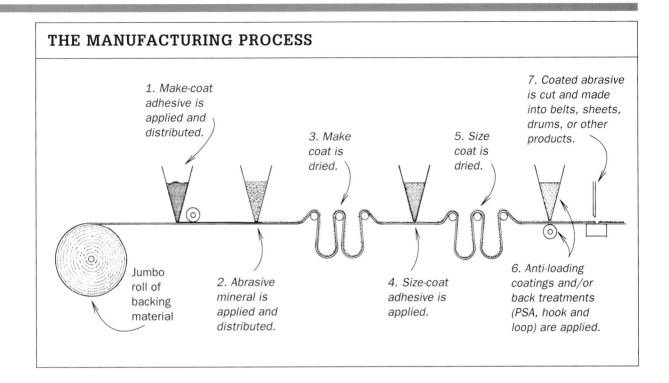

1. Make-coat adhesive is applied and distributed.

3. Make coat is dried.

5. Size coat is dried.

7. Coated abrasive is cut and made into belts, sheets, drums, or other products.

Jumbo roll of backing material

2. Abrasive mineral is applied and distributed.

4. Size-coat adhesive is applied.

6. Anti-loading coatings and/or back treatments (PSA, hook and loop) are applied.

20% to 25% higher efficiency than sandpapers made by the gravity method.

Finally, the jumbo roll is ready to be made into abrasive products. The big roll is slit into narrower widths for belt, sheet, and drum stock. Discs are punched out in a die press. Stock destined for abrasives for power tools is then flexed. Flexing cracks or partially breaks the glue bond in order to make the belt or disc more supple, so it will conform more easily to curved work. Products are then packaged and shipped off to distributors and hardware stores to await purchase–and use by you and me.

NATURAL MINERALS

Even though most modern woodworking supply catalogs are teeming with the latest and greatest that abrasive technology can offer, natural abrasives—old standbys such as emery, flint, and garnet—are often still readily available and may be useful to you in your woodshop.

Emery A naturally mined ore, emery grit is basically an oxide of iron that is dark gray and relatively hard and tough. Cloth sheets or rolls of emery (or crocus, a ferrous oxide similar to emery) are not intended for woodworking uses, but rather to shape and polish

Reading the Back of a Sheet of Sandpaper

If you're a cryptographer, breaking a secret code is undoubtedly a source of great pleasure and accomplishment. If you're a woodworker, trying to decipher the confusing code of mixed numbers and letters on the back of the average sheet of sandpaper is just a pain in the grit. The back of the average sheet, belt, or disc of sandpaper is loaded with information (see the photo below). If you know the code, it can tell you not only the brand and grit of the paper, but also the abrasive mineral, the backing weight, the coatings, and more (for specifics, see the information on the facing page).

What's printed on the back of the paper is often your only clue to the kind of sandpaper you're buying (or already have on hand); the looks and color of the abrasive don't tell you much. The same kind of abrasive can come in a plethora of different colors. For example, aluminum-oxide sandpaper comes in all the colors of the rainbow; the color depends on the maker, the brand, the bond type, and so forth. Color is often used by makers of cheap imported papers to fool unwary buyers: I've seen sanding belts that closely resembled resin-coated aluminum oxide that were really garnet bonded with hide glue, colored to mimic more expensive production products.

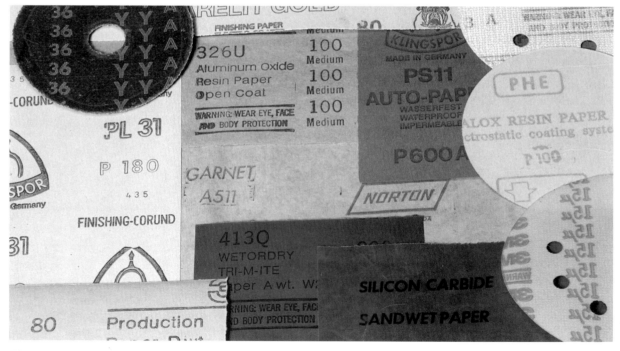

The printing on the back of a sheet of sandpaper can be almost as cryptic as the writing on a mummy's tomb. Fortunately, there is some sense to these notations, and cracking the code will tell you what you need to know about the properties of each abrasive product you use.

Information you're likely to see:

The logo or name of the manufacturer or distributor

- Carborundum
- Klingspor
- Norton
- Pasco
- Sungold
- 3M
- Uneeda

The brand name of the sandpaper and/or its numerical designation (which can tell you the kind of grit mineral used)

- Adalox = aluminum oxide (Norton)
- Crystal Bay = emery (3M)
- Durite = silicon carbide (Norton)
- Garnet is always garnet
- Norzon = zirconia alumina (Norton)
- Production = aluminum oxide (3M)
- Regal, Cubitron = ceramic aluminum oxide (3M)
- Regalite = ceramic/aluminum-oxide mix (3M)
- SG = ceramic aluminum oxide (Norton)
- Three-M-ite = aluminum-oxide cloth, belts (3M)
- Tri-M-ite = silicon carbide (3M)
- 216U (Production RN) = friable aluminum oxide (3M)

The grade number (specifying the grit size), usually printed periodically across the paper

- 80, 100, 120, 150, 180, 220, 600, P220, etc.

The weight of the backing material

- Paper: A, C, D, E, F
- Cloth: J, X, Y
- Film: 1 mil, 2 mil...7 mil

The name of the anti-loading (stearated) coating on the paper

- Dri-Lube (Carborundum)
- Fre-Cut (3M)
- No-Fil (Norton)

Whether the paper is open coat or closed coat

- OpenCote (3M)

Whether the paper is waterproof

- Tufbak (Norton)
- Wasserfelt (Klingspor, German)
- Wetordry (3M)

You may also find:

A string of numbers and letters that tells when the product was produced, the batch number, and similar manufacturing information of little importance to woodworkers

A PSA or hook-and-loop designation

- Hookit, Stikit (3M)

On 3M products, a product identification number that consists of three numbers followed by a single letter:

1st number = mineral type (Norton uses this designation too)

- 1 = garnet
- 2 and 3 = aluminum oxide
- 4 = silicon carbide
- 5 = alumina zirconia
- 6 = diamond
- 7 = ceramic

2nd number = backing weight

- For papers: 1 = A; 3 = C; 4 = D; 5 = E; 6 = F
- For cloth: 1 = J; 3, 4, 5 = X (standard, regular, extra stiff); 6 = Y
- For film backings: 1 =.3 mil; 2 = .5; 3 = 1 mil; 4 = 1.5 mil; 5 = 2 mil; 6 = 3 mil; 7 = 5 mil

3rd number = coding number

- 1 = closed coat;
- 2 = open coat;
- 3, 4 = internal codes;
- 5 = Fre-Cut-coated;
- 6 = internal code

Letter = family designation; how the paper was made

- D = phenolic resin make and size coats on cotton cloth
- N= glue make and size coat
- Q = wet/dry designation
- RN or U = glue make coat, resin size coat

metal. When used on wood, it tends to leave deep scratches because of the shape of its particles. Worse, because of its composition (which is essentially the same as rust), it can easily discolor tannin-rich woods, such as oak and walnut, with dark streaks if bits of grit get trapped in the wood's open pores. The best uses for emery in a woodshop are for sharpening tools (see the sidebar on p. 93) and for shaping or polishing metal hardware.

Flint A real holdover from long ago, when it was the only kind of sandpaper made, flint-coated sandpaper (typically manufactured in the Orient) is still sold at variety and discount stores. Flint, which is basically beach sand, is grayish white in color and is quite soft (see the photo below left). Its particles are neither tough or sharp, so flint paper cuts wood poorly. Further, particles are poorly graded (see p. 21) and don't hold an edge well, so the paper wears out very quickly. Because the mineral is cheap, construction of sandpaper made with flint is usually also cheap. Because inexpensive glue is used to bond the grit to the backing, the mineral comes off readily. Despite its low cost, flint sandpaper is a very poor choice for woodworking—or just about anything else.

One of the original sandpapers, flint paper is still available in many hardware stores and home centers. It is the least expensive of abrasive papers, but it performs poorly and wears out quickly.

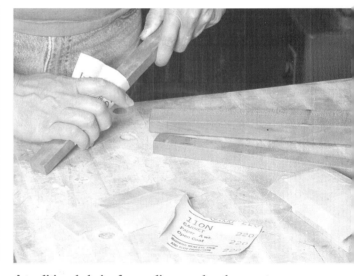

A traditional choice for sanding woodwork, garnet paper is still in popular use today, although it wears out more quickly than most artificial abrasive minerals. You can use worn garnet paper to burnish a final sanded surface.

Garnet A gemstone that is technically an amalgam of iron, aluminum, and silicon, garnet is a reddish-brown semiprecious mineral. Garnet sandpaper (commonly known as "cabinet paper") is still a fixture in many contemporary woodworking studios, despite the plethora of modern synthetic abrasives, and with good reason. Garnet grit particles are extremely sharp, so the sandpaper cuts aggressively when new. The sharp grit facets tend to cut into a wood surface very cleanly, creating little shavings of wood instead of mushy swarf (swarf is the debris produced by the cutting action of the abrasive grains). As the paper wears down, the garnet particles fracture along natural cleavage lines, exposing sharp new cutting edges. This keeps garnet paper cutting coolly, which makes it good to use in operations where burning of the wood is a concern, such as when sanding the end grain of dense hardwoods.

Unfortunately, garnet is not a hard or tough mineral, so particles don't hold an edge for long. The particles dull and round over as they are used, breaking down more quickly when sanding hard woods, such as oak or maple, than soft woods, such as pine or butternut. Because garnet wears out much more readily that any of the artificial abrasive materials, it's a poor choice for power sanding operations. It's also not an economical choice for production woodworking, since frequent paper changes are required. If you continue sanding with dulled paper, you're less likely to remove scratches left by a previous coarser grit and end up with an imperfect final surface.

But garnet's lack of toughness isn't entirely a bad thing. As garnet particles dull, they actually begin to burnish the surface of the wood instead of cutting into it. This means that a well-used piece of garnet sandpaper of any given grit yields a surface smoothness that's more like one created using a finer-grit paper (see the photo at right on the facing page). This is one reason many woodworkers like to take a final pass with used garnet paper just before finishing the raw wood. This technique is best reserved for hand sanding, so surfaces are burnished evenly (see p 103).

SYNTHETIC MINERALS

In the late 19th century, American inventors started synthesizing artificial abrasive minerals, such as aluminum oxide and silicon carbide. These minerals are much tougher and longer lasting than any of the natural abrasives, such as flint and garnet.

By far the most prevalent grit minerals found in woodworking shops today (both hobby studios and production shops), synthetic grits perform better than natural minerals, and usually at a lower cost. They are also essential for many modern power-sanding operations with portable and stationary machines, where high heat and pressure degrade natural minerals quickly. And, when prepared with anti-loading coatings (see p. 30), synthetic-grit abrasive papers excel at operations that can gum up sandpaper quickly, such as sanding oily or resinous woods and leveling and rubbing out finishes.

The toughness of aluminum oxide makes it one of the most versatile of woodworking abrasives and a good choice for most hand- and power-sanding tasks.

Aluminum oxides The most popular of all woodworking abrasives, aluminum oxide is the mineral you'll find most often on abrasive sheets, drums, belts, and discs commonly available to woodworkers. Known in the abrasives industry as ALO for short, this mineral has a good balance of hardness, sharpness, and toughness, which makes it a great all-around woodworking abrasive. Most aluminum-oxide particles are shaped like a wedge, which allows the grains to penetrate the hardest and densest hardwoods at high rates of cut, without excessive fracturing. This quality, combined with a good degree of particle toughness, makes aluminum-oxide abrasives a good overall choice for power shaping and smoothing operations using powered hand or stationary tools (see the photo at left). Aluminum oxide yields a very consistent scratch pattern, with particles that eventually round over (as garnet does), but last much longer than garnet because of their superior hardness.

Widely available at both hardware and home-supply stores and catalog suppliers, aluminum-oxide sandpapers comes in a full range of grit sizes, from 12 grit to sub-micron, making them suitable for both heavy-duty operations, such as abrasive planing, and delicate jobs, such as polishing a final finish. If you do metalwork, coarser aluminum-oxide grits are particularly well suited for grinding materials with high tensile strength, such as carbon steels, alloy steels, and tough bronze.

The one big bugaboo is picking the right type of grit. Within the overall family of aluminum-oxide minerals, there are at least two dozen individual varieties. At one extreme, basic brown aluminum oxide is a fairly cheap mineral with relatively poor working properties; at the other extreme, industrial-grade "friable" aluminum oxides are remarkably durable (see the sidebar on the facing page). That's why two different aluminum-oxide sandpapers can perform so differently. To add to the confusion in identifying like products, coatings can make aluminum-oxide particles just about any color. The best advice when shopping for aluminum-oxide sandpapers is to beware of cheaper products that are bonded and coated with animal hide glue (see p. 28). These papers don't hold up nearly as well as better-quality coated abrasives that are designed for production applications. Once you find a paper you like, stick with the same brand and numbered product to be sure you'll get the same performance.

Friable Grits

Some kinds of aluminum-oxide minerals, as well as ceramic minerals (described on pp. 14-15), are manufactured with a special property called friability. As a friable mineral particle heats up during sanding, it breaks down, at a controlled rate, to reveal sharp new cutting edges. Unlike garnet, which fractures but dulls quickly, friable minerals stay sharp longer and continue to cut aggressively for the life of the sheet, belt, drum, or disc.

This is how a friable mineral works: As a particle dulls and rounds over, heat caused by sanding friction builds up and eventually causes a fracture line to form. When the particle shatters, a new cutting edge forms, as shown in the drawing at right (imagine the rounded bottom of a glass soda bottle breaking off to become a sharp, jagged edge). The result is that friable minerals cut very quickly

and last an incredibly long time. Some products are rated to last 4 to 5 times longer than regular aluminum-oxide papers, but I find this estimate to be very conservative—10 to 12 times longer isn't unrealistic. This translates into more time between paper changes, saving time and trouble and offsetting the relatively high cost of these abrasive products. Further, the grains of a friable mineral stay so sharp that the sanding swarf from even well-used paper looks like perfect little shavings from an impossibly small hand plane. This clean cutting action keeps the grit from heating up excessively, so the backing material doesn't degrade as quickly. These qualities make friable-grit abrasives the top choice for really demanding power sanding jobs, such as abrasive shaping or thicknessing rough lumber.

HOW FRIABLE GRITS WORK

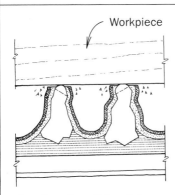

As mineral particles dull during sanding, they fracture.

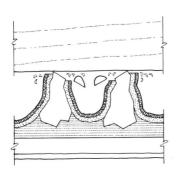

Fractured tips break off, revealing new, sharp facets that cut more aggressively.

Silicon carbide Silicon carbide, known by the acronym SIC in industry, is an artificial carbide synthesized from coke and silica sand in an electrolytic process. Bluish-black in color, silicon-carbide grains are very sharp and almost as hard as diamonds. The sliver-shaped particles have a great ability to cut aggressively on wide variety of materials with only light working pressure. But due to the mineral's hardness, the grit particles are rather brittle and not very tough. Therefore, silicon-carbide abrasive papers don't last as long as aluminum-oxide papers. But because they resist heat well,

Silicon carbide is a very hard mineral that's commonly available in very fine grits, bonded to waterproof paper backings. These papers are a great choice for wet-sanding a finish.

silicon-carbide abrasive products hold up well during demanding power-sanding operations such as abrasive shaping, surface leveling, and thicknessing.

Silicon carbide is one of the only readily available papers that will cut hardened steel, so it can be used for sharpening woodworking tools (see the sidebar on p. 93). In the metalworking trades, silicon-carbide abrasives are popular for grinding nonferrous materials such as brass, copper, bronze, and aluminum, and are the grain of choice for certain finishes on stainless steel. Silicon-carbide papers are also terrific for polishing polyester finishes, which are rock hard when cured, including the ultraviolet-cured finishes now common in the commercial furniture and cabinet industry. Auto-body shops often use silicon-carbide abrasives to level and smooth automotive primers, lacquers, and sealers.

Because silicon carbide is so hard and brittle, it's easy to crush into small particles that have a consistent size and grading (see p. 21). Therefore, sililcon-carbide papers are available down to the super-fine grits—commonly to 2500 grit. The grit is typically bonded to waterproof paper backings (see p. 24), which make them suitable for wet-sanding tasks, such as polishing a finish (see the photo at left).

Ceramics

One of the more recently developed synthetic abrasives, ceramic minerals are made by infusing glass-like ceramic materials with metal compounds. One type of ceramic abrasives, alumina zirconia (AZ in abrasive vernacular) was originally patented by Norton as "zirconia alumina" and sold under the name Norzon. There are also ceramic products, such as 3M's Regal or Cubitron, and ceramic aluminum oxides, such as Norton's SG. Another product is 3M's Regalite, which is a ceramic/aluminum-oxide mix.

All ceramic minerals have terrific working properties: They are extremely hard, very sharp, and very tough. Though not quite as hard as silicon carbide, ceramics are still hard enough to cut very aggressively on most materials, including the hardest of hardwoods (i.e., ebony and lignum vitae). When used with portable power sanders, the aggressiveness of ceramic minerals can take some getting used to; a good bit of operator finesse is required to avoid deep scratches and sand-through on veneered surfaces (see the photo on the facing page).

In addition to their other good properties, ceramics are friable abrasives, which means that the heat generated by normal use triggers controlled fracturing of the blocky grains to expose new sharp cutting edges (see the sidebar on p. 13). This makes ceramics a good choice for heavy stock removal, such as abrasive shaping using a disc in a right-angle grinder or abrasive planing with a stationary drum or wide-belt sander. Ceramics are also capable of handling the tremendous amount of heat that builds up on the platens (the metal plate that backs up the belt) of many portable and stationary belt sanders (even a small portable belt-sander platen can exceed 400°F during heavy sanding). Their heat resistance makes ceramic abrasives a good choice for power-sanding hardwood end grain without burning.

Two drawbacks of ceramics are their limited range of available grit sizes and their high cost. Because ceramic grains are so tough and hard, it's very difficult to crush them any finer than about 150 grit; you must switch to other abrasive minerals for fine sanding or polishing duties. Ceramics are typically a lot more expensive than other abrasive products (excluding diamond-coated abrasives, which are extremely expensive), but they generally last at least five times longer than other abrasives. In a production shop, using ceramic abrasives can actually save you money because you don't have to pay for time spent on paper changes. In the hobbyist's woodshop, less expensive mixed ceramic/aluminum-oxide abrasives are a great choice for portable belt sanders and stationary edge, belt, and drum sanders, where they'll perform very well and wear out slowly.

Structured abrasives

All natural abrasives and ordinary synthetic grains have irregularly shaped crystals. A relatively new breed of synthetic abrasives, called structured abrasives, has grains that are perfectly consistent in

The aggressive sanding characteristics of ceramic abrasives occasionally create problems, such as sanding through the delicate face veneers on hardwood plywood.

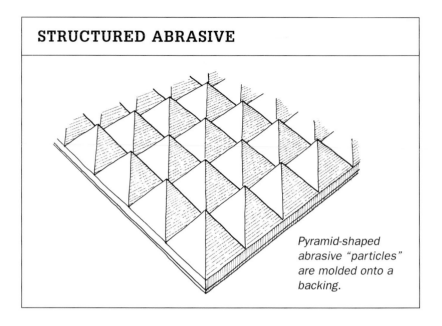

STRUCTURED ABRASIVE

Pyramid-shaped abrasive "particles" are molded onto a backing.

shape and distribution. That is because they are, in effect, "molded" onto the backing material. The only product I've seen so far, 3M's Apex, has a surface with row upon row of tiny pyramids that look like a King Tut condo project (see the drawing above). Structured abrasives are frightfully expensive and currently used only in industry. Will they ever become affordable and available to small-shop woodworkers? Only time will tell.

Sizes and Grades

Once a natural or synthetic mineral has been crushed into tiny rocks (called grains), the grains must be sifted and sorted into particles of the same approximate size. This is so that once the grains are bonded to sandpaper, they will make scratches of the same size and depth, forming an even scratch pattern on the sanded surface.

The reason for separating out abrasive grains into like-sized particles is simple enough. However, there are quite a few different systems used worldwide for sizing and specifying abrasive grit. The chart on pp. 18-19 lists and compares the relative sizes of various grits (in fractions of an inch and microns) and their specification in each system.

The four most common grading systems are ANSI, FEPA, JIS, and micron. The ANSI (American National Standards Institute) PS-8 grading system is also often identified on grit charts as the

CAMI (Coated Abrasive Manufacturers Institute) scale. The grit numbers range from 12 to 2500 (coarse to fine). The FEPA (the French European P scale, called P grading for short) is used for classifying European abrasive products. The grit numbers range from P12 (extra coarse) to P1200 (ultra fine). The JIS (Japan Institute of Standards) grading system is a Japanese system used for abrasives produced in the Orient. The grit numbers ranges from 240 to 3000 grit. Micron grading is used by manufacturers to specify the actual size in microns of very fine abrasive grits, ranging from 60 microns to .1 microns.

Additionally, you'll sometimes see sandpaper grits sized by the aught system (5/0, 2/0, 0/0, etc.), which is mostly outdated but occasionally seen on flooring abrasives. You'll also sometimes see grit sizes identified by generic names, such as "Very fine," "Medium," or "Coarse." Such grit names are individually specified by manufacturers, and are not part of a controlled grading system (so a "very fine" garnet paper might actually have a slightly finer grit than an aluminum-oxide paper that's also called "very fine."

Unfortunately, the proliferation of grading systems and specifications can make shopping for sandpaper seem as complex as buying computer equipment! For example, the following five sandpapers (each specified by a different grading system) all have grit that's about the same size: 400 grit (ANSI), 10/0 (aught), P800 (FEPA), 23.6 micron (micron), and "super fine" (generic name). And papers numbered similarly may or may not have grains that are the same size (for example, P220 paper and ANSI 220 grit are about the same, yet P1200 is about the same grit as ANSI 600).

The good news is that the majority of abrasive products available through hardware stores, home centers, and woodworking suppliers in the United States will have an ANSI grit number or, less frequently, a P-grading specification stamped on the back (see the sidebar on pp. 8-9). I've chosen the ANSI grit numbers to specify abrasives grit sizes throughout this book.

SIZING THE GRIT

All grit-sizing systems depend on a precise and consistent method of separating grains into the various grit sizes. Depending on the physical size of the grains, one of four different methods is likely to be used: screen grading, air classification, water classification, or Coulter counting.

Screen grading is most commonly used sorting system for abrasive grains between 12 grit and 220 grit. As its name implies, it uses sieve-like screens with a regular pattern of holes in them to sift and sort grains into the different grit sizes. The numbers in the

Approximate Grit-Size Equivalents

ANSI scale	Average diameter (in.)	Micron grade	FEPA scale	Average diameter (microns)	JIS scale	Aught size	Generic description
	0.00000394	0.1					
	0.0000118	0.3					
	0.0000197	0.5					
	0.0000394	1.0					
	0.0000787	2.0					
1500	0.000118	3.0					Micro fine
	0.000158	4.0					
	0.000197	5.0					
	0.000236	6.0					
1200	0.00026						
	0.00035	9.0					
1000	0.00036						
	0.00047	12.0			3000		
800	0.00048						Ultra fine
	0.00059	15.0			2000		
600	0.00062		P1200	15.3			
					1200		
					1000		
500	0.00077		P1000	18.3			
	0.00079	20.0			800		
400	0.00092		P800	21.8		10/0	Super fine
	0.00098	25.0			600		
360	0.00112		P600	25.8			
	0.00118	30.0			500		
			P500	30.2			
320	0.00140	35.0	P400	35.0		9/0	Extra fine

Approximate Grit-Size Equivalents (continued)

ANSI scale	Average diameter (in.)	Micron grade	FEPA scale	Average diameter (microns)	JIS scale	Aught size	Generic description
					360		
	0.001575	40.0					
			P360	40.5			
280	0.00172	45.0			320	8/0	
			P320	46.2			
					280		
	0.00197	50.0					
240	0.00209		P280	52.5		7/0	Very fine
	0.00217	55.0					
		60.0			240		
220	0.00257		P220	65.0		6/0	
180	0.00304		P180	78.0		5/0	
150	0.00363		P150	97.0		4/0	
120	0.00452		P120	127.0		3/0	Fine
100	0.0055		P100	156.0		2/0	
80	0.00749		P80	197.0		0	Medium
60	0.01045		P60	260.0		½	
50	0.0139		P50	326.0		1	Coarse
40	0.0169		P40	412.0		1½	
36	0.02087		P36	524.0		2	Extra coarse
30	0.02488		P30	622.0		2½	
24	0.02789		P24	740.0		3	
20	0.03535		P20	984.0		3½	
16	0.05148		P16	1324.0		4	
12	0.07174		P12	1764.0		4½	

Information for this chart was provided by Lyle Rawlins (Pacific Abrasive Supply Co.) and Dub Parker (3M).

ANSI system refer to the number of holes per inch in each sifting screen (100 grit equals a 100-hole-per-inch screen). An abrasive grain that is graded as 100 grit is small enough to pass through a #100 screen, but too large to pass through the next screen size down (#120). Grains that are smaller than 100 grit freely pass through the #120 screen, and so are separated out (see the drawing below).

Abrasive grains in the 240-grit to 600-grit range are typically sorted by a method know as air classification: Fine grain particles are blown through a device that's something like a dust-collection cyclone, which separates heavier (coarser-grit) grains from lighter (finer-grit) grains by cyclonic separation.

The water-classification method is reserved for sorting extremely fine abrasive grains (smaller than 15 microns), and uses the process of sedimentation, whereby larger grains settle more quickly than smaller grains.

A more sophisticated sorting method employs a device called a Coulter Counter, which actually measures the size of individual particles. This provides a much more accurate means of sizing grains, which makes for a higher-quality abrasive product that performs to exacting tolerances. As we'll see in the next section, consistency is an important measure of how well an abrasive paper works.

SCREEN GRADING FOR ABRASIVE PARTICLES

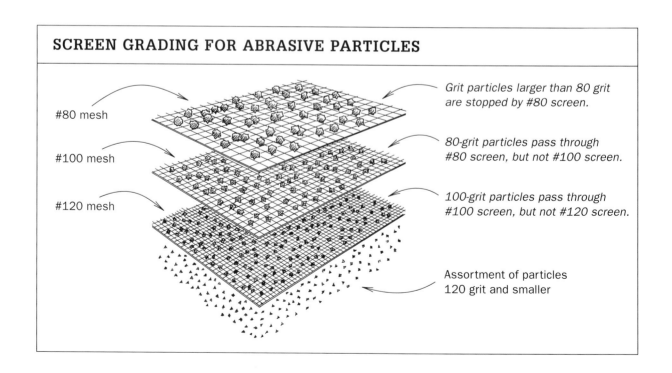

#80 mesh

#100 mesh

#120 mesh

Grit particles larger than 80 grit are stopped by #80 screen.

80-grit particles pass through #80 screen, but not #100 screen.

100-grit particles pass through #100 screen, but not #120 screen.

Assortment of particles 120 grit and smaller

GRADING THE GRIT

In addition to sizing grit, each of the systems described in the previous section is also a grit grading system. That is, each grit size corresponds to an ideal grain size—the actual size of the particles you'll find on, say a piece of 240-grit sandpaper aren't all exactly equal to the defined size of a 240-grit grain: 0.00209 in. diameter (see the chart on pp. 18-19). That's where the grading of the particles comes in. Each grading system specifies what percentage of larger or smaller grains is permissible for any particular grit size. This is known as a grading tolerance.

Why should we care about the tolerances of the sizes of grains on a piece of sandpaper? Because grains that are smaller or larger than grains of the specified size are undesirable and, in part, spoil the performance of the abrasive product. Larger-than-specified grains (known as clinkers or rocks) ruin the consistency of the scratch pattern by making deeper scratches than those left by the specified grit (see the drawing below). Smaller-than-specified grains leave smaller scratches that are obscured by the specified grit and are inconsequential; they only take up room on the paper.

Grading tolerances vary from system to system, in great part due to the grain-sorting methods specified by the system. The screen-grading system (most commonly used for consumer abrasive products) does a pretty good job of sifting out like-sized

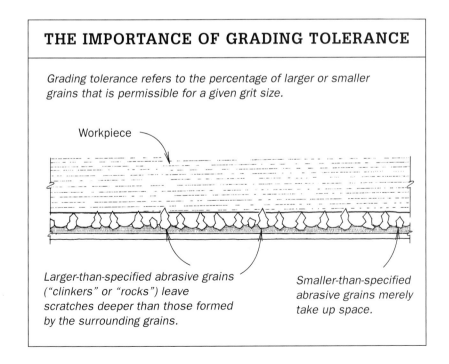

THE IMPORTANCE OF GRADING TOLERANCE

Grading tolerance refers to the percentage of larger or smaller grains that is permissible for a given grit size.

Workpiece

Larger-than-specified abrasive grains ("clinkers" or "rocks") leave scratches deeper than those formed by the surrounding grains.

Smaller-than-specified abrasive grains merely take up space.

grains. However, grading screens do let through a small percentage of larger-sized grains at each grit size. These larger grains are capable of passing through a screen that's sized to stop them because of their long or narrow shape (a thin person can dive through a hula hoop that a fat person couldn't fit through).

Of all the grading systems, micron grading maintains the highest tolerances, and that's the system employed for grading the ultra-fine and micro-fine micron papers that are used for demanding jobs such as optical polishing. But such precision comes at a price: Micron-graded papers are considerably more expensive than papers graded by other means. They are rarely required for sanding bare wood, but are reserved for more exacting sanding jobs, such as leveling and polishing a finish (see pp. 78-81).

Backing Materials

Once you have sifted and sorted grains of abrasive grit into like sizes, you can use a handful of loose particles to abrade a surface: Very-fine-grit powders and compounds are commonly used for rubbing out and polishing a finish (see pp. 74-75). But for wood-sanding purposes, it's far more desirable to attach the grit particles to some sort of backing material. Grit applied and glued to a backing is, in fact, the very definition of a coated abrasive.

Although we commonly refer to most coated abrasives as "sandpaper," paper is only one of the backing materials in common use for modern abrasive products. For woodworking, three are commonly used: paper, cloth, and film. Two other backing materials, fiber-reinforced paper and screen, are seen only occasionally in woodworking abrasives. These are reserved for special sanding tasks, as described later in this section.

The abrasive mineral and its size are the first determinants of how a sandpaper performs. But the "weight" of the backing (its thickness and stiffness) also affects sanding performance. Backing weight, in great part, determines how durable a sheet, belt, drum, or disc will be, and hence how long the grit will cut before the abrasive product wears out. Heavier backings are more resistant to stretching, so belts and drums tend to last longer. They are a better choice for discs when power sanding sharp-edged wood parts, where a lightweight backing material would be apt to tear or wear out quickly.

The weight of the backing also affects how aggressively the abrasive grit will sand: the heavier the backing, the more stable a substrate for the abrasive grains to bond to. Hence, heavier backings tend to stabilize glued-on grit particles better, so their cutting edges make better contact with the work surface and cut more quickly.

The backing's stiffness or flexibility determines how easily it will conform to curves. A paper with a heavy backing is likely to be a poor choice for hand-sanding moldings or carvings, since the stiff-backed paper won't easily let you work in tight corners and crevices.

To help you decide which type and weight of backing are right for your needs, consult the charts on pgs. 24, 25, and 26, which list backing materials common for woodworking abrasives, along with their weights and characteristics. Individual backing materials are discussed below.

PAPER

Paper, a vintage backing material, is still the most popular backing material for everything from light hand sanding to medium- to heavy-duty power sanding with portable power tools. It is an inexpensive, reasonably durable backing for a wide range of uses, and it's easy to work with. On the down side, lighter weights of paper tear easily, and moisture can cause them to curl or ruin them entirely (see pp. 100-102).

Standard paper backings for woodworking come in five basic weights (see the chart on p. 24). A-, C-, D- and E-weight papers are quite commonly available, and you may find F-weight paper in very heavy-duty industrial abrasive products, though it's rare. (Why no B-weight paper? It was offered at one time, but supposedly wasn't different enough from A-weight or C-weight papers to have become popular.) Paper weight is measured by what a ream of paper (480 sheets of 24-in. by 36-in. paper) weighs, in pounds. The higher the weight of the paper, the stronger and stiffer it is, and the more resistant to tearing and mineral shedding (the mineral grains being knocked off).

For general wood shaping, smoothing, and polishing purposes, A-, C-, and D-weight paper backings are adequate—E and F are too inflexible for most uses. Choose an A-weight paper when the most flexibility is needed, such as for contour or detail sanding. You can get away with using A-weight papers for power sanding with finer grits if you work carefully and avoid sanding sharp edges and corners. You can also prolong the life of A-weight paper by using a stiff backup pad when power sanding (see p. 144). But for heavy-duty power sanding, use C-weight or D-weight papers whenever possible.

Backing Materials: Paper

Backing designation	Weight of backing (pounds per ream)	Flexibility
Standard papers		
A	40	Very flexible
C	70	Moderately flexible
D	88	Moderately stiff
E	130	Very stiff
F	165	Extremely stiff
Wet/dry papers		
A	58	Moderately flexible
C	90	Moderately stiff

Wet/dry papers

Wet/dry papers are waterproof papers. They are the same thickness as standard paper backings of the same letter designation, but are actually heavier because of their latex coating (which is what makes the paper repel water). Besides adding weight, the latex coating does make wet/dry paper somewhat stronger than a regular paper backing. While many regular paper-backed abrasives can be used wet for a short time, wet/dry paper is the logical choice for jobs such as rubbing out a finish using a water-based lubricant (see p. 79), or for sharpening or honing chisels or other bladed tools (see the sidebar on p. 93). The most commonly available wet/dry sandpapers use silicon-carbide minerals.

Fiber-reinforced paper

Fiber-reinforced paper is made by bolstering heavy-weight paper with cloth fibers and treated for strength and durability. It's used mostly as a backing for heavy-duty abrasive products such as coarse-grit discs for right-angle grinding, as well as sanding drums. It's also a popular backing for belts for electric floor sanders.

CLOTH

Loom-woven cloth materials offer a strength and durability that you won't find with plain paper backings. This durability is especially important when using sanding belts, which receive wear on the back as well as the front. This is why most belts for portable and stationary belt sanders are made from woven cloth. The cloth is commonly made from cotton mixed with synthetic fibers. Polyester fabrics are used for applications where extreme strength is required, such as for grinding metal and glass.

Cloth backings for woodworking are commonly available in three weights (see the chart below): J, X, and Y, sometimes designated as JWT, XWT, and YWT (the WT simply means weight). J is the lightest, thinnest, and most flexible of the three. It's good for applications where a sheet or belt must bend around or conform to curved surfaces, such as on a pneumatic sanding drum or for profile sanding (see p. 188).

The next heavier-weight cloth, X, has a nice blend of strength and medium flexibility that makes it the most popular belt choice for both portable and smaller-sized stationary sanders. The heaviest (Y) belts are best reserved for really heavy-duty power-sanding operations where high amounts of pressure and heat are generated, such as with a stroke sander or a thicknessing sander.

Backing Materials: Cloth

Backing designation	Fabric	Flexibility
J	Jean-like cloth typically woven from cotton or a cotton/poly blend	Thin, very flexible
X	Drill cloth, strong cotton or poly blend	Slightly thicker, moderately flexible
Y	Duck cloth woven from heavy yarns	Thick, relatively stiff

Backing Materials: Film

Backing designation	Thickness (mils)
1	0.3
2	0.5
3	1.0
4	1.5
5	2.0
6	3.0
7	5.0

FILM

The most expensive of the backing materials, films are thin plastics such as polyester (Mylar is one trade name for polyester). Film backings were developed for high-tolerance operations, such as polishing optical lenses and computer hard disks. Film backings are excellent for such precise tasks because they are extremely flat and even in thickness. The flatness of the substrate allows each bonded abrasive grain to cut in the same plane, which yields an extremely even scratch pattern for consistent smoothness.

Like other backing materials, polyester films come in several weights. These weights are numbered 1 to 7 (see the chart at left). The numbers represent actual thickness, in mils (a mil is $\frac{1}{1000}$ in.). Coarser grits typically come on the heavier backings, while ultra-fine and micro-fine grits are available on the thinner films.

While fairly common in production woodworking, film-backed abrasive products are generally too expensive for every day bare-wood sanding tasks. However, more and more woodworkers are favoring them for final smooth sanding on fine-grain hardwoods, and for leveling and polishing a finish.

SCREEN

Sanding screens—pieces of plastic mesh coated on all surfaces with abrasive grit—were designed primarily for sanding drywall in house construction and remodeling. The gypsum inner core of drywall produces a white powder that loads (clogs the abrasive grains of) standard sandpapers very quickly. For this reason, sanding screens have found favor among some woodworkers for sanding painted surfaces and leveling primers, for fine-sanding gummy woods (such as teak and pine), and for smoothing solid-surface materials (such as Corian).

Bonds and Coatings

By definition, a coated abrasive has mineral grains that are glued to a backing material. Gluing is a two-part process, including a make coat and a size coat that serve to bond and secure the grains (see the sidebar on pp. 6-7). Additionally, an abrasive may receive an anti-loading coating, to make it more resistant to gumming up with swarf (sanding debris) during use, and/or a back treatment, to make it easier to mount and use. All these processes significantly affect the way an abrasive product performs and how long it lasts, as can the density of abrasive grains on the backing.

CLOSED COAT VS. OPEN COAT

Even before the abrasive grains are glued to their backing, an important decision is made that affects the cutting performance of the final product: how densely to apply the mineral. Covering the backing material 90% to 95% virtually blankets the backing with abrasive grains, creating what's referred to as a "closed-coat" paper. Alternatively, a 50% to 70% covering produces what's called an "open-coat" paper (see the photo at right).

Closed-coat sandpapers provide the greatest number of abrasive points on a surface, for the most aggressive sanding. This is why closed-coat abrasives are preferred for heavy-duty operations, such as grinding away lots of metal in a short time. For woodworking applications, though, more isn't usually better. This is because sanding swarf needs a place to go immediately after it's been abraded, before it leaves the surface of the sandpaper. The tiny open spaces between grains on a sheet of open-coat sandpaper provides relief for swarf, just as the gullets on a sawblade provide clearance for chips cut by the blade's teeth. In contrast, a closed-coat abrasive is more likely to load and eventually burn and glaze the surface of the abrasive. The heat generated reduces the life of the abrasive belt, disc or drum as well.

Because they are less likely to load up, open-coat sandpapers are the better choice for sanding soft, gummy woods, such as pine and jelutong, or oily, resinous woods, such as teak and rosewood. Open-coat papers are also a blessing for sanding or polishing clear-finished and painted surfaces (see p. 87).

While open-coat abrasives are clearly a better choice for most woodworking operations, you'll still find lots of closed-coat products in woodshops today. Part of this is due to misconception: Because open-coat papers usually cost the same as closed-coat papers, many woodworkers feel they are getting "less grit for the buck" if they buy open-coat products. Also, because closed-coat products are ubiquitous in the metalworking and auto industries (where so many woodworking abrasives come from), you sometimes find closed-coat sanding products in woodworking supply catalogs or hardware and home supply stores (if you're unsure about what you're buying, ask the dealer or manufacturer). If you do use closed-coat abrasives for heavy-duty power sanding, it's important to run them at slower speeds (see pp. 137-138) and to clean them more often (see pp. 96-97) to reduce loading and burning.

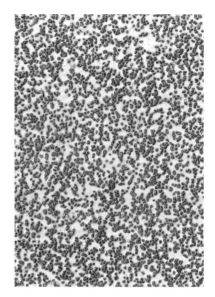

The surface of open-coat paper is covered only 50% to 70% with abrasive mineral. The spaces between grains provide clearance for sanding swarf, making the paper less susceptible to loading than closed-coat paper, which is entirely covered with abrasive mineral.

MAKE-COAT AND SIZE-COAT ADHESIVES

Because of all the stress and strain abrasive grains are subjected to during sanding (especially power sanding), a two-part process is necessary for gluing them to their backing (see the drawing below). The first step, the make coat, bonds the particles to the backing. The second step, the size coat, flows an extra layer of adhesive over and around each particle, further anchoring the particles to the backing and helping them resist sanding forces. The choice of adhesives affects the strength and flexibility of the sandpaper as well as how it will perform and how long it will last.

Two types of adhesives are commonly used for coating abrasives: hide glue and resin. Either may be used for make or size coats, and in various combinations. A filler, such as calcium carbonate, is sometimes used with other adhesives as a size coat. The chart on the facing page gives a quick comparison of strength and flexibility for various adhesive-bond systems.

Hide-glue bond Animal hide glue (known simply as "glue" in abrasive-coating vernacular) is by far the cheapest of the coating adhesives. Its virtues are that it provides an inexpensive and flexible means of bonding and fixing grit particles to a backing. Its flexibility makes glue-bond papers great for hand-sanding curves or small details (garnet paper is usually glue bonded). But more significantly, the glue's flexibility allows abrasive grains to deflect

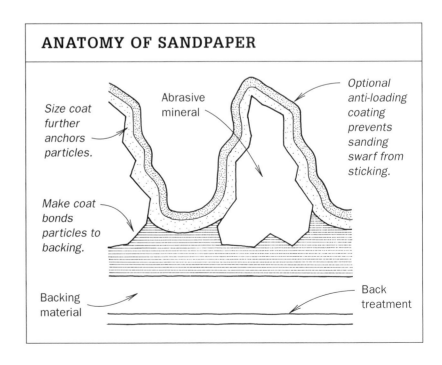

ANATOMY OF SANDPAPER

Size coat further anchors particles.

Abrasive mineral

Optional anti-loading coating prevents sanding swarf from sticking.

Make coat bonds particles to backing.

Backing material

Back treatment

Abrasive-Bond Systems

Make adhesive	Size adhesive	Type or trade name/designation	Strength	Flexibility
Hide glue	Hide glue	Gluebond, GB	Weakest	Most flexible
Glue and filler	Glue and filler	GLB; Grit-Lok-Bond (3M)	↑	↑
Hide glue	Urea resin	Resinite; RN, RES (3M)		
Urea resin	Urea resin	Resin bond; RB	↓	↓
Phenolic resin	Phenolic resin	Waterproof, WOD Wetordry (3M)	Strongest	Stiffest

somewhat under sanding pressure, so glue-bond sandpapers tend to leave a scratch pattern that's finer than the scratch pattern left by a resin-bond paper of the same grit.

Because hide glue is heat sensitive, glue-bond paper is a poor choice for power-sanding applications. It is also water soluble, so it isn't used by itself on wet/dry papers.

Hide glue can be used for both make and size coats or used as a make coat with a filler or resin size coat (papers may be also be coated with varnish, to make them waterproof). Mixing hide glue with a filler (which has no adhesive properties of its own) creates what's called a "modified glue bond." The filler makes the bond tougher and more heat resistant. Some manufacturers use fillers with resins as well.

Resin bond In contrast to animal glues, bonds made with either urea-formaldehyde or phenolic resins generally offer greater resistance to heat and are more durable. This makes them the best all-around bond system for power-sanding operations (with a few caveats, as we shall see). On the down side, resin-bonded papers are less flexible and have a tendency to leave a harsher, more scratchy finish in fine grits than glue-bonded papers.

Urea-formaldehyde resin is a thermosetting adhesive, which makes it especially good for machine sanding belts and drums, which must handle high heat. It is often used as make and size coats on high-quality products using ceramic grit minerals. Sometimes used as a size over a hide-glue make coat (referred to as RN construction in the trades), urea-formaldehyde resin actually chemically alters hide glue to make it water resistant.

Resin-bonded abrasives are a good choice for tough, long-lasting sanding belts. Unfortunately, the thermoplastic resins used to bond the grit tend to load up when sanding off excess wood glues and most wood finishes.

Although they're less flexible than urea-formaldehyde resins, phenolic-resin make and size coats are often used for high-performance applications, such as belts for thicknessing sanders. Tough and durable, phenolic resins are highly water resistant and provide good anchorage for minerals, thereby increasing the life of the abrasive product. Besides being the stiffest of bond systems, phenolics also have the unfortunate affinity to load, especially when sanding plastic coatings, such as PVA wood glues (yellow or white carpenter's glue) and clear wood finishes (see the photo at left). Also, phenolic-resin-coated belts that are 80 grit and finer are difficult to manufacture with an anti-loading coating.

ANTI-LOADING COATINGS

A treatment that is often applied to the surface of sandpaper over the size coat is an anti-loading coating. These soapy, white powdery coatings are metal salts, such as zinc stearate or calcium stearate, with names such as Fre-Cut (3M) and Dri-Lube (Carborundum). An anti-loading coating acts as a lubricant between the sandpaper and the wood, thereby reducing the heat produced while sanding—a real plus in power-sanding applications.

Besides attenuating heat, anti-loading coatings decrease the tendency of abrasive papers to load up with dust and swarf (sanding residue). This helps tremendously when sanding bare wood surfaces, especially hard, oily woods, such as teak. Anti-loading coatings are also helpful when leveling or polishing a finish or scuff sanding between coats. Most finishes are thermoplastic, and the heat generated by sanding makes their swarf into little semi-molten balls, which readily gum up the mineral grains or stick to the surface of the work.

One of the few shortcoming of anti-loading coatings is that they wear off fairly quickly (which is one reason you won't find them on super-long-wearing ceramic abrasive products). Also, when sanding a finish, bits of stearate powder that remain on the surface can cause contamination, so it's important to clean the surface off before topcoating (see pp. 69-70).

BACK TREATMENTS

Besides the coatings that go into manufacturing the "working side" of a piece of sandpaper, there are treatments for the back side. Some, which are intended for use with a sanding block or the pad of a portable power sander, make it quicker and easier to mount a sheet or disc to a backing. Others, such as anti-static coatings, affect the way the abrasives themselves work.

Pressure-sensitive adhesives You can use just about any glue to stick a piece of sandpaper to a block or pad. The only problem is, how do you get it off again when the paper wears out? Pressure-sensitive adhesives, known in the industry as PSAs, are usually high-strength acrylic glues applied to the back of some sanding products, like sticky-back paper rolls or the discs for random-orbit sanders (see the photo below). While sticky enough to bond paper to just about any smooth backing, they don't set and dry like most glues. This means that when the paper is spent (or when you want to change grits), you can peel off the old sheet or disc and stick another one on. PSA-backed abrasive products are quick to change and relatively cheap, which makes them a staple in production woodworking shops. However, they have their share of problems. Pressure-sensitive adhesives must be heated to room temperature before use—they don't stick worth a darn in an environment cooler than 40°F. Further, they tend to stick aggressively to vinyl backing pads on random-orbit sanders, so they can be a bear to get off if not removed immediately after use. Also, the sticky coating picks up dust like a magnet and reduces or defeats its ability to stick to a backing, so PSA-backed abrasive products must be stored with care in dusty shops. (For more information on using and storing PSA sandpapers, see pp.100-102.)

Sandpaper backings coated with pressure-sensitive adhesive (PSA) are quick and easy to stick down to sanding blocks or backing pads. PSA discs are the abrasives of choice for random-orbit sanders used in production woodworking.

Hook-and-loop-type backings are convenient for portable power tools, such as a detail sander. The hooked backing pad holds the loop-backed paper firmly in position, yet paper can be changed, and reused, readily.

Hook-and-loop fasteners There are few garments, pieces of luggage, or sports accoutrements that have escaped the application of hook-and-loop style fasteners (Velcro, manufactured by Velcro Industries B.V., is the most common brand). Many abrasive products also use a hook-and-loop mounting system. A woolly material (the loop part) on the back of the sandpaper, engages its counterpart "hooky" material on the face of the sanding block or backing pad. The loops and hooks cling to each other with surprising force when pressed together, yet release (with a satisfying ripping sound) when you peel the paper from the block or pad. Hook-and-loop backings are commonly used on discs for random-orbit sanders and triangular-head detail sanders (see the photo at left).

Though more costly than PSA discs, hook-and-loop discs have become de rigeur for many small-shop woodworkers because of the ease with which you can change grits and because you can reuse the peeled-off disc without its becoming ruined by dust (the common fate of used, but not spent, PSA discs).

ANTI-STATIC COATINGS

A sandpaper backing treatment that's become available to small woodworkers only recently, anti-static coatings were developed years ago for industrial sanding belts that build up high amounts of static electricity during heavy use. A static charge developed by a spinning belt can not only zap the operator (static sparks can even start fires), but the positive charge also tends to make dust, which is negatively charged, cling to the belt. This "static cling" encourages loading and defeats dust collection to some degree. An anti-static coating (usually graphite) applied to the belt backing helps cut down static, so the belt releases dust particles more readily, making dust collection a lot more efficient.

Products Made from Coated Abrasives

In the factory, coated abrasive is manufactured in long, wide sheets (called jumbo rolls), which are cut, stamped, punched, or otherwise fashioned into smaller sheets or discs, belts, drums, rolls, flap wheels, and other products (see the photo on the facing page). While most of this process is of little interest to you and me, there is one aspect of fabrication that is worth scrutiny: how the ends of a continuous sanding belt or sanding drum are joined together. This simple splice has a lot to do with the performance and longevity of the product.

Abrasives come in many shapes and sizes. Once an abrasive paper has been manufactured into a jumbo roll, various products may be cut out and made into sheets, discs, belts, drums, rolls, and flap wheels.

BELT AND DRUM SPLICES

You'll find various types of splices joining the ends on sanding belts and drums—butt splices, zigzag splices, and lap splices (see the drawing on p. 34). As with everything else in life, each has its pluses and minuses.

Butt splices The simple butt splice joins the ends of a belt or drum together the way a butt joint connects the corners of a cabinet frame: The two blunt-cut ends of the belt fabric just butt up together, secured on the front or back by a piece of tape. Since the ends don't overlap, you can run these belts or drums in either direction. (If a butt-spliced belt has directional arrows printed on the backing, it's probably because the belt was made from a jumbo roll that was pre-printed for lap-spliced belts. It's usually okay to ignore the arrows and run the belt either way.) Reversing the belt allows you to get more life out of the abrasive: When you use the cutting edges of each grain from both sides, the abrasive wears more evenly. You'll also find it's easier to clean a belt clogged with sanding swarf if you reverse it first (see p. 98).

Depending on how a belt or drum is manufactured, the seam may run straight across or at an angle. Of these, the angled butt is a bit stronger, because a longer piece of tape joins the ends. However, the straight butt is more resistant to damage at the edges. (Regardless of the direction you run an angled splice, one edge always has the pointed end of the splice running forward, where it can snag on sharp edge of the work and tear.)

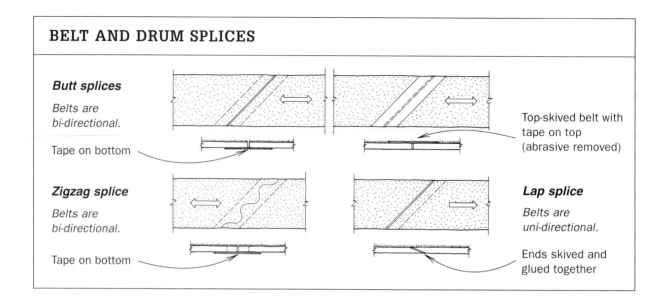

BELT AND DRUM SPLICES

Butt splices

Belts are
bi-directional.

Tape on bottom

Top-skived belt with
tape on top
(abrasive removed)

Zigzag splice

Belts are
bi-directional.

Tape on bottom

Lap splice

Belts are
uni-directional.

Ends skived and
glued together

Because tape is applied to the back of the belt to make a splice, thicker cloth tapes cause a rhythmic bumping during sanding as the splice passes between the sander's platen and the work (the bump is somewhat less abrupt with angled splices). The bumping can leave sanding marks on the wood when using a portable belt sander, or make it more difficult to do precise work on a stationary machine. Most better-quality belts use a very thin, strong plastic tape, which makes the bumping much less noticeable.

Another way to minimize butt-splice bumping is to "top skive" the belt (remove abrasive mineral in the area of the splice) and apply tape to the working side of the belt. This leaves the backing smooth (and smooth running), but creates the weakest and most vulnerable of all splices. Don't choose this type of splice if you intend to use the belt for heavy sanding duties.

Zigzag splices On a zigzag-spliced belt, the ends are cut in a sine-wave pattern and butt-joined together. The zigzag creates a mechanical joint along the splice (see the photo on the facing page). And the little interlocking tabs allow better adhesion for the backing tape, making for a very strong splice. The tabs also prevent belts from "hinging" at the splice (constantly bending and unbending the splicing tape), which helps them to last longer when run across the smaller-diameter rollers of portable sanders.

Because the ends are butted, zigzag-spliced belts can be run in either direction. To prevent bumping, a very thin (2-mil), strong tape is applied to the backing, and the seam is usually compressed. Just as with butt splices, the joint in a zigzag splice may run square or at an angle across the belt, the latter being stronger.

Lap splices Lap splices are made by overlapping and gluing the ends of the belt together. It's the strongest way to make a belt or drum joint, but it's also the least flexible and most prone to bumping. Bumping can be reduced by making the lapping ends thinner, a process called skiving (see the drawing on the facing page). Unlike butt-spliced and zigzag-spliced belts, lap-spliced belts are uni-directional—that is, they may be run in only one direction—which limits their useful life.

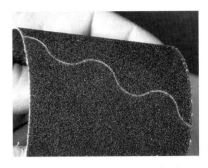

The undulating cut at the ends of a zigzag belt splice creates a strong mechanical joint, yet allows the belt to run as smoothly as one with a butt splice, which is weaker.

Other Abrasive Products

Besides sandpaper, there are lots of other coated abrasive products that easily find a useful role in the woodshop. Among the most popular products are non-woven plastic abrasives, foam-backed abrasive pads, steel wool, and metal-backed abrasives, all of which are discussed below. There are still other bonded-grit media, such as diamond files, honing stones, and grinding wheels, which are beyond the scope of this book. For information on these tools, see Leonard Lee's *The Complete Guide to Sharpening* (The Taunton Press, 1995).

NON-WOVEN PLASTIC ABRASIVES
Unlike standard sandpapers, which have abrasive minerals glued to a flat backing, non-woven plastic abrasive pads are truly three-dimensional abrasives. They consist of a freeform matrix of polyester or polyester/nylon fibers, to which are glued abrasive grains. Rather than just coating the surface, the grains are blown into the matrix of the fibers and dispersed throughout in random fashion. This construction creates a cushioned abrasive pad that's comfortable to hold and easy to form to fit the surface of the work.

Non-woven abrasive pads are great for a wide variety of tasks, such as fine sanding, cleaning, polishing, and deburring wood as well as metal and plastic. They can be cut to whatever size you want with ordinary scissors, and they conform readily to irregular shapes, so they are ideal for smooth-sanding moldings, turnings, or

Non-woven abrasive pads are easy to hold and conform readily to round or irregular surfaces. They're good for smoothing or dewhiskering shaped parts, moldings, and turnings.

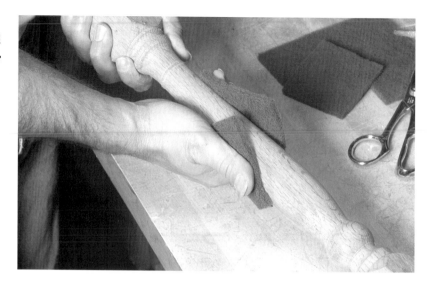

carved details (see the photo above). Their versatility, relatively low cost, and user-friendly qualities have made non-woven plastic abrasives, such as 3M's "ScotchBrite," a staple in most woodworkers' supply cabinets.

Because the abrasive grains in a non-woven plastic abrasive pad are bonded to flexible fibers, they cut less aggressively than regular sandpapers. This is not a bad thing. Sanding with these pads leaves a finer, softer scratch pattern than you would get from regular sandpaper of the same grit. The softer scratch pattern means that finer-grit non-woven abrasives are a good choice for final-sanding bare wood, such as when dewhiskering a surface (see pp. 65-68) or for polishing a finish or scuff sanding between coats. Also, their thickness and porosity makes non-woven plastic abrasives much less susceptible to surface loading than regular sandpaper. Disc-shaped pads are great to use on a random-orbit sander (they stick directly onto hook-and-loop system backing pads) and are unlikely to cause deep scratches or swirl marks. Use coarser-grit pads for stripping a finish. Since they are made from plastic, the pads are waterproof, so wet sanding is no problem. And they are safe to use when working with water-based finishes, where steel wool can create problems (see p. 38).

Abrasive pads come in different degrees of coarseness. Color-coded in black, green, maroon, gray and white, from coarse to extra fine, this color grading system seems to be fairly consistent among manufacturers. (Remember, though, that because of the cushioning effect of the pad, each grit produces a scratch pattern equivalent to regular sandpaper that's one or two grits finer.) Black pads have an 80-grit silicon-carbide mineral bonded to heavy-filament nylon and are designed for removing paint and stripping finishes. Green pads (impregnated with 180-grit aluminum-oxide mineral) and maroon pads (with 280-grit aluminum oxide) are great for sanding and polishing bare wood and scuff-sanding finishes. Gray pads, with a 360-grit aluminum-oxide mineral, are fine for polishing a finish or to soften the sheen of a glossy finish (see pp. 81-82). Gray pads are also good for applying wax; the abrasive action helps clean off old wax and gunk on the surface. White pads, which contain only non-abrasive talc, may be used for final polishing and for buffing.

Besides rectangular pads, non-woven plastic abrasives come in other handy forms, such as random-orbit discs, mandrel-mounted polishing discs (for sanding contours and moldings) and small flap wheels. One style of flap wheel (made by 3M) has interspersed segments of maroon ScotchBrite and cloth-backed aluminum-oxide sandpaper, so the wheel sands and polishes at the same time.

FOAM-BACKED ABRASIVES

Unlike non-woven plastic abrasives, which have grits throughout their thickness, foam-backed abrasives have just one or more surfaces coated with abrasive grit. The grit is size coated with a durable resin adhesive that not only keeps the grit from falling off, but is also waterproof, so the pads can be washed off if the surface loads up). Foam-backed abrasives are handy for sanding curved parts and surfaces where their foam core molds easily to the shape of the part. The foam provides a cushioned grip (and disperses heat), so they're comfortable to use for extended periods.

Foam-backed abrasives come in the form of thin pads and thicker blocks (see the photo below). The pads have abrasive applied only to one surface; the rest is just soft foam that's easy on

Foam-backed pads and blocks are essentially sponges that have been coated with mineral grit. They are available in a wide range of grits.

the fingers. Because they are thin, these pads can conform to very small radiuses and get into very tight areas, such as the details on a carving. Foam blocks are usually rectangular semi-rigid sponges that are coated with abrasive material on their four longest sides. While not as flexible as thin foam pads, blocks provide a more rigid backing and support, which is better for sanding flat or slightly curved parts and surfaces, or for rounding over edges. Some blocks have one edge angled at 45° for sanding in grooves and corners.

STEEL WOOL

As much a mainstay of the traditional woodshop as sandpaper, steel wool is still preferred to more modern non-woven plastic abrasives by many woodworkers. Depending on its coarseness, steel wool may be used for jobs as varied as removing an old finish, dewhiskering bare wood prior to finishing, and polishing a finish to a rich satiny luster. Steel wool is available in seven grades, from #3 (very coarse) to #0000 (ultra fine). The coarse and medium grades (#3 to #0) are good for stripping finishes or cleaning metal parts (including taking the rust off machine tables). Fine grades (#00 to #000) are good for smoothing or dulling a high-gloss paint or varnish finish. Ultra fine (#0000) is best for rubbing out a final finish to a satin luster. You can buy steel wool in a long roll rather than as separate pads (see Sources of Supply, which begins on p. 209). Some woodworkers prefer rolls because they can tear off and use only as much as they need at a time.

Steel wool's chief shortcoming is that loose fibers can snag on sharp edges, small splinters, or even on the fibers of coarse-grained woods, such as ash and red oak. Worse, a light oil that's applied to most steel wools to prevent rusting can deposit on bare wood or finished surfaces and contaminate the finish; for this reason, you should buy de-oiled steel wool whenever possible (see Sources of Supply). Steel wool is also a no-no if you are applying water-based finishes, as discussed below.

BRONZE WOOL

Whenever you apply water to a wood that has a high tannin content, such as oak, maple, or ash, any stray bits of steel wool embedded in the surface are likely to react and cause black streaks. This can easily happen when dewhiskering or finish-sanding wood in preparation for a water-based finish. One way to avoid problems is to use a non-woven plastic abrasive pad; another is to use bronze wool. As you might guess, bronze wool is just like steel wool, only it's made from filaments of bronze (an alloy of copper and tin). Since it is nonferrous, bronze wool doesn't react with tannin and water. It's available in three grades (fine, medium, and coarse) but can be hard to find locally. Check your local boatyard or marine supply, or see Sources of Supply.

MICRO-MESH

A unique product that consists of a flexible fabric backing coated with ultra- to micro-fine grits, Micro-Mesh, which uses a proprietary grading system, is available in grits from 1500 (30 microns) down to 12000 (1 micron). A layer of resilient material between the mineral grains and the backing provides a cushioning effect and improves the scratch pattern. Micro-Mesh can be used in lieu of fine non-woven plastic abrasive pads and steel wool for sanding bare wood. Wrapped around a flexible foam-rubber block, small sheets of Micro-Mesh can be used dry or with lubricants for leveling, rubbing out, and polishing a fine finish. They are also great for cleaning up the surface around shellac-stick burn-ins and other finish repairs. In the super-fine grits, Micro-Mesh can be used to polish plastic laminates, such as Formica, as well as clear plastics. The sheets can be washed to remove sanding swarf and reused indefinitely.

SANDING CORDS AND TAPES

Imagine taking a piece of string or tape and covering it with abrasive grit and you've got a picture of sanding cords and tapes. They allow you to get into the nooks and crannies of a turned form, such as fillets, coves, and V-grooves (or into grooves and tight corners on a non-turned part, for that matter). Sanding cords and tapes come in a various diameters and widths, so you can refine and smooth details with lots of control and precision. The coarser grits are good for cleaning up torn grain or deep scratches, while the finer grits allow smooth final sanding.

METAL-BACKED ABRASIVES

One final product worthy of mention is the metal-backed abrasive plate. Depending on the brand, these thin sheets of metal have been coated with carbide particles or acid etched, creating thousands of sharp "grit" edges. Metal-backed abrasives cut very aggressively and last for a long time. (One maker, Sandvik, claims that its "Sandplates" last up to 100 times longer than regular sandpaper.) When they become loaded, you clean the surface with a brass wire brush (see the photo at right). Metal-backed abrasives come in coarse, medium, and fine grades, and in various forms, including hand files and sanding blocks. The coarser-grit files are terrific for hand-shaping work, while the sanding blocks are a reasonable replacement for sandpaper when leveling and smoothing wood.

Unlike single-use sandpaper, metal-backed abrasive plates are durable and may be reused indefinitely. When the abrasive grains becomes clogged, the surface can be cleaned with a brass wire brush.

2

Shaping, Leveling, and Smoothing Bare Wood

There are three chores in a woodshop that sandpaper does best: shaping, leveling, and smoothing bare wood. Shaping is the process of grinding wood using coarse-grit sandpapers; it is useful for tasks such as rough-forming parts for furniture, carvings, and sculpture. Leveling removes dents, defects, and excessive roughness to flatten a surface in preparation for smoothing. Smoothing removes and refines scratches to clean up a bare wood surface before finishing.

You can use just about any abrasives or methods and do a fair job of shaping, leveling, or smoothing wood. But you'll get better and more consistent results—and spend a lot less time sanding—if you use the appropriate abrasive techniques and materials. The information in this chapter will help you select the right sandpaper grits and sanding techniques for the job at hand.

Abrasive Shaping

Coarse abrasives can provide an effective way of shaping complex parts without the need for special carving tools or the skills required to use them. Rapidly removing wood by splitting and cleaving using gouges, planes, or drawknives can be risky, as any false move may split off parts you wanted to keep. Sandpaper, on the other hand, abrades wood in a chosen area regardless of grain direction; as long as you don't sand off too much, you remove only the areas you choose.

TOOLS AND GRITS FOR GRINDING

Abrasive shaping can be done by hand, but it is generally accomplished using portable power tools—and a few stationary machines as well. Among the arsenal of portables that may be used for grinding wood, three versatile tools stand out: the right-angle grinder, the portable belt sander, and the narrow-belt sander (see the photo below). Equipped with a coarse-grit disc or belt, these tools are capable of forming a great variety of shapes, from smooth, large-radius curves and spheres to small dimples and concavities. In the hands of an experienced user, these tools can remove stock faster than can be done with a spokeshave, scorp, gouge, or other carving tool. For smaller or more intricate work, a die grinder (or Dremel tool) may be fitted with small-diameter sanding drums and discs. These smaller tools allow access to hard-to-reach areas for shaping or refining details on moldings, carvings, and sculpture.

These three tools—the right-angle grinder (foreground), the narrow-belt sander (center), and the light-weight belt sander (background)— are well suited to the tasks of shaping wood parts and grinding away wood rapidly.

If the workpiece itself is manageable in size, it's often desirable to bring the work to the tool rather than the other way around. If you work carefully and safely, a stationary drum, edge, or disc sander can be used to shape small parts freehand (see pp. 146-147). Regardless of the power-sanding equipment you choose, make sure to protect your respiratory health. Fit the tool or machine with proper dust collection, and/or use a mask or air-cleaning device; see pp. 148-155 for details.

Since the whole idea of abrasive shaping is to grind away wood rapidly, coarse-grit papers are essential. It's typical to use 24-grit or 36-grit sandpapers for the roughest work, stepping up to 50 to 80 grit for subsequent refinement to prepare for smoothing. The high density of abrasive grains allows closed-coat abrasive products to grind wood aggressively, but they also load up and burn more quickly. If this poses a problem, try slowing the tool down. You'll want to switch to open-coat abrasives when grinding gummy or resinous woods. Slower tool speeds are also a good idea, as grinding will generate less heat, thus reduce burning and loading (slower speeds can actually quicken stock removal and extend abrasive life; see pp. 137-138). Whether you use an open-coat or closed-coat sandpaper, you'll get the best performance from high-quality products coated with a resin-on-resin system (see p. 29). Resin make and size coats keeps large abrasive particles from coming off during the rigors of hogging off wood.

If you plan to use bladed woodworking tools—chisels and carving tools—or rasps and rifflers to add detail or to refine shaped parts, it is very important to clean the surface of the wood thoroughly after abrasive grinding. This is because any grains of grit that remain embedded in the surface (especially on open-pore woods, like red oak) will quickly dull and/or nick sharp tool edges. Give the workpiece a thorough vacuuming first, using a stiff-bristled brush to scrub particles form pores and crevices. Then don a face mask and eye protection and use high-pressure compressed air to dislodge embedded grits (see pp. 69-70).

SHAPING CURVED PARTS

When abrasive-shaping a curved or shapely part, start by rough-sawing away as much waste as you can before grinding. Roughing out will save a lot of time (and sandpaper) and create a lot less sawdust to have to deal with. If you're making small-radius three-dimensional forms (such as newel-post finials or the head of a figure), it's efficient to create the shape by forming several facets, then grinding away their edges (see the photo on the facing page).

Each time you grind away an edge, you create a smaller facet that forms new edges. Repeat the process until the shape approaches the curve you want. Working this way not only removes stock quickly, but also reduces the contact area between the wood and the sandpaper, thereby minimizing heat and loading.

For panels and parts that curve in only one direction, here is a neat trick you can use to help regulate how deep to grind on different areas: Cut a series of kerfs across the workpiece to define the shape of the final curved surface (see the drawing below). The kerfs can be cut on a table saw or radial-arm saw, or with a portable circular saw (alternatively, you can drill a series of holes as depth guides, in lieu of kerfs). As you work the abrasive tool across the surface, the kerfs provide a graphic indication of how much stock you have removed, and when to stop grinding when you have attained the desired depth of cut.

As you get closer to the final shape, take smaller and smaller cuts to create smooth, continuous curves. If you're power sanding, a nice way to do the final refinement and smoothing on curves is with flexible sanding devices, such as a pneumatic drum, flap wheel, or brush-backed sander (see pp. 173-174 and pp. 206-208).

You can rough-shape a three-dimensional form quickly by creating and refining a series of small facets, as shown here with a flap disc in a right-angle grinder. Once the rough form is achieved, the facets may be rounded over to a smooth curved surface.

DEFINING A CURVE WITH KERFS

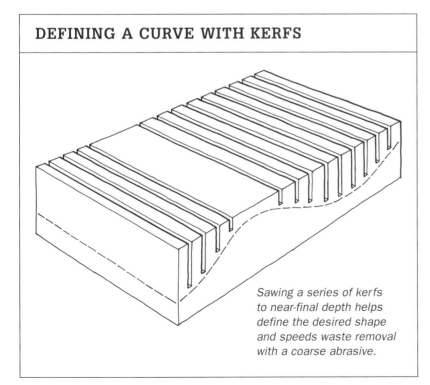

Sawing a series of kerfs to near-final depth helps define the desired shape and speeds waste removal with a coarse abrasive.

Leveling a Surface

Before you can sand a surface smooth, you must make it level and free from defects such as dings, dents, and tearout. If you have a stationary drum or wide-belt sander that's properly adjusted, getting flat, defect-free parts usually isn't difficult. Thickness planers don't have a problem creating flat surfaces (as long as you joint out the cup in boards or panels before you plane them). However, even sharp planer knives or hand-plane blades can cause deep tearouts on figured or squirrely-grained woods. Defects left after planing are best removed by abrasive means: sanding by hand and/or with portable power sanders.

The point of leveling is to sand below all defects and end up with a flat, consistent surface that's ready for further smoothing. This sounds simple, but it can be infuriatingly difficult to achieve, because the natural tendency is to handle defects locally by sanding them directly (see the drawing below), which causes dimples. Dimples really spoil the appearance of prominent surfaces such as tabletops and cabinet door panels. To maintain flatness, you must sand the entire surface of the part down to just below the depth of the defect. Since tearouts typically go $\frac{1}{32}$ in. deep and can be much deeper—$\frac{1}{16}$ in. or more—you can end up removing a tremendous amount of material! Quick stock removal is best accomplished by leveling in multiple passes.

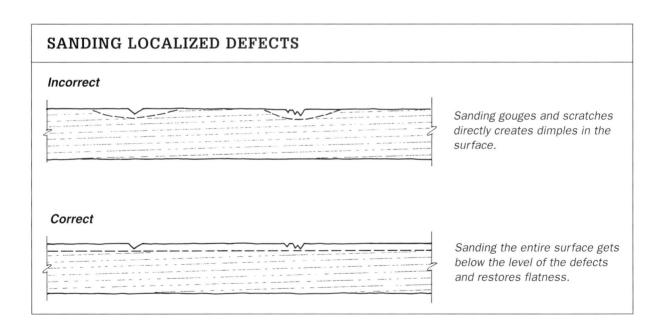

SANDING LOCALIZED DEFECTS

Incorrect

Sanding gouges and scratches directly creates dimples in the surface.

Correct

Sanding the entire surface gets below the level of the defects and restores flatness.

LEVELING IN THREE PASSES

For the quickest stock removal, level a surface by sanding at an angle relative to the direction of the grain (see the sidebar on pp. 46-47). While choice of the coarsest grit to start with depends on the condition of the wood surface, as discussed on pp. 48-50, leveling unplaned wood typically starts with 40-grit or 50-grit paper for the first pass, 80-grit paper for the second, and 120-grit paper for the third, as needed. Ideally, you want to remove 70% of the waste with the first pass, 20% with the second, and the remaining 10% with the third. The three-pass technique helps you remove stock evenly as you go, leaving a level surface devoid of deep scratches and ready for painting or smooth sanding.

Regardless of whether you sand by hand or by machine, maintaining flatness requires you to work consistently and evenly across the whole of a surface, especially if it is a large panel or tabletop. One key to quick stock removal while maintaining flatness is a large, rigid backing for the abrasive. A stiff, flat backing helps keep more abrasive grains in contact with the workpiece for more aggressive sanding, while the large surface area of the block or platen helps distribute sanding pressure evenly. For hand sanding, it's a good idea to use a sanding plane (see the photo below and pp. 115-117).

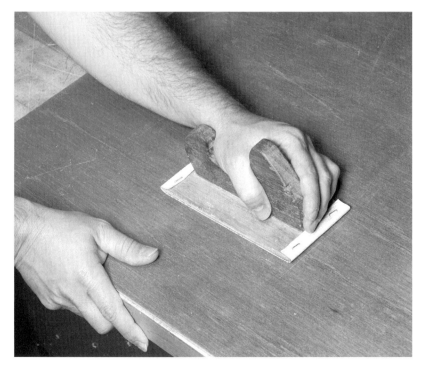

A sanding plane can help you level and smooth a large surface, while keeping it flat. You can make a sanding plane from scrap wood and simply staple on the sandpaper.

Sanding across the Grain for Quick Stock Removal

Most of us have been taught to sand wood with the grain, but this isn't always the best technique. When you want to hog wood away quickly, such as when doing abrasive shaping, leveling, or even during the coarser-grit stages of smooth sanding, you'll remove stock more rapidly by sanding at a 45° to 60° angle across the wood's grain (see the photo below). At this orientation the abrasive grains aggressively remove large bundles of wood fibers, rather than just slicing between the bundles, as they would when sanding with the grain. An angled attack also removes stock more quickly than sanding perpendicularly across the grain, which slices fibers, but doesn't remove them as well.

You'll work most efficiently by changing sanding direction after each pass (see the drawing on the facing page), because that way you'll be able to see when all the scratches from the previous pass are gone; any remaining scratches appear as little crosshatches. Take the first pass sanding in one direction at an angle across the grain, then change grits and take the

The fastest way to remove a lot of stock is to sand at an angle across the grain. A power sander run across the grain this way will quickly shape parts or flatten rough surfaces.

For power sanding, a wide, well-balanced belt sander is just the ticket . You can add stability to a narrow or poorly balanced belt sander by fitting it with a sanding frame (see p. 160). While capable of removing stock quickly, random-orbit sanders don't sand evenly enough to keep large surfaces flat. If you're faced with a really large job, such as sanding a whole kitchen's worth of cabinet doors, it's worthwhile to rent time on a wide-belt sander (if you don't own one) at a local cabinet shop.

second pass sanding at an angle across the grain in the other direction. If your sanding schedule calls for more grits, continue to alternate directions on subsequent passes. On your final smoothing pass (or last couple of passes), sand with the grain to remove the cross-grain scratches left by the previous pass.

This technique works when performing any sort of straight-line sanding action, either by hand with a sanding plane or when machine sanding with a belt sander or in-line pneumatic sander. It even works when running stock through a stationary wide-belt or drum sander (see p. 140). It doesn't apply to disc, orbital, and random-orbit sanders, since their sanding action is rotary, not straight.

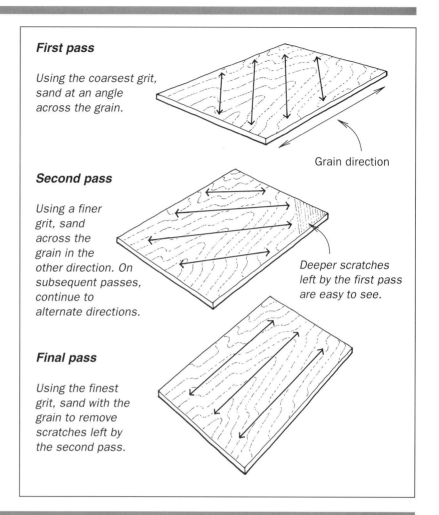

First pass

Using the coarsest grit, sand at an angle across the grain.

Grain direction

Second pass

Using a finer grit, sand across the grain in the other direction. On subsequent passes, continue to alternate directions.

Deeper scratches left by the first pass are easy to see.

Final pass

Using the finest grit, sand with the grain to remove scratches left by the second pass.

FLUSH TRIMMING

Abrasive leveling is also useful for flush trimming, such as when evening up the overhanging edge of a cabinet face frame flush with the cabinet side. Flush trimming can be done with a hand plane or with a flush-trimming bit in a router, but abrasives get the job done without tearing out or burning the wood. You can also use abrasives to flush up adjacent surfaces, such as the surfaces of two boards glued edge to edge. Before any trimming job, it's prudent to scrape off any beads or drips of excess glue that have dried on the surface. You can sand away the glue, but it's likely to load up the sandpaper. One insidious problem to watch out for when trimming face frames on plywood-sided cabinets is sand-though of thin face veneers (to learn a method for preventing this, see pp. 111-112).

Abrasives technicians say that the biggest mistake most woodworkers make when leveling is not starting with a coarse enough grit to sand out defects. Most of us (I admit, I used to think this way too) shy away from coarser sandpapers because we think we'll save time by not having to use as many different grades of sandpaper. Unfortunately, this approach is misguided. Woodworkers often don't sand a piece thoroughly enough because it's taking them too long to sand out defects with a finer-grit paper. For example, removing a $\frac{1}{32}$-in.-deep defect with 120-grit paper alone can take much, much longer than leveling in three passes using 50-, 80-, and 120-grit papers.

Dealing with Subtle Defects

Leveling a surface with sandpaper can usually eliminate surface defects that are easy to spot, such as dents, dings, and areas of torn grain. But there are other defects, such as surface glazing, knife marks, and sticker stain, that can be hard to spot. Unfortunately, they're all too apparent after the finish has been applied, and they're hard to remedy.

Glazing and ripple

Thicknessing or jointing lumber on a machine with dull knives can glaze the wood's surface. A glazed surface won't absorb water-based glues properly, so that glued-up parts may be weak or even fall apart. Surface glazing also retards the absorption of stains and finishes, which can create a blotchy look. Dull or misaligned planer/jointer knives leave a subtle wavy surface pattern, where each knife pass compresses wood in a small arc (see the drawing below). Dull or gummed-up knives and cutters can also cause burns and scorching.

In most cases, you can remove surface glazing and washboard by abrasive leveling. Run the parts through a drum or wide-belt thicknessing sander, or sand them with a portable belt sander (see p. 160). In the case

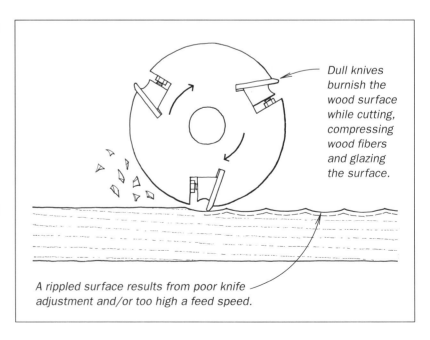

Dull knives burnish the wood surface while cutting, compressing wood fibers and glazing the surface.

A rippled surface results from poor knife adjustment and/or too high a feed speed.

While overly fine papers are a time-consuming choice for leveling, you don't want to use paper that's any coarser than necessary either. Unlike smoothing, where you want to sand every part to the same degree, you can level the various parts of a project with papers of different coarseness, depending on how rough or smooth the parts are to begin with and what specific imperfections you are trying to remove.

The coarsest grit you use on any part should remove all machine and tool marks, including knife chatter marks, burning, and tearouts. The rougher the surface left by previous operations, the coarser the grit you'll need to level below them. Wood with torn grain or other surface defects requires a coarse initial grit—

of surface burns, it's usually better to take another pass on the planer (or shaper/router table, if a molded edge) rather than trying to sand, as burns, like beauty, often run more than skin deep. And don't forget to refit your machines with sharp knives, and endeavor to keep them that way!

Sticker stain

One defect you'll have difficulty sanding out is sticker stain. Present as a bluish-gray streak or patch on the surface of light-colored woods, such as maple and birch (see the photo below left), sticker stain is caused by a fungus that grows in the area of contact between a sticker (a short stick used as a spacer in a stack of boards being dried) and a plank. On raw wood, sticker stains can be very faint and hard to detect, but they become annoyingly clear after finishing, even under a fairly dark wood stain.

You can get rid of sticker stains by thicknessing the wood down below the stain. But even a slight sticker stain may go deep into the wood—easily $\frac{1}{8}$ in. to $\frac{1}{4}$ in. or more! Who wants to pay for 4/4 stock and end up with boards that are $\frac{5}{8}$ in. thick? It's best to avoid sticker-stain problems entirely by not buying or using boards that show even the slightest sign of sticker staining in the first place.

Sticker stain is a problem that often goes unnoticed until stain or finish is applied. These light bands of fungal discoloration (indicated on this poplar board by the pencil) can be nearly impossible to sand out; avoid or cut around them whenever possible.

try 80 grit for softwoods, 60 grit for hardwoods. Figured wood is especially susceptible to tearout, as are woods with interlocked grain (where grain direction changes in adjacent sections, so you can't avoid planing some sections against the grain). It may be a good idea initially to start with these parts thicker than you need, because you can lose a lot of wood during leveling.

Defects also include small dings and dents created by dropped tools or slipped clamps. Setting work down over glue drips that have dried onto a workbench surface is another common cause of small surface dents (avoid these by keeping your benchtop clean). Fortunately, dents can usually be removed by steaming them out with an ordinary household iron applied over a damp cloth—a faster and easier solution than leveling.

For how to handle defects that are not so easy to see as dents, see the sidebar on pp. 48-49.

Sanding Wood Smooth

Making a wood surface smooth is usually a two-part process. First, you level the surface and eliminate all defects, as described above. Second, you remove coarse scratches left from leveling by replacing them with progressively finer scratches (the very definition of the smoothing process). Leveling alone may yield a surface that's smooth enough to prime and paint. But if your project will receive a clear finish, smoothing is necessary to achieve a surface that shows no scratches, only the beauty of the wood's natural grain.

The basic idea of smoothing is to go over the surface several times, each time with a finer grit of sandpaper that removes all the scratches left by the previous grit. Scratches that remain at any stage will only become more prominent as the surface surrounding the scratch is sanded finer. Each successively finer grit leaves a shallower, denser scratch pattern than the grit preceding it. With this goal in mind, it's important to begin with a surface that's flat and defect free. If yours isn't, you should go back and level it (see p. 44) before proceeding with smooth sanding. Alternatively, you might want to consider smoothing wood by scraping it, or using a combination of scraping and sanding, as discussed in the sidebar on the facing page.

Sanding vs. Scraping

In the hands of a skilled user, a well-honed hand scraper is a sensitive yet formidable tool for leveling and smoothing wood. A scraper can remove small scratches and minor surface defects, leaving the wood with a silky-smooth surface that's ready for finish.

Unlike sandpaper, which smooths a surface by creating an even pattern of very fine scratches, a sharp hand scraper actually shaves thin layers of wood cells from the surface (see the photo below right). Because the fibers are sliced rather than abraded, a hand-scraped surface often has a distinctly different tactile feel than a sanded surface, a feel that many woodworkers and fanciers of fine woodwork covet. Even better, scrapers are quiet to use. They don't wear out quickly, like sandpaper, and they create wispy shavings in lieu of clouds of lung-choking dust. Further, the edge of a scraper can be cut and filed to various profiles for use on moldings and shaped edges.

What's to discommend scrapers? Probably their biggest single drawback is that a even a simple straight-edged scraper blade can be tricky to sharpen correctly. Forming a sharp, even "burr" on the edge is a skill that many find frustratingly elusive (especially on scraper edges that are shaped to match moldings). And although a rectangular scraper blade can have four useful edges (two on each long edge), you can go through a lot of sharpenings in a single session if you have a large area to scrape down.

If you're not yet ready to throw your sandpaper away (and, probably, this book with it) to become a scraper worshiper, you might want to try smoothing wood by combining scraping and sanding. One effective technique is to use abrasives for leveling wood and preliminary sanding, and reserve scraping for final surface smoothing. Alternatively, you may wish to final-scrape only the prominent surfaces of your project—a tabletop or desktop, a chair back or bench seat—and fine-sand the rest. Either of these approaches offers the user the tactile experience of a scraped surface, and the maker the expediency of sanding most of the piece. Just be aware that a scraped surface tends to take finishes (especially stains) differently than a sanded one. Therefore, it's a good idea to experiment before splitting up the smoothing operations on your project.

A well-tuned scraper can produce a fine cut that yields neat little shavings. Scraping may be combined with sanding to produce an impressively smooth surface.

Dense, fine-grained hardwoods such as rock maple reveal fine-grit sanding scratches even when they run with the grain.

CHOOSING YOUR FINEST GRIT

Unless sanding is your life (in which case, I'd suggest you consider getting a new life), you don't want to spend any more time sanding than you have to. While sanding to ultra-fine 1000-grit will virtually guarantee a super-smooth final surface, you don't usually have to sand anywhere near that fine to get results that are visually and tactilely satisfying. Some factors to consider when deciding how fine to sand include the species of wood you're working with, the choice of finish and whether or not you'll stain the wood first, and even the visual prominence or importance of the part relative to the rest of your project.

Type of wood It's a fact of life that some woods sand better than others. Hardness, texture, and resin content are among the many characteristics of a species that affect how well the wood will sand and how fine a grit it will take to obtain an acceptable degree of smoothness.

Generally speaking, the harder the wood species is, the more it resists abrasion and the more it will show sanding scratches. So the harder the wood, the finer the grit of sandpaper you have to use for a final pass to eliminate visible scratches in the surface. In contrast, softwoods and softer hardwood species are easier to abrade and hide scratches more readily.

Grain has an even greater effect on sanding. Coarse-grained woods, such as red oak and ash, have large cells and open pores that tend to hide scratches, while fine-grained woods that lack visible pores, such as maple, ebony and holly, are more apt to show scratch patterns left by sanding. You can sand large-pored woods, such as red oak or mahogany, with 150-grit paper and hardly notice scratches under most finishes. In contrast, very fine-pored, dense hardwoods, such as maple, holly, ebony and cherry, tend to show even very fine scratches (see the photo above left). You'll probably want to sand these woods down to at least 320 grit or 360 grit. When power sanded (with an orbital or random-orbit sander), fine-grained woods are more likely to show to swirl marks (see pp. 108-109). And light-colored woods, such as birch and maple, show deep scratches prominently when stained with certain kinds of stains. To prevent this, they should be sanded as fine as 220 grit or 240 grit.

Woods that have a high resin content (hemlock and spruce), pitch or latex pockets (pine or jelutong), or extractives and oils (rosewood and teak) may be difficult to sand with fine-grit papers because their natural stickiness tends to load the sandpaper. This is especially true if you machine-sand these woods beyond 180 grit to 280 grit; the heat generated tends to liquefy resins and make them gum up the sandpaper. You can reduce loading somewhat by using open-coat sandpapers and cleaning the paper often as you sand (see pp. 96-99).

Type of finish The scratch patterns left by smooth sanding show up differently under different kinds of finishes, so your choice of finest grit should depend, at least in part, on your choice of finish. As a rule, solvent-bases finishes are more forgiving than water-based finishes. This is because of the way each type of finish forms a film. As solvents in a solvent-based finish evaporate, the film flows into the fine surface scratches, filling and hiding them. In contrast, water-based finishes dry by coalescence to form a high-viscosity film that doesn't readily flow into small scratches. Instead, this film traps air and refracts light, which tends to make scratches more visible (see the drawing below). Therefore, most surfaces coated with a water-based finish should be sanded to at least 220 grit, while 180 grit is likely to be acceptable for wood coated

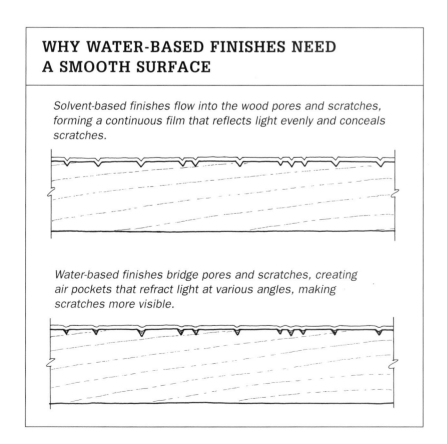

WHY WATER-BASED FINISHES NEED A SMOOTH SURFACE

Solvent-based finishes flow into the wood pores and scratches, forming a continuous film that reflects light evenly and conceals scratches.

Water-based finishes bridge pores and scratches, creating air pockets that refract light at various angles, making scratches more visible.

with a solvent-based finish. Solvent-based finishes that are applied in very thin coats (such as nitrocellulose lacquer) may require finer surface preparation, especially on fine-grained woods; sanding down to 320 grit or 400 grit probably isn't excessive.

Oil finishes, such as Danish oil, seed oils (tung, linseed), and long-oil varnishes are penetrating materials that soak into a wood surface rather than forming a film on top. They tend to show scratches as minute dark lines where the oil darkens the scratch-damaged cell wall. Projects that will be finished with oil should be sanded to a very fine grit. Sand to at least 400 grit, and perhaps even 600 grit if the wood is dense and fine grained. Many woodworkers do their final sanding when they apply the oil (see p. 66); some oil finishes recommend this right on the can.

If you're a purist who likes the look and feel of unfinished wood (or a wax-only finish), then feel free to sand to as fine a grit as it takes for a satisfying silkiness: 600 grit or finer; whatever your fingertips tell you is right.

Staining is another element of finishing that can affect final grit choice. If you're planning on applying a pigmented stain, sanding the wood with a too fine a grit can dramatically lighten the final color. This is because pigmented stains create color by embedding zillions of little particles of ground minerals (pigments) into the surface of the wood. These particles stick to a rough surface better than a smooth one. Too fine a sanding removes scratches but also tends to burnish the wood and make it less absorptive—and not accept stain as readily (see the photo below). Therefore, it's ill advised to sand finer than 220 grit or 240 grit in preparation for a pigmented stain. However, end grain tends to take stain darker than side or face grain. By sanding end grain finer, you can lighten the final color a bit, to even up the look of end-grain surfaces that are adjacent to side grain or face grain.

A finely sanded surface can stain less dark than one that has been sanded to a coarser grit. Pigment particles stick better to a rough surface (such as the left half of the board, which was sanded to only 100 grit) than to a smooth one (such as the right half, which was sanded to 320 grit).

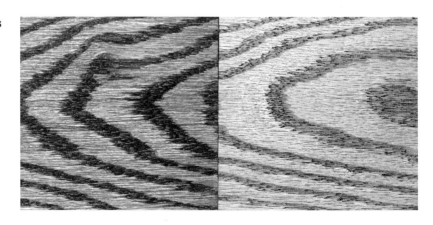

Visual importance of the surface All parts of a project do not have to be sanded to the same degree. If you're trying to earn your living working wood, you might consider this shortcut: Sand highly visible surfaces (e.g., tabletops and drawer fronts) to a finer grit than less visible surfaces (e.g., bookcase backs, table aprons, the undersides of a desktop). But watch out if you're planning on staining the entire piece: A surface sanded to a finer grit is likely to absorb stain less readily than a coarse-sanded surface. You can use this to your advantage if you're trying to match the color of two adjacent parts that will be stained, say a cabinet face frame and a door or drawer front, with the wood on one much lighter than the other. If you sand the lighter-wood part with a slightly coarser final grit, it will stain a darker color.

DEVELOPING A SANDING SCHEDULE

Once you've chosen your coarsest grit paper for leveling and finest grit for smoothing, you need to decide how many grit-change steps you need in between. The progression of grits you use is referred to by professional woodworkers and finishers as a sanding schedule.

Sanding schedules are one of the most controversial topics surrounding the abrading of wood. Some woodworkers swear that you must never skip a step between two grits; others follow rules of thumb about what grits to skip at different degrees of fineness. One popular guideline says to jump no more than 100 points in grit between coarse and medium papers, and 200 points in grit when moving between fine and very fine papers. Another bit of sanding wisdom says to jump no more than two paper sizes at a time, except in the last two stages before the finest grit (three stages if you're power sanding); and not to jump at all when hand sanding.

Since the refinement of sanding scratches is the name of the game in getting wood smooth, any sanding schedule should include a progression of grits that, at any stage of sanding, expediently remove the scratches left by the previous grit. The key word here is *expedient*. While 600-grit paper can be used to sand out 80-grit scratches, it'll take eons longer than if you were to use several sanding steps instead (for example, 80, 120, 180, 280, 400, and 600 grit). You don't want to skip too many steps between any two grits, but there is no hard-and-fast rule that your sanding schedule must use all the grits that exist.

So exactly what grits should your sanding schedule follow? It depends a great deal on the kind of wood you're using and how you choose to sand it smooth. Softer woods (pine, butternut, soft maple) abrade readily, so you can skip grits and still remove scratches expediently. In contrast, really hard woods (rock maple, cherry, holly) abrade less quickly, so you'll probably want to include more steps in your sanding schedule.

If you prefer power sanding, you'll likely want to take larger steps between grits than if you sand by hand. Power sanders, especially random-orbit machines, remove stock more aggressively than hand sanding does, and hence can remove coarser scratches with relatively finer paper quickly.

The best advice is to experiment: Try sanding a couple of different test pieces from coarse to fine, following different sanding schedules on each one. Inspect the test pieces carefully after each sanding stage (see pp. 59-61) to see how well scratches have been eliminated. If you're a professional woodworker gearing up for production, you'll also want to keep track of how long it takes to get scratches out at each stage and how long sanding takes overall. When in doubt (and when the quality of your final surface is a high priority), don't jump too far between grits. Adding more steps to a sanding schedule might take you more time (and use up more sheets of sandpaper), but you're much less likely to end up with scratches that will spoil a flawless finish.

TIPS FOR SANDING WOOD SMOOTH

If you've ever read anything before about sanding wood smooth, you probably already know the mantra: *Sand wood with the grain.* But as we've already seen (see the sidebar on pp. 46-47), you'll smooth a wood surface a lot more quickly (when sanding with a straight-line action) by sanding at an angle across the grain with successively finer grits, sanding with the grain only for the final few passes with the finest-grit papers. Any stray scratches left by your last sanding passes are likely to be camouflaged by the grain of the wood (which is probably the reason for the "sand only with the grain" mantra in the first place). Woods with a busy, well-defined grain pattern, such as oak and ash, and woods with highly linear grain, such as quartersawn Douglas fir, are best at hiding scratches (see the photo on the facing page).

Sanding techniques vary, depending on whether you choose to sand by hand (see Chapter 5) or by machine (see Chapter 6). But there are some general considerations that apply in both cases. These include how to smooth sand quickly and evenly, how to sand tricky end grain, and how to protect areas that will be joined if you sand parts ahead of assembly.

Some woods are just naturally forgiving when it comes to concealing the fine scratches left by sanding. Woods with busy grain patterns, such as ash (top), or woods with highly linear grain, such as quartersawn Douglas fir (bottom), don't show scratches readily.

Sanding parts evenly The first step toward a flawless finish is an evenly sanded bare wood surface. That means that the entire surface of a part must be abraded to an equal degree. As most sandpaper wears out, the biggest problems can come when sanding large surfaces, such as big cabinet sides and tabletops. If you sand these surfaces by starting at one end of the top and working toward the other, the sandpaper won't cut nearly as aggressively at the end as it does at the beginning. As it wears out, it will leave a progressively finer scratch pattern, and it won't remove scratches left by the previous sanding grit as well. Hence you can end up with panels and tops with deep scratches or areas that won't accept stain and finish evenly.

Fortunately, it's easy enough to stave off unevenness by changing to fresh sandpaper more frequently. Alternatively, you can switch to a tougher, longer-lasting abrasive, such as a friable aluminum oxide or ceramic mineral (see pp. 14-15). With these you can sand large surfaces with fewer paper changes. Whatever abrasive you use, be sure to inspect the surface for coarse scratches at the completion of each sanding stage, as described on pp. 59-61, before proceeding to a finer grit.

Sanding end grain End grain is harder to abrade than side grain or face grain, so it's difficult to achieve a smooth surface when you sand the two at the same time, say, where a stile and rail converge in a cabinet frame. The sandpaper will cut the side grain faster than the end grain, which can leave a difference in level between the two parts. To counteract this tendency, use a stiff backing block or pad, and keep even pressure as you sand across the parts.

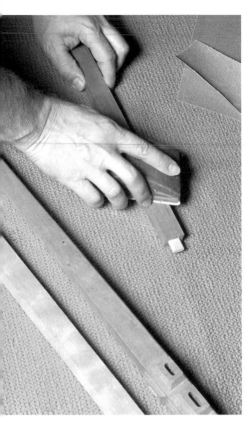

Sanding parts before assembly is often easier than sanding them after they have been glued up.

Sanding parts before assembly Most woodworkers view sanding as the last onerous step that stands in the way of finishing their project. Because it can be a tedious, dusty task, most people put off sanding until the very last moment, when all bare wood parts have been completely—or at least partially—assembled. Depending on the complexity of the project, this can make it more difficult to sand less accessible areas. You can end up with parts that are inadequately sanded, or with cross-grain scratches on adjacent parts.

Often it pays to sand parts ahead of assembly. Raised or flat panels for cabinet doors and drawer fronts are much easier to sand before they are inserted in their frames. If panels will be held in place with moldings, the assembled frames can be sanded ahead of time as well.

Fixed shelves, dividers, and pigeonholes usually have to be sanded ahead of assembly, since there just isn't enough room to get at them after they're assembled. If you forget, however, you may still be able to sand them using a detail sander (see pp. 164-165).

Parts of a frame or other assembly, such as table or desk legs and aprons or chair legs and seat frames, are often best sanded individually (see the photo at left). This both prevents cross-grain scratches and helps to preserve details, such as a beaded or shaped edge on a chair leg. In contrast, cabinet face frames (where adjacent rails and stiles are flush) should be sanded after assembly.

Whether intricate or simple, moldings that hold parts in place or add decoration are almost always best sanded before they are mounted. This is especially true for thin moldings that are surface mounted on panels across the grain, making it nearly impossible to sand the molding without scratching the panel.

Sometimes, it is much easier to sand a very thin or delicate part as it is lying down on your workbench or held in a vise than in final assembly. Fretwork or scrollwork must be carefully supported as you sand, and thin panels may overflex or vibrate to destruction (when orbital sanded) without proper support. Drawer pulls and applied ornaments are clearly easier to sand before they are mounted to an assembled project.

A thin layer of masking tape applied before sanding helps protect joint surfaces from abrasion, which might ruin their tight fit.

Protecting bonding surfaces When you sand bare wood parts ahead of assembly, it's best to avoid surfaces that will be joined, such as tenon faces and mitered ends, as well as boards to be glued edge to edge. Even when supported on a stiff backing block or pad, abrasive papers tend to sand the edges of small parts more readily than the center, resulting in a slightly convex surface. This can ruin the wood-to-wood contact on joint surfaces, which compromises joint strength on assemblies bonded with yellow or white woodworking glues. You can protect joint surfaces during sanding by covering them with masking tape (see the photo above). 3M's Long Mask #2090 is one brand that is durable enough to withstand light machine sanding. You can also temporarily clamp a scrap of wood or plastic laminate over the joint surfaces as you sand the part.

INSPECTING A SANDED SURFACE

You'll do a better job of smooth-sanding your work if you take the time to inspect your work as you sand it. Examining for defects and deep scratches at each stage of sanding—from leveling to final smoothing—will save you the time and trouble it takes to go back and resand problem areas later, as well as ensuring a flawless surface. Deep scratches, either left by previous coarse sanding or from accidents, will usually darken and become more apparent when stained; they become painfully apparent under a high-gloss finish. If surface inspection is put off to just before finishing, you're likely to have to revert to a coarse-grit paper to remove defects, then repeat all subsequent sanding stages. Finding scratches early allows you to remove them by backing up just a single stage and resanding with the next coarser grit.

Your most powerful aid for detecting cross-grain scratches, dings, and dents is a strong light. A bright light source placed at a low angle will quickly reveal even the tiniest of surface variations, which are usually masked by the flat illumination from standard overhead shop lights. While any light source can be used for inspection—a flashlight, a drop light or a desk lamp—the brighter the bulb, the better. Super-bright quartz-halogen lamps provide dazzling illumination for their size, and are inexpensive to purchase as clamp-on work lights. In a pinch, you can even set your project up in front of your late-model car's head lamps, which are also likely to have halogen bulbs.

To inspect a surface, shine the light across it at a low angle while viewing it at a low angle from the side opposite the light source (see the photo below). Defects will reveal themselves as small, hard shadows, indicating little lumps (glue drips, splinters, areas of raised grain) or valleys (dents, dings, deep scratches, cracks).

You can also use a bright light to evaluate the trueness and evenness of a surface. Trueness refers to how close an overall surface is to a geometric ideal: how perfectly flat a top is, or how evenly curved a bowed cabinet side is. Evenness refers to smaller irregularities in a surface, which can be caused by uneven sanding (such as dimples that result from sanding only a small area) or from improper sanding of wood with soft earlywood (see pp. 106-107). Deviation from trueness is like an ocean swell; while unevenness is like smaller ocean waves.

Checking a surface for defects before or after finishing is much easier if you use a bright light source, such as a quartz-halogen work lamp. Place the work surface between you and the light, and observe the light reflected from the surface as shown.

You can evaluate the flatness of a smooth-sanded surface with a simple white card with a geometric pattern of dark straight lines drawn on it. Irregularities in the reflection of lines from the card reveal a lack of trueness or unevenness in the surface.

Check the surface by setting a test card (a small white card lined with a simple pattern of lines on it) and illuminating it with a bright light. Using a low viewing angle, observe the reflection of the line pattern. Subtle curvatures in the overall pattern indicate a lack of trueness, while smaller, more localized deviations in the pattern indicate areas of unevenness (see the photo above). While this test works best on a finished surface, you can check a bare wood surface by first wetting it with mineral spirits. This test can reveal irregularities in, say, a desktop that's been belt-sanded flat. The bare wood top might appear flat, but look like a ridged potato chip after a high-gloss finish has been applied.

You can restore the trueness and evenness of a flat surface by resanding it judiciously. If flat parts are unassembled (and you have access to the equipment), you could run any panels, tops, or shelves through a drum or wide-belt sander. A better solution would be a well-tuned belt sander fitted with a sanding frame, as described on p. 160.

3

Sanding to a Great Finish

Putting on a coat of finish is usually the last step in completing your project. The shaping, leveling, and preliminary smooth sanding of parts have been completed (see Chapter 2), and the project is usually at least partially assembled. You might think you're almost done with the work, but you'd be cruelly deceived. The final preparations in getting the clean, bare wood ready for finishing can have as much of an impact on the appearance and quality of your piece as all the previous work you've done. These preparations include the detection and repair of new or remaining defects and the dewhiskering of surfaces to remove any grain fuzziness. Once finishing begins, abrasives are carefully employed to scuff-sand and level between coats and rub out and polish the final surface. These steps may take a little time, but amount to insurance that your final finish will be flawless, bringing your project to a beautiful conclusion.

Surface Evaluation and Repair

When committing a wood project to a finish, it's important to do a thorough final inspection of all sanded surfaces before the first coat of stain or sealer goes on. Any machining defects, such as planer marks and burns, will have been removed during leveling (see pp. 48-49), and deep scratches revealed and repaired by careful inspections during smooth sanding (see pp. 55-59). But small dents, gouges, and glue drips or smears often creep in between the time you assemble your project and finish it. It's a lot better to discover them now, rather than after the first coat goes on, when defects are more difficult to remedy. Shining a bright light across the surface at a low angle while scrutinizing the surface from the side opposite the light source (see pp. 59-61) reveals defects as small, hard shadows, indicating glue drips or rivulets, as well as dents, dings, and cracks.

Although not exactly a welcome sight, small dents don't have to be sanded to be removed. In most cases, you can remove them by steaming them out with an iron set over a damp cloth. But gouges and dings (where surface fibers have been torn and broken, as opposed to just compressed as with dents) must be filled or sanded out. Deep gouges must be patched or puttied, while shallow gouges can usually be sanded out. Just remember that you have to level the entire area around the defect again—simply sanding out a deep gouge leaves a dimple or depression around it (see the drawing on p. 44), which may be highly visible if the repair is in a prominent area, such as the front of an upper cabinet door, or on a tabletop.

Any beads, drops, or rivulets of glue that remain on the surface of your project will create spots and blotches at finish time by preventing the proper absorption of stains and finish. Since the piece has already been smooth-sanded (and dried glue gums up fine sandpaper quickly), it's best to pop off offending glue drips with a sharp chisel or scraper (see the photo below). Scraped areas benefit from a little touch-up sanding with fine sandpaper. Glue smears and other forms of surface contamination, unfortunately, are tougher to deal with. Some contaminants—especially wax and silicone—are nearly impossible to sand away.

Small glue drips and runs can be removed from a wood surface with a sharp chisel. Use your thumb to keep the tip of the chisel flat, popping off the drip or run with a slicing motion.

You can detect hidden glue smears by wiping bare wood surfaces with a rag that has been dampened with mineral spirits or naphtha. Here, a gluey thumbprint is revealed in the center of the wetted area.

GLUE SMEARS AND SURFACE CONTAMINANTS

Unlike beads of glue, which tend to set atop a surface and are easy to scrape off, glue smears present an insidious problem. Just touching bare wood with a gluey finger can leave a near-invisible smear that won't show up until the finish is applied. Smears are even more problematic if you're working with an open-grained wood, such as oak, walnut, or mahogany. Glue can get into the open pores and remain, even after the surface has been sanded.

You can check for the presence of glue smears by wiping down bare wood surfaces with a little mineral spirits or naphtha (see the photo at left). This mild solvent can also reveal the presence of other surface contaminants, such as wax or silicones, that can ruin finishes as well (see the discussion below). After the wood has been dampened with the solvent, contaminated areas appear as light spots or streaks. Alternatively, you can check for contaminants when dewhiskering, as described below, but subtle problems won't be as apparent.

A sharp scraper will remove small glue smears on a wood surface. But glue that has been absorbed into the grain is best handled by power sanding, using a portable belt sander fitted with a fine paper. A 220-grit or 240-grit belt will allow you to sand below the glue while keeping the surface level. After the repair, you'll need to repeat all the stages in your sanding schedule through to your finest-grit choice.

If you've handled bare wood parts after final sanding, or if you're working on a hot day (and may have gotten sweat on the wood), it's a good idea to do a final wipe-down of your piece with a rag dampened with a solvent, such as naphtha or mineral spirits. The solvent will remove any surface contamination that might prevent a perfect finish.

CONTAMINANTS YOU CAN'T SAND AWAY

While sandpaper removes a multitude of sins (including glue smears), it won't do a thing to rid a wood surface of contaminants such as wax and silicones. These can cause stains that are extremely difficult—or impossible—to remove.

Contamination from waxes, such as carnauba or paraffin (which many woodworkers rub onto tool tables to reduce friction), can be detected when wood is wetted for dewhiskering (as described in the next section). Waxy areas don't absorb water readily, so they remain drier and lighter in color. You can usually remove traces of wax by lightly scrubbing down the wood surface with a rag dampened with mineral spirits or with a commercial wax remover.

The worst chemical offenders are dry lubricants, spray polishes, and rust preventives that contain silicones. While silicones do a great job of lubricating cast-iron tool tables, they're terrible when they get onto bare wood surfaces. Once they soak into the wood, you don't stand a chance of getting them out, and they wreak havoc with both water-based finishes and traditional finishes, such as nitrocellulose lacquers, where they're responsible for creating fisheyes. Here, the best solution is to avoid all products that contain silicones.

Dewhiskering

Wood is composed of bundles of fibers that are sheared at the surface by all regular woodworking operations: cutting, planing, shaping, and abrading. Unfortunately, abrasives do a relatively poor job of shearing wood fibers cleanly, and hence some fuzziness remains at the surface, even after fine sanding. This fuzz may not be apparent when the wood is dry, because the fibers tend to lie flat with the surface (woolliness, a more serious grain fuzzing problem, is discussed on p. 107). You will notice the fuzz when the wood is moistened or exposed to humidity: The loose wood fibers swell and stand up to varying degrees, creating a surprisingly rough surface on coarse-grained woods such as oak and ash. You can feel this "raised grain" right through a thin film of finish (see the drawing below).

RAISED GRAIN UNDER A FINISH

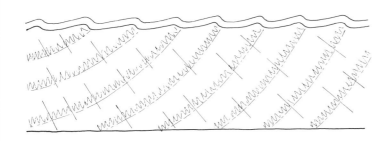

Moisture can penetrate a finish and raise the wood's grain, leaving a nubbly surface.

Wet-sanding a Danish-oil finish with 400-grit paper is an expedient way to dewhisker the surface at the same time that you're applying the first coat of finish.

The best way to deal with fiber fuzzing is to dewhisker the surface before finishing by moistening the wood to raise the grain and then sanding the loose fibers away. The resulting surface is smooth and should stay that way, even if the finished piece is exposed to moisture in the future. An added advantage of raising the grain is that it makes it easier to spot subtle defects—tiny dings, dents and scratches—you might have missed before.

Many woodworkers think that dewhiskering is necessary primarily for surfaces to be coated with water-based finishes. While it's true that water-based finishes do raise the grain readily, solvent-based finishes also raise grain slightly. Film-type solvent-based finishes, such as nitrocellulose lacquer and sanding sealer, just mask the fuzz under the relatively thick coat of finish. The bottom line is that you're likely to see a smoother final surface if you raise the grain before applying practically any kind of finish.

There are times, though, when you can skip dewhiskering altogether, such as when preparing the wood for painting, or when the surface is to be packed with a pore filler prior to top-coating. Any raised-grain fuzziness will be smoothed out when the primed or filled surface is sanded. When applying an oil finish, you can combine dewhiskering with the application of the finish: Danish oil can be wet-sanded with a very-fine-grit paper, such as 400 grit, while the first coat is soaking into the wood. Thus, any grain raised by the oil will be sanded smooth (see the photo at left). Some of the resulting wood-fiber-and-oil slurry may be packed down into the pores of open-pore woods, but most is removed when the excess oil is wiped off. For other finishes, you can combine dewhiskering with final sanding with your finest-grit paper to save a step in surface preparation for finishing.

You have a choice of several different ways of dewhiskering, all of which are commonly practiced by woodworkers. The exact method you choose will depend on your choice of abrasives (sandpaper, steel wool, or non-woven plastic abrasive) and on how much of a hurry you're in to get on with finishing.

FOUR WAYS TO RAISE THE GRAIN

The most common method for raising the grain (though not necessarily the best) is to wet the wood surface thoroughly with clean water. You can spray it on with an atomizer or wipe it on with a clean rag. Take care to moisten the surface of the wood evenly. If water droplets splatter onto adjacent dry surfaces, small water spots (where the grain has raised only in the area of the drop) can develop that will show up through a stained or clear finish. If you see drops on a dry surface, simply wet that surface evenly.

Once the surfaces are wet, you usually have to wait for the wood to dry completely before sanding can begin. This can take anywhere from one hour to overnight, depending on the humidity of your shop. If you sand the wood while it is still damp, the fibers won't shear cleanly, and the grain is likely to raise again when the finish is applied.

If you can't wait for water-dampened wood to dry before you dewhisker, you can wipe down the bare wood with denatured alcohol. It won't raise the grain quite as much as water does, but it does an adequate job for preparation under film-type finishes, and the surface will be dry enough for final sanding very quickly.

Here's another way to save some time when dewhiskering without waiting overnight. Working in a warm, dry shop, lightly wipe down all surfaces with a damp (not wet) rag or sponge, then wait 15 minutes to a half-hour before sanding. The moisture from the rag or sponge is usually enough to raise the grain without the wood itself absorbing too much liquid. Make sure to use only clean, clear water and a clean rag or sponge. If you're wiping down wood with really big pores, such as oak or ash, don't use a loosely woven rag because the fibers could easily snag.

If you want to dewhisker wood in a New York minute, an even speedier method is to heat the surface after wetting it with water. Some pyrotechnically gifted woodworkers use a propane torch or blow torch as a heat source, claiming that the method raises wood fibers better than just letting the wood dry naturally (I've seen no

You can speed up the drying of a surface wetted with water in preparation for dewhiskering by heating it gently with a heat gun.

evidence of this in my experiments). A safer way to dry wood quickly is to use a heat gun (as shown in the photo on p. 67), the same kind used to soften house paint prior to scraping it off. If you try this method, use a medium heat setting and keep the heat gun moving briskly to avoid scorching the wood, especially near sharp edges and details where the wood is very thin. Practice on scraps at first, if you're nervous about incinerating your project. Alternatively, use a gun-style hair dryer set on high.

KNOCKING DOWN RAISED GRAIN

After the wood has been wetted and dried, you're ready to sand the entire surface to remove the loose fibers. Some woodworkers like to apply a thin sealer coat of shellac or even a hide-glue size to the surface ahead of this final sanding. The sealer can help to lock the fibers in place, so they aren't as apt to raise after final sanding.

For a dewhiskering abrasive, you have several choices. You can use the finest paper you've chosen for your sanding schedule (see pp. 52-55), or you might substitute a medium-grade non-woven plastic abrasive, such as 3M's gray ScotchBrite. In either case, you'll do a better job of shearing the raised fibers off (instead of just pushing them back down) if you sand at an angle across the wood's surface (see the sidebar on pp. 46-47). Don't sand too enthusiastically; you just want to shear off the stiff, standing surface fibers, not create new fibers that will fuzz later, when the finish is applied. Plastic abrasive pads are particularly good for working on curved or round parts and fine details; the flexible pads wrap around them easily (see the photo at left).

Steel wool is another popular material for knocking down grain. I've seen gunstock makers rub down a raised surface with a loose ball of fine (#00 or #000) steel wool, working it with the grain. They claim that the steel-wool strands actually hook under raised, loose wood fibers and pull them off, yielding a surface less likely to fuzz up again than one that has been sanded conventionally. In my experience, I've found the tendency for the metal strands to snag more annoying than useful. If you do prefer steel wool, avoid surface contamination by using only de-oiled steel wool, and avoid discoloring streaks by using bronze wool on tannin-rich woods ahead of a water-based finish (see pp. 38-39).

Because they mold readily to curved surfaces, non-woven plastic abrasives are great for dewhiskering moldings or other detailed parts.

Cleaning the Surface

Now that your wood project is dewhiskered and feels as smooth as a baby's cheek, only one task remains before you can apply the finish: Dust, sanding grit, and wood powder must be removed from the surface. If you don't clean them off, they'll end up in your stain and top coat, resulting in a dirty-looking surface that's nubbly to the touch.

On dense, closed-grain woods, such as maple and cherry, cleaning the surface is relatively easy with a standard shop vacuum fitted with a brush-style accessory tip. Open-pore woods, such as walnut and mahogany, can be a bit tougher to clean. Their large pores tend to trap grains of grit and small wood particles, in the same way cracks in a floor trap dirt. It can take a little more coaxing to get the debris out, a task best done by blowing out the pores with compressed air or wiping them with a tack cloth.

One way to remove embedded dust is to blow it out with high-pressure compressed air. But before you do, a couple of precautions must be taken. First, wear goggles to keep particles out of your eyes. Your compressed-air supply must be perfectly dry and filtered clean, as you can easily contaminate a surface with oil (used to lubricate the compressor) or oily water from condensation in the tank or air line. A moisture trap should be mounted at the compressor and an in-line filter fitted between the end of the air line and the blow gun (see the photo at right). Make sure to empty the container on the trap and replace in-line filters periodically. Also, drain the compressor tank often, especially if you work in a humid climate. Never use an air hose for blowing off that's been used with air tools; the oil used to lubricate them usually gets into the hose and will sputter out if you use a blow gun. And don't ever blow dust off by mouth; there isn't enough force to blow particles out of the wood's pores, and you'll likely just spray the surface with fine droplets of spittle.

If you can, blow off your piece outside or in a room that's segregated from your finishing space. Fine dust blown off your project ends up in the air, where it will eventually just settle on your project again, probably when the finish is still wet. What's worse, fine particles (smaller than 10 microns) can stay aloft for hours and cause respiratory problems. (For more on dust in the woodshop and how to control it, see p. 148.)

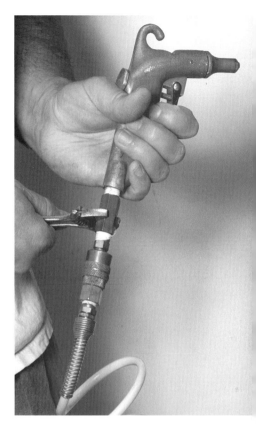

Mounting an in-line filter to the inlet of a blow gun helps to ensure that the compressed air used to blow away fine dust from wood surfaces prior to finishing will be dry and clean.

USING A TACK CLOTH

A tack cloth (also called a tack rag) is a piece of cheesecloth or muslin fabric that's impregnated with a sticky substance. Wiping this sticky cloth across a dusty part picks up grit and debris on the surface and does a pretty good job of pulling it out of pores and crevices as well. Tack cloths come in two varieties: oil impregnated, which is coated with polybutylene, and PSA, which has an acrylic pressure-sensitive adhesive. Oil-impregnated cloths (the ones most commonly found at hardware stores) can contaminate a surface and cause finishing problems if some of the oil wipes off—which is likely if you wipe hard. Contamination causes fisheyes to form in water-based lacquer finishes and white spots or localized softness under solvent-based lacquers. PSA tack cloths, on the other hand, will not leave behind contaminants, which is why I prefer them. However, they cost more than oil-impregnated cloths and are available primarily at auto-supply stores (see the sidebar on pp. 94-95).

Regardless of the type of tack rag you choose, use a light touch. Turn and fold the cloth often during wiping to reveal fresh sticky portions of the cloth that will continue to pick up dust. Keeping the cloth warm helps it to stay tacky. You can extend the life of tack cloths by keeping them from drying out between uses: Store them in a sealed plastic bag or glass jar. Throw away a dried-out cloth that has no tack left. Just make sure to deposit discarded oil-impregnated cloths in a sealed metal container, as they can spontaneously burst into flame.

You can dispense with the tack rag before applying water-based dye stains and clear coats by wiping surfaces thoroughly with a clean rag lightly moistened with clean water. If the wood surface has been previously dewhiskered, this slight moistness won't raise the wood's grain again.

Scuff Sanding between Coats

Once the finishing process begins, most film-type wood finishes (lacquers, varnishes, polyurethanes) require a light scuff sanding (also called touch sanding) between coats. Scuff sanding can remove debris that floats onto the finish as it is drying. Particles of wood dust, as well as insects and other debris, can land on a wet finish and stick. This problem is worse with slow-drying finishes (such as traditional spar varnishes), which can take hours to dry to the touch, giving ample time for debris to embed. With each new coat, more debris accumulates. Scuff sanding between coats leaves a smooth surface that will require much less work to rub out and polish later (see pp. 74-86).

Scuff sanding with a padded sanding block will flatten streaks, runs, and roughness that result from uneven brushing or orange peel from poor finish flow-out after spraying. This is an important step, since subsequent coats of finish build upon whatever surface they're applied to (flat or rough), and tend to magnify irregularities and defects rather than concealing them. This is true even with evaporative finishes, such as lacquer and shellac, which dissolve the coat that they're applied on top of.

One thing scuff sanding will not do is promote better inter-coat adhesion. It's a common misconception that scuff-sanding a finish will give subsequent coats a better "bite." Coats of finish bond to each other on a molecular level—not a mechanical level. Therefore, it's only necessary to scuff-sand to remove unevenness or surface debris, with two exceptions: Vinyl sealers have a surface that oxidizes quickly. If you wait more than a few hours between coats, you should scuff-sand the surface to remove oxidized material. The only other case in which scuff sanding would be necessary is if you want to top-coat a finish that's more than six or eight weeks old.

MATERIALS AND METHODS

Scuff sanding a finish is much like sanding bare wood, but with some important differences. While some resinous woods can cause some loading up of the sandpaper, loading (see the photo below) is *always* an issue when scuff-sanding a finish. The reasons are

When scuff-sanding, little bits of finish become trapped in the abrasive grit, forming lumps called corns. Besides gumming up the paper, making it cut less effectively, corns can damage the finished surface.

twofold: First, you are sanding an uncured finish that is still soft; second, an uncured finish, because of its thermoplastic nature, is likely to bond readily to the surface of resin-bond abrasive papers (especially when heated from the friction created by power sanding). Bits of sanded-off finish (swarf) commonly form into little clumps on the surface of the sandpaper. These clumps, called "corns," reduce the sanding efficiency of the paper and can actually cause scratches and streaks in a soft finish, such as nitrocellulose lacquer.

There are several ways to minimize loading when scuff-sanding. First, use only sandpapers with an anti-loading coating (see p. 30). These waxy stearate coatings not only prevent paper from gumming up, but also act as a dry lubricant that helps reduce the heat produced by sanding friction. This is especially important when scuff-sanding, because fresh coats of finish are soft and easy to damage.

Choice of grit depends, in great part, on the kind of finish. Finishes that form a more brittle film, such as shellac or lacquer, can be scuff-sanded with 400-grit, or even 600-grit, paper. Choose a coarser grit (220 or 240 grit) if you're using a finish with a more elastic, flexible film, such as spar varnish. These rubbery finishes sand well with waterproof silicon-carbide papers but, since this type of paper usually lacks an anti-loading coating, you must use a lubricant. Mineral spirits or VM&P naphtha is a good choice, since their solvents evaporate rapidly and don't leave any harmful residue. If the surface is really rough with heavy orange peel or brush marks, switch to a 220-grit, or even 180-grit, sandpaper. Wrapping the sandpaper around a foam block or heavily padded sanding block will help you keep the sanding pressure light and even on flat or slightly curved surfaces (see the photo at left on the facing page). Switch to non-woven plastic abrasive pads for scuff-sanding moldings, turnings, or small details. If the finish you're scuffing is quite flat and free of serious defects or roughness, you can also use non-woven plastic abrasive pads backed up with a big, flat sanding block or plane.

If you're working on a primed, painted, or a heavily varnished piece, scuff sanding with an 80-grit to 100-grit (medium) foam sanding block is a good alternative to regular sandpaper (see pp. 37-38). Professional painters like foam blocks because they're comfortable to hold. And, although they're not treated with an anti-loading coating, the cushioning effect of foam tends to make them less likely load up. If they do load, they can be washed out and reused numerous times (see the photo at right on the facing page).

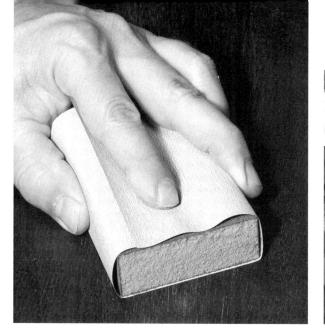

Wrapping the sandpaper around a foam block or a stiff sponge will help you keep the pressure light and even when scuff-sanding flat or slightly curved surfaces.

Foam sanding blocks are handy for scuff-sanding a finish. Because they're waterproof, they can be washed off in soapy water when they become loaded with sanding swarf.

If you find the abrasive grit on a new foam sanding block cuts too aggressively, you can rub a pair of new blocks together *lightly*, to dull the abrasive slightly (heavy rubbing simply sheds abrasive and reduces the life of the blocks).

Regardless of whether you use sandpaper, foam sanding blocks, or non-woven plastic abrasives, always scuff-sand with a light touch. Sanding direction isn't important; any fine scratches deposited in the surface will be either dissolved or covered up by subsequent finish coats. Just don't sand in any one spot for long—it's terribly easy to sand through most finishes back down to raw wood. This is ruinous if the wood has been stained because the area of the sand-through will be lighter in color, and hard to restain to match. Also, removing more finish than necessary is counterproductive to building a thicker film of finish. If you scuff-sand off nearly as much as you applied, you're just taking a step forward and a step back.

After each scuff sanding, clean all surfaces before applying the next coat of finish by blowing the surface off with high-pressure air or by wiping with a clean rag lightly moistened with naphtha. Cleaning removes not only sanding dust and stray abrasive grains, but also the waxy stearates (anti-loading coatings) that rub off the sandpaper and can hinder the adhesion of subsequent finish coats.

Rubbing Out a Finish

Unless you have enough skill to create a perfect finish right from the spray gun, brush, or applicator pad, almost every matte, eggshell, or semigloss finish needs to be rubbed out in order to have a surface that's satisfying to the eye and smooth to the touch. Rubbing out is typically done to all the large, visible surfaces of a piece, such as carcase sides, tabletops, cabinet doors, and drawer fronts. (Smaller components, such as table legs and chair stretchers, aren't usually rubbed out.) But rubbing out the final coat of finish can mean different things, depending on the final surface sheen that's desired—matte, satin, or gloss.

The process which we can generically call rubbing out can have up to three distinct stages: leveling, compounding, and polishing (see the drawing below). The first stage, leveling, employs fine-grit

RUBBING OUT A FINISH

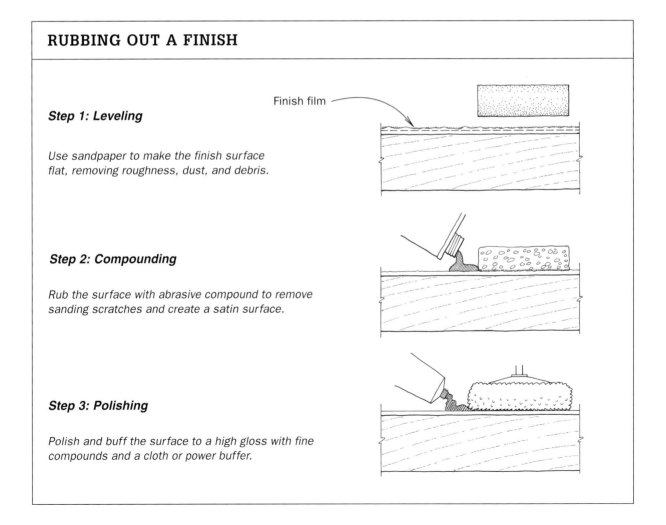

Finish film

Step 1: Leveling

Use sandpaper to make the finish surface flat, removing roughness, dust, and debris.

Step 2: Compounding

Rub the surface with abrasive compound to remove sanding scratches and create a satin surface.

Step 3: Polishing

Polish and buff the surface to a high gloss with fine compounds and a cloth or power buffer.

sandpapers to remove dust and debris and to make the finish surface truly flat. The second stage, compounding, is the process of rubbing the surface with abrasives in order to refine the scratch pattern left after leveling. The third stage, polishing, uses special compounds with very fine abrasives that remove fine scratches and swirl marks and leave the surface ready to be buffed.

The higher the gloss you wish to attain, the more stages of rubbing out you need to perform: Each stage uses progressively finer abrasive media that leave a progressively finer scratch pattern. The more refined and less visible the scratch pattern gets, the more reflective (and less refractive) the surface. A surface that's been leveled has a relatively coarse scratch pattern that creates a matte finish. A leveled, then compounded surface has a finer scratch pattern appropriate for a satin or semigloss finish. A leveled, compounded, and polished surface has no discernible scratch pattern and reflects like a mirror, for a shiny, high-gloss finish. In short: Matte finishes require the least work, gloss finishes the most.

Traditionally, rubbing out a finish was done with fine ground minerals, such as pumice and rottenstone, which were mixed with lubricants (often paraffin or mineral oil) and rubbed over the surface. Unless you're a whiz at this or a proponent of traditional finishing practices, you'll find these materials difficult to use. I consider these materials and methods arcane, and don't use them in my work. (Traditional rubbing out is well described in Michael Dresdner's *The Woodfinishing Book,* published by The Taunton Press in 1992.)

The procedures for rubbing out that are outlined below are aimed at the amateur wood finisher (even many professional woodworkers are amateurs when it comes to wood finishing). These procedures are simple to follow and require little in the way of special skills, yet yield predictable, attractive results without years of practice—and without "instructive" failures.

BEFORE YOU BEGIN

You'll have more success with rubbing out if you consider a few things before beginning the finishing process. Getting the desired look and feel in a finish begins with choosing one that rubs out well, then applying it thick enough for rubbing out safely. Timing is also critical: You must let the finish cure before rubbing, or your project's crowning glory will turn into a murky mess.

The whitish goo at the bottom of a can of satin or semigloss finish is flattening powder, which is added to create a dull sheen. To ensure an even luster, you must mix the finish thoroughly before use.

Choosing the right finish Some finishes rub out better than others. In general, hard, brittle finishes, such as nitrocellulose lacquer and shellac, rub out better than softer, more flexible finishes, such as varnish and polyurethane. Finishes designed to be very flexible and tolerate the sometimes extreme movement of solid wood exposed to the elements, such as spar varnish and exterior polyurethanes, have films that deform when abraded instead of scratching cleanly. Thus they rub out poorly. Indoor finishes (alkyd varnishes and interior polyurethanes) tend to be harder, and thus abrade and rub out more readily. Really tough finishes, such as commercially used catalyzed and UV-cured polyesters, cure hard as a rock and require lots of elbow grease to rub out. At the other extreme, oil finishes, which are mostly absorbed into the wood, need no special rubbing out at all. They produce a warm, glowing final surface all by themselves, a quality that makes them popular with many woodworkers, especially hobbyists.

Among the lacquers, water-based formulations are the most difficult to rub out well; their relatively flexible films tend to deform and deflect scratches rather than abrading cleanly. Acrylic lacquers (made for automotive finishing) are the easiest to abrade simply because they are designed to be rubbed out—this is a standard part of painting a car. Be cautious when adding retarders or "slow" thinners to spray lacquers. Retarders prevent blushing and help the finish flow out better, but also make it cure more slowly (see pp. 77-78) and not rub out as well. Brushing lacquers also tend to have lots of retarder in them.

Another important consideration when selecting a finish is its inherent glossiness. Most film-type finishes, by themselves, produce a glossy film; matte, satin, and semigloss finishes have different amounts of flattening powders added to them to create a duller sheen (see the photo at left). While it is possible to polish a matte finish to a high gloss or to rub out a gloss finish to give it a more satin-like appearance, you generally want to choose a finish that has about the same degree of gloss or dullness as the final surface luster you're aiming for. Because flattening powders tend to make a finish cloudy, a good trick when working up a satin finish is to build all but the last couple of coats with gloss finish. The better film clarity of the gloss material helps the beauty of the wood shine through, while the satin top coats provides enough film thickness for rubbing out.

Building a thick enough film One common pitfall in rubbing out is starting with a film that's too thin. Rubbing out removes finish, and if the film isn't thick enough, you might rub right through the film down to bare wood. It can take quite a few coats of finish to form the relatively thick film that's needed. (Films get thinner as they dry, and you want the dry thickness to be 4 mils to 5 mils.) Unfortunately, the exact number of coats is hard to specify: It depends on the kind of finish, the thickness of each coat, and the amount of rubbing you will do. You'll remove at least 1½ mil just to level a finish and double that to take it all the way to a high gloss. To be safe, put an extra coat or two on a project you plan to rub out. The best insurance is to prepare a finish sample (coated the same as your project will be) and try rubbing it out. If you rub through the sample, put another coat or two on your project.

Waiting for the finish to cure A finish must be entirely cured before rubbing out can begin. The chart below provides general guidelines for the drying times of a number of popular wood finishes. Being cured is different from just being dry to the touch. A thick film of finish may feel completely dry, but may still be soft inside. This is especially true of polymerizing finishes, such as polyesters and oils, which dry from the outside in. Curing time depends on many variables, including the type and composition of the finish, the thickness of the film, and, for evaporative finishes

Approximate Cure Times for Wood Finishes

Finish	Minimum cure time before the finish can be rubbed out
Catalyzed finishes (polyesters, cross-linked nitrocellulose, and other industrial finishes)	2 days
Acrylic lacquer	3 to 5 days
Nitrocellulose lacquer	5 to 7 days
Shellac	7 days
Water-based lacquer	14 days
Polyurethane	14 days
Water-based varnishes	14 days
Spar varnish	Too flexible to rub out properly

(such as lacquer and shellac), the temperature and humidity of the finishing room. The rate at which a finish film is built up can also affect the rate of cure. A dozen coats of lacquer sprayed on over a period of days will cure much more quickly than half that number all applied on the same afternoon. (Faster curing time is one reason the label on the can usually instructs you that it's better to apply several thin coats than a single thick one.) Lacquers that contain lots of retarder also take a longer time to cure.

Because of all these variables, the range of cure time can be enormous. Many water-based lacquers have slow-evaporating solvents and may take two weeks to cure, while catalyzed polyesters, designed for high-production commercial woodworking, may take only two days.

You can get away with rubbing out a satin or semigloss finish that isn't 100% cured, but you'll work much harder and not get as good a result. The best way to be sure that your finish is cured is to check your finish sample. After the projected cure time has passed, test the sample by scuff-sanding it with 320-grit or 360-grit paper. If the paper doesn't load up readily with mushy finish swarf, your project is probably ready for rubbing.

LEVELING FOR A MATTE FINISH

Regardless of the final surface sheen you're after, leveling is the first step in rubbing out any finish. Leveling removes inconsistencies from poor finish flow-out, such as roughness, brush marks, and orange peel, to surface debris such as dust and bugs. The amount of leveling required depends on how well the surface has been previously handled: how well it was prepared (smooth, level, dewhiskered) and scuff-sanded between coats, and how evenly the final top coat went on. If you're really good with a spray gun or if you've rubbed on a quick-drying finish (gels, French polishing), you may be able to proceed directly to compounding and polishing, or just apply a final coat of wax.

Probably the easiest and quickest way to level a finish is by using very-fine-grit papers and working in three passes, using progressively finer grits to refine the scratch pattern left by the previous pass. Regardless of the kind of paper you choose, or whether you sand wet or dry (see the sidebar on the facing page), the grades you use will depend on how rough the surface is to start.

For a rougher initial surface, you might start with 400 grit, followed by 600 grit and 1000 grit. You'll have to be careful with the relatively coarse 400-grit paper, but you'll work a lot faster than

Leveling Wet or Dry?

In the old days, rubbing out a finish meant mixing up a messy slurry from powdered minerals—rottenstone or pumice—and oil. Going the more modern route and leveling a finish with abrasive papers lets you choose to sand wet or dry. Even dry sanding requires lubricity, so you should use sandpaper with anti-loading coating. The coating serves as a lubricant, not only keeping the paper from gumming up with finish swarf, but also reducing the risk of heat damage to the finish film.

Dry sanding is less messy than wet sanding, and, since the surface won't be covered with a slurry, it's easier to monitor your progress. Aluminum-oxide papers that are open coat and have an anti-loading coating are great for working dry when rubbing out a variety of common finishes (lacquer, shellac, and varnish). I also like 3M's Imperial Microfinishing film-backed wet/dry papers, which are available from auto-body supply stores in grades down to 9 microns (about 1000 grit); 3M's Imperial "lapping films" come graded down to 0.3 microns (about 2500 grit). Silicon-carbide wet/dry papers work well on very hard finishes, such as UV-cured polyesters.

Regardless of the kind of sandpaper you choose, don't skimp on paper changes. Fresh, sharp grains cut faster and leave a more regular scratch pattern than you can obtain using dull paper.

What are the advantages to wet sanding? You'll get a slightly shinier finish (a finer scratch pattern) wet sanding than dry. Besides preventing loading, the lubricant also floats away sanding swarf that might otherwise stick into the finish, causing streaks.

Many finishers prefer to use naphtha or mineral spirits as a lubricant for leveling because they are easy to clean up and leave no residue. Plain water with a few drops of liquid dishwashing detergent in it also works just fine, but if you accidentally sand through the finish film you're liable to raise the grain of the wood.

if you started with a finer grit. The surface left by the 1000 grit will be smooth enough for a matte finish, and it will require only hand buffing with a soft cloth (see p. 84). For a satin or semigloss finish, the 1000-grit surface will be ready for compounding, as described on pp. 81-83.

If your initial surface is fairly clean and flat, you can skip the 400 grit and start with 600-grit or even 800-grit paper. If a high-gloss finish is in your plans, work down to 1500-grit paper. You can rub a 1000-grit surface to a high gloss, but it takes less work to refine scratches by sanding ahead of compounding than to remove them by compounding alone.

If you sand by hand, support the paper by wrapping it around a firm block. You can use a traditional cork block or a large rubber block, but I've gotten the best results using a foam pad designed specifically for rubbing out with wet/dry sandpaper. A #20 pad is made from a fairly dense foam that's sized for half a sheet of sandpaper; it's big enough to keep the paper flat and distribute pressure evenly, which is especially important for even leveling of large surfaces. These pads are available at auto-body supply stores.

If you prefer to level a finish with a power sander, you can use a random-orbit sander for small surfaces, but these machines tend to leave a less-than-flat surface on large panels. To keep big surfaces flat, it's better to level with a half-sheet-sized orbital sander or better yet, a straight-line sander (see the photo below). If you prefer to wet-sand, always choose a pneumatic unit to avoid the hazard of electric shock. Never wet-sand with an AC-powered sander.

Sanding in three passes The quickest way to level a finish is by taking three passes with progressively finer grits. Just as when sanding bare wood, sanding across the grain from two directions on the first two passes makes it easier to see if you've removed the scratches from the previous pass completely (see the sidebar on

An air-powered straight-line sander works with a straight, back-and-forth motion. It does an excellent job of leveling large finished surfaces while maintaining flatness.

pp. 46-47). Even though the finish has no grain of its own, taking the final sanding pass with the grain of the wood tends to hide any errant scratches left by the previous passes.

You must take care when sanding (especially power sanding) at the edges of a surface, where most film finishes are naturally thinner because of surface tension. You may want to anticipate this, and apply the finish a little heavier around the edges of a surface than at the center. On large, highly visible surfaces, such as tabletops (where repairs would be harder to hide), it's not a bad idea to go around the circumference of the top first, rubbing a short section (6 in. to 8 in.) in from each edge while keeping the backing pad flat. You can then work over the top, feathering your strokes in near the edges. Use long strokes and liberal pressure; you won't rub through as long as you're working on a thick enough film. To level safely on curved panels, use maroon or gray non-woven plastic abrasive pads, working with the grain.

As you proceed with leveling, it's important to monitor your progress. If you're wet sanding, the slurry created by the finish swarf and lubricant will make it hard to see the condition of the surface; wipe off the haze occasionally with a rag or your hand. A rubber squeegee is very handy for clearing large panels and tabletops. You'll know you're done leveling when the surface is uniformly dull and flat, with no bright dimples (low spots) or obvious deep scratches. If it's a prominent surface, such as a large tabletop, check it for evenness (see p. 61).

If your choice for a final finish is matte, all that remains after leveling is simply a little buffing with a dry rag, and maybe applying a light coat of wax. If you're planning on a satin, semigloss, or gloss finish, you're ready to refine the luster on your leveled surface by compounding.

COMPOUNDING FOR A SATIN FINISH

The next step to a more lustrous finish is to use rubbing compounds, steel wool, or non-woven plastic abrasives to refine the scratch pattern left from leveling. This process is known in the abrasive trades as "compounding." Compounding leaves the surface with a satin or semigloss sheen (depending on what compound or abrasive is used and how it is rubbed). If you're after a high-gloss finish, compounding should be followed by polishing and buffing (described on pp. 83-84).

If you are seeking to achieve a simple satin finish, the easiest route is to avoid messy compounds and simply rub the leveled surfaces with a fine (gray) non-woven plastic abrasive. (Although gray non-woven plastic abrasive is a relatively coarse 360 grit, the cushioning effect of the pad creates a round-bottomed scratch that diffuses light more readily than scratches created by regular coated abrasives, so the surface will look and feel shinier.) If you prefer, use #0000 steel wool instead.

Use a lubricant to reduce heat and improve the cutting action of the plastic or steel-wool pad. For a lubricant, you can use soap waxes, such as Wol-Wax (pronounced "wool-wax") or oil soap, such as Murphy's, which, when diluted with water, produces foamy suds. These products are easier to clean off than oil lubricants, which are commonly used with traditional compounds, such as pumice and rottenstone. The only caveat with oil soaps is that on open-grained woods (like unfilled walnut, mahogany or ash), they can leave a whitish residue that's hard to get out of the pores. For these finishes, professional finisher Michael Dresdner recommends using a "black wax:" a dark brown wax-based liquid, such as No. 61 Dull Wax (see Sources of Supply, which begins on p. 209). Alternatively, you can use regular brown or cordovan-colored shoe polish, thinned with naphtha to form a thin paste.

For a finer, more professional-looking semigloss finish, rub out surfaces with an automotive-type rubbing compound, such as 3M's Imperial or Meguiar's 1 machine glaze (see the sidebar on pp. 94-95). These create a fine abrasive slurry that's self-lubricating and breaks down as you rub, further refining the scratch pattern. If you're unsure of which product to use after leveling, better rubbing compounds usually tell you what size of scratch (in grit size) they'll remove. All these compounds do create a mess, so you'll want to avoid using them on unfilled finishes where they're difficult to clean out of the pores.

The automotive compounds can be worked in by hand, using a gray non-woven plastic abrasive pad as an applicator, or with a power buffing machine fitted with a foam pad (see the photo at left and the sidebar on p. 85). In lieu of a power buffer, you can rub with a random-orbit sander fitted with a gray non-woven plastic abrasive pad backed by a cork or rubber block; if the sander has a hook-and-loop backing, the abrasive pad will stick directly to it. But be aware that the circular rubbing action of the sander will create a subtly different surface sheen than sanding back and forth by hand. Even though the finish has no "grain," the direction of rubbing will affect the way the surface looks when viewed from different angles. Rubbing with a straight-line motion (with the wood's grain) yields a slightly softer look than rubbing with a circular motion. Experiment on a scrap panel to see which you prefer before tackling your project.

A power buffer fitted with a foam pad is a fast, professional way to compound a finish to a consistent semigloss sheen.

Before compounding, thoroughly clean off any residue left after leveling. Apply a liberal amount of lubricant or automotive compound and simply begin rubbing. If you're working by hand, rub the surface vigorously, working with the grain and using overlapping strokes. Take care not to rub through at the edges of large surfaces (see the drawing on p. 85). When the surface has attained a consistent sheen, compounding is complete.

After you're done rubbing, remove any lubricant or remaining compound from the surface. Many automotive compounds are "self-cleaning," which means that they dry after rubbing and can be brushed or blown off the surface. Use a wooden toothpick to remove any dried residue that has accumulated in crevices and details; it will show up more when dry. Some wax-based lubricants tend to leave a smeary film on the surface that readily shows up fingerprints; take these off by rubbing the surface lightly with #0000 steel wool dampened with water or with a rag dipped in naphtha or mineral spirits.

POLISHING AND BUFFING A HIGH-GLOSS FINISH

Compounding leaves you with a satin finish that's pleasant to the touch. If you want a shinier, sparkling surface, the next step is to polish the finish using special polishing compounds. Compounding leaves an ultra-fine scratch pattern in the finish; these scratches are visible with a hand lens if you look carefully. Polishing is also an abrasive process but one that uses micro-fine abrasive compounds that break down as you polish. The latter stage of polishing actually burnishes the finish, leaving no visible scratch pattern and (if things go well) a gleaming, mirror-like surface.

Before you get your expectations up, be forewarned: It's hard to work up a perfect gloss surface. Gloss finishes show even the slightest imperfections, which is why most woodworkers prefer semigloss and duller finishes—they're more forgiving. Gloss finishes usually don't look very good on non-filled surfaces, so you'll need to fill and seal the wood before top-coating. You'll also remove more finish when rubbing to a high gloss, so the film must be thicker to start with, which means more top coats.

There are dozens of different auto finishing polishes, such as Meguiar's Mirror Glaze 2 and 3 machine glazes, and 3M's Finesse-it, that are excellent for polishing a clear wood finish. As with the rubbing compounds, polishing compounds are applied directly to the finish surface and are then "rubbed" by buffing. Most are self-cleaning compounds that dry and can simply be brushed or blown away after polishing.

Buffing can be done by hand, with a soft cloth diaper or a lint-free polishing cloth (available from an auto-body repair supply store; see the sidebar on pp. 94-95). Hand buffing is fine for smaller surfaces (or if you have a lot of energy to work off). But for large tabletops and big panels, nothing beats a power buffer fitted with a convoluted foam pad or lamb's-wool bonnet (see the sidebar on the facing page).

As when compounding, large surfaces are buffed by working in a small area at a time, and then blending in your strokes between areas. When you've covered the surface once, work over the entire surface again, taking long strokes to blend in any remaining marks. As the compound begins to dry, use lighter pressure.

You can polish a surface using only one polishing compound, or for even greater shine, you can buff with one compound (such as Meguiar 2), then repeat with the finer #3 compound. But first, either change bonnets or clean the bonnet before proceeding to the finer compound. You can clean a lamb's-wool (or synthetic lamb's wool) bonnet by running it against a cleaning rake (available from auto-finish supply stores). Alternatively, run the spinning bonnet against a sharp edge, such as the end of a hardwood stick clamped in a bench vise (see the photo below). You can clean foam applicator pads by washing them out with soap and water.

You can clean finish and compound residue from the face of a lamb's-wool bonnet by running the spinning bonnet against the sharp end of a hardwood stick clamped in a vise.

Using a Power Buffer

You can polish a surface entirely by hand, but a power buffer takes a lot of the sweat out of rubbing out a finish with compounds, as well as polishing and buffing a surface to a high gloss. Most power buffers made for finishing are right-angle-drive portable electric machines that take a 7-in. backing pad. This pad is made to accept a bonnet of convoluted foam, lamb's wool, or synthetic lamb's wool. Don't confuse power buffers with similar-looking 7-in. right-angle body grinders: They are too fast and will generate too much heat for rubbing out. And save the orbital waxer/polishers sold at hardware and auto-supply stores for spiffing up your automobile; they're too slow for serious work on wood finishes.

A power buffer uses the rotating bonnet to apply rubbing, polishing, or glazing compound to the finish surface. With lamb's-wool bonnets, the natural or synthetic wool (which has its own abrasive quality) abrades the finish right along with the action of the compound.

While a power buffer can save you a lot of time, it can also get you into trouble faster than you can say "rub through." A bonnet creates a surprising amount of heat, which can quickly ruin a finish film. Reducing the speed on a variable-speed machine also reduces heat by slowing down the bonnet's abrasive action. Always start the machine while the bonnet is in contact with the surface. Dropping the running bonnet on a surface can create streaks and gouges. As you work, keep the buffer moving at all times and try to keep only a semicircular portion of the bonnet in contact with the surface. When you wish to stop buffing, pull the bonnet off while it's running. If you buff near an edge, tilt the buffer so that the part of the bonnet that's doing the work is rotating away from the edge, instead of into it (see the drawing below). Most important, let the weight of the machine do the job; don't press down hard. Work in small areas at a time—a couple of square feet at the most—and blend in your strokes as you go.

POWER BUFFING NEAR AN EDGE

When buffing a surface at the edge of a top or panel, tilt the buffer; the part of the bonnet that is doing the work (shaded area) should spin away from the edge.

Removing swirl marks If you're creating a very high-gloss polish by hand, it's likely at this stage that your efforts have resulted in a shiny surface compromised only by slight streaks (formed by very slight differences in pressure or cutting action). If you've used a power buffer, the finish will probably have some swirl marks. These are usually so slight that you can easily live with them, unless you're creating a black piano finish, in which case they're painfully visible. (Those of us who have owned a black car know all too well that black really shows up the most minute scratches and smudges.)

If you really want to go all out and remove even the faintest swirl marks or streaks for a world-class gloss surface, use an automotive liquid glazing compound, also called "swirl mark eliminator" as a final polish. These products contain special resins that actually fill in the microscopic scratches, and hence create an even more lustrous shine. However, you should avoid products that contain silicones, which can wreak havoc by causing fisheyes if the finish requires future repair.

To use a swirl-mark eliminator, fit your buffer or random-orbit sander with a clean convoluted foam pad (see the photo below). Dip the pad in the glazing compound, and run the pad across the surface, working just as with other polishes. After the compound dries, run the pad over the surface a few more times, to burnish the finish. Blow or wipe off the residue and stand back. And be sure to wear your sunglasses when admiring that sparkling surface.

Swirl-mark eliminator, applied with a clean convoluted foam pad, will fill in whatever tiny scratches yet remain, leaving a gleaming finish.

Removing an Old Finish

Many people reach immediately for sandpaper when faced with a refinishing job. But that's almost always a bad idea, for several reasons. First, it can be slow, tough work, depending on the hardness of the finish. Second, sanding an old piece down to bare wood will destroy the patina (the surface aging), and a lot of the character of the piece with it. Finally, if you don't know much about the piece, you could be in for a nasty surprise if the wood was originally stained, faux finished, or veneered. Many hobbyists have set out to refinish a lovely "rosewood" furniture bargain, only to discover that it is really faux-finished pine or birch.

It's far more prudent to use a chemical stripper to soften the finish so that it may be removed. Once the viscous stripper has been applied and allowed to do its work, putty knives, scrapers, and stiff-bristle brushes are best for removing the gunk from flat surfaces. On curved parts, turnings and carvings, coarse (maroon-grade) non-woven plastic abrasives are terrific. You can wrap the pad around the surface and rub off the softened finish. A sharp stick is useful for excising the goo from fine grooves and details.

If you eschew chemical strippers (either the nasty methylene chloride ones for their harmful fumes, or the "safe" ones because they don't work too well), you can still get paint and finish off without abrasive papers. Non-woven plastic abrasive pads can remove finishes more deftly (and with less damage to the wood underneath) than sandpapers. A coarse (maroon) rotary disc chucked in a portable drill or random-orbit sander will remove most softer finishes (nitrocellulose lacquer, shellac, varnish) with fair expedience (see the photo above right). For thicker finish films or paints, extra-coarse black plastic abrasive pads are just the ticket.

Unfortunately, some finishes, like commercial polyesters, are so tough that neither chemical strippers nor plastic abrasive pads will budge them. You have no option but sanding. Use a silicon-carbide abrasive, which is one of the hardest minerals. Choose a waterproof backing and use with soapy water as a lubricant (a few drops of liquid dish detergent in about a pint of water is about right). Be prepared to put in a lot of effort—these finishes are super hard!

You can remove most paints and finishes fairly quickly and deftly by using a coarse non-woven plastic abrasive disc mounted on a random-orbit sander or chucked in a portable drill, as shown here.

4

Tips for Handling Sandpaper

The way you treat a new car, computer, or compact disc has a lot to do with how well these items will perform and how long they will last. Woodworking abrasives are really no different: The way you prepare, handle, clean, and store your sandpaper has a whole lot to do with how convenient it will be to use and how well it will do its job.

Making the best use of abrasives also requires that you know how to recognize and remedy common sanding problems, such as cross-grain scratches, washboarding, and woolly grain. Power sanding can dish out an even more frustrating series of dilemmas, such as excessive paper loading, swirl marks, burning, streaking, and veneer sand-through. Learning how to avoid or deal with these problems help you get the best performance—and longest life—out of your coated abrasives.

Preparing Abrasive Paper for Use

Some abrasive products, such as belts, discs, and drums, are ready to use right out of the box. Others, such as sheet goods and rolls, usually must be cut to size before they're ready for use. And some abrasives need to be broken in before sanding to improve their working properties.

CUTTING SHEETS TO SIZE

Most sandpaper sheets you buy in the hardware store or from a woodworking supply catalog are 9 in. by 11 in., and you must cut or rip them to size before using them. While you can do this any old way (just don't ruin your spouse's favorite pair of scissors), here are a couple of methods that should save you time and bother. If you prefer to work by hand, see p. 134 for a strategy for folding a sheet into a handy sanding pad.

Orbital sanders require fractional sheets of sandpaper, usually quarter or half sheets. You can get half sheets by folding the paper in half lengthwise, abrasive side out, and cutting it with a knife. Abrasive minerals will dull a knife edge quickly, so it's a good idea to dedicate an old paring blade or pocketknife for this job. Fold and slice in half again for quarter sheets.

A much quicker way to size full sheets of paper is to rip them to size. If you have a metal machine table or worktable with relatively sharp edges, you can rip sheets cleanly without folding them first. Mark the position of the corners for both the half sheet and quarter sheet on your table with a marker pen and line up the edge of the paper, abrasive side up, before you rip. Pull the paper down with a smooth, continuous motion, starting from one edge. This method works only with paper backings that are no heavier than C weight. Fabric-backed abrasives can usually be torn evenly along the weave of the fabric by ripping carefully across the sheet from one edge to the other.

A quick and versatile tool for accurately tearing sheet sandpaper to size is a commercially made jig, as shown in the photo below. The

A sizing jig can shorten the time it takes to cut sheets of sandpaper to size for portable power tools or for hand work.

tool has a single sharp blade that cuts paper-, fabric-, or film-backed abrasives easily and cleanly. Lines are marked for creating all typical—and many atypical—paper sizes; you simply place the paper abrasive side down and slide it under the tool's blade, then line up the edge of the paper with the mark for the desired dimensions, and pull up to rip the paper to size.

If you're a professional woodworker (or you just hate to cut up sandpaper), many abrasive and woodworking product suppliers sell precut quarter- and half-size sheets, which are just right for most orbital and finish sanders. Another possibility is to fit your sander with a special pad and use a PSA roll dispenser (see the photo below). The pad, which replaces the stock felt backup pads found on most orbitals, has a smooth rubber surface designed for sticky-back PSA papers. The roll is one-quarter sheet in width, so you just tear off the length needed for your sander, stick it to the pad, and you're ready to sand. Paper changes are also much faster—you peel off the used sheet and stick on the new one. There's no fooling around with clamps or clips, which would be necessary when changing regular sheets.

This roll dispenser holds two rolls of quarter-sheet-width PSA sandpaper neatly, so you can quickly tear off the length you need. PSA sheets stick to a special pad designed for the sticky paper.

Stretching a sheet of sandpaper back and forth over the sharp edge of a benchtop or machine table makes it more flexible and easier to work with.

BREAKING IN SANDPAPER

As part of the manufacturing process, most coated-abrasive products undergo a flexing operation designed to break the bond bed (the make and size coats) in a controlled way. This makes belts for power sanding tools and machines more flexible and prevents cracking and shedding of the mineral. For sanding a flat surface using a sanding block or a portable power tool, sandpaper doesn't need more flexing. But for sanding curved or irregular surfaces, a little additional flexing will allow the paper to conform to the work surface more easily. Flexing can be done with sheets to be used for hand or power sanding or with discs to be used with flexible backup pads in right-angle grinders or random-orbit sanders.

To flex the abrasive, pull it over the edge of a benchtop or machine table (see the photo above). For more flexibility, turn the disc or sheet 90° and repeat the operation; for still more, turn it 45° and repeat again. Since some of the abrasive mineral is shed by the process, flexing reduces paper life somewhat, so don't overdo it.

GLUING SANDPAPER DOWN

There are many situations in which sandpaper is glued down to sanding blocks, planes, and sticks for hand sanding parts, and to flat sufaces, for sanding small parts, leveling boxes, and more (see the sidebar on the facing page). Sandpaper with a PSA (pressure-sensitive-adhesive) backing is terrific for such applications; all you do is cut off the length you need and stick it down. PSA-backed paper is available in rolls from some mail-order suppliers (see Sources of Supply, which begins on p. 209). Automobile body-shop equipment and supply stores also carry PSA-backed paper, as well as many other abrasive products that are helpful in woodworking (see the sidebar on pp. 94-95).

If you don't have a roll of PSA paper handy, don't despair. You can glue most paper- or film-backed abrasives down to either porous or nonporous surfaces using a spray craft adhesive such as 3M 77, which is available at art and craft supply stores. Spray a light coat of the adhesive onto the back of the sandpaper and wait until the glue is tacky (5 to 30 seconds), before pressing it onto the desired surface. Another good method for gluing sandpaper down is adhesive transfer tape. A special applicator deposits the sticky part of the tape without the backing, leaving a snail-slime-like trail (see the photo below). The product is available from a well-stocked stationary store or office supply.

You can turn regular sandpaper into sticky-backed paper by applying adhesive transfer tape or spray adhesive to the backing.

Other Uses for Sandpaper in the Shop

Besides sanding, coated abrasives come in handy for sharpening tools and increasing the holding power of clamps. Here are some tricks you can teach this versatile material.

Sharpening tools

You probably already have a nice stash of whetstones for sharpening and honing bladed tools, but if you don't, coated abrasive papers make a very handy and effective substitute. Ceramic or aluminum-oxide sandpaper in the 120- to 220-grit range is great for quickly reconditioning a nicked or uneven edge, or for flattening the back of a blade. Because silicon-carbide papers are

commonly available in very fine grits—down to 1000 grit or finer—they're terrific for putting a keen final edge on high-speed-steel (HSS) blades. (You'll still need special grinding wheels and diamond stones to sharpen carbide cutters.)

Before you can hone a keen edge, you have to stick the sandpaper down to a reliably flat backing. You can use a machine table for this, but it's more practical to use a sheet of ¼-in.-thick glass (see the photo below left). Have the edges ground off at a glass shop, or wrap them with a thick layer of tape, so you won't cut yourself. PSA paper rolls make for quick stick-down, as does spray craft adhesive on the back of a waterproof or film-backed paper. You can stick down several strips, each with a different grit, to one glass sheet to create a sharpening and honing center. You can use light oil for a sharpening lubricant, but water that has a few drops of liquid detergent works at least as well, and won't get your hands (or your work) oily.

Improved clamping

Clamps will be less likely to slip off the work as they're tightened if you glue a small piece of 150 grit or 180-grit paper to the clamp faces. PSA-backed paper won't work for this job, because

To prevent hand-held parts from sliding out of position, mount sandpaper to the positioning surfaces of the fences and bases of your jigs.

it creeps under pressure; use regular yellow or white glue instead. Alternatively, you can glue sandpaper to the protective blocks you use with the clamps. This works really well for beveled or mitered workpieces, where clamps tend to slip off.

Sandpaper is particularly useful for boosting your grip when holding parts in a jig or fixture. For example, strips of sandpaper glued to the fence faces on a mitering jig (see the photo above) help the operator keep hand-held parts from creeping out of position during the cut. Similarly, sandpaper glued under the spots where quick-action clamps or C-clamps clasp parts into a jig or fixture will improve the effectiveness of their hold.

Chisels and plane blades can be sharpened with sandpaper, using soapy water as a lubricant. Here, two grits of silicone-carbide PSA-backed sandpaper (one light, one dark) are mounted on a thick sheet of glass.

The Automotive Connection

We woodworkers groan and moan about how difficult it is to get a smooth, even finish on a big dining table, but pity the poor auto-body repair person! The finesse required to sand, rub out, and polish wood is trivial compared to the skill it takes to obtain a perfect finish on an expansive solid-color metal surface (such as a trunk lid or hood). There's no wood grain to hide scratches or swirl marks. As consequence, the sandpapers, sanding tools, rubbing compounds, and polishes made for the automotive industry tend to be of better quality than those commonly available to woodworkers.

Fortunately, you and I do have access to many of the automotive supplies that can make rubbing out and polishing a finish—as well as sanding bare wood smooth—a lot easier.

You might find a few of these products (such as high-quality polishing compounds) at well-stocked auto-supply stores. But you'll do much better to seek out an auto-body supply store in your area. Check your local commercial phone directory under "Automobile body shop equipment and supplies." You'll even find these stores in many small towns (after all, crunched fenders are everywhere). Unlike most mail-order industrial suppliers, which require large-quantity orders—and often only

An auto-body repair equipment and supply store can be a treasure trove for woodworkers searching for high-quality coated abrasive papers, discs, and wheels as well as compounds and accessories for rubbing out and buffing.

sell wholesale—auto-body supply stores will usually sell small quantities of most products to anyone.

Here's just a sampling of the kinds of products you're likely to find (see the photo on the facing page).

For sanding wood:

- High-quality random-orbit sanding discs, with either premium-grade aluminum oxide or exceptionally durable ceramic minerals.

- High-quality pneumatic orbital and random-orbit sanders (called jitterbugs) as well as straight-line sanders and sanding accessories, such as backing pads (see p. 144).

- Silicon-carbide belts for portable belt sanders. Originally designed for grinding glass, these expensive belts have very tight mineral tolerances (for a very even stock removal) and are waterproof. They're particularly good for wet-sanding Corian countertops, when leveling seams between pieces that have been glued together, or for cleaning up cut edges.

- File sheet rolls, for air files used in autobody work. The 2¾-in.-wide rolls come with PSA coating on the back, making them extremely handy for all manner of custom-made sanding blocks. PSA rolls are great for making your own sanding sticks, blocks, and planes (see pp. 126-127).

For rubbing out and polishing a finish:

- Finishing film discs, which are designed for sanding auto paint without a lubricant. These have an anti-loading coating that serves as a lubricant and also keeps finish from gumming up the disc; they are really handy for rubbing out a clear lacquer or polyurethane wood finish. Most auto-body supply stores also carry micron-graded abrasive discs and papers.

- Professional-grade rubbing and polishing compounds with very tightly controlled grit tolerances, for aggressive cutting with very even scratch patterns (such as 3M's Imperial and Finesse-it). Meguiar Mirror Glaze machine glazing compounds and swirl removers (found in many auto-parts stores) are also excellent.

- All manner of buffing and polishing pads, including lamb's-wool (and synthetic lamb's wool) bonnets, foam applicators, and backing pads. Also lint-free polishing cloths, surface cleaners, waxes, and more.

Prolonging Paper Life

Sandpaper is by nature a disposable product. Once the abrasive minerals have dulled or the backing has worn out, the sheet, drum, disc or belt is ready for the dumpster. But there are a few simple things you can do to forestall the inevitable demise of your abrasive products. Regular cleaning and proper storage can have a profound effect not only on how long sandpaper lasts, but also on how well it performs during its useful life.

CLEANING ABRASIVES

You'll get longer service from each piece of sandpaper if you clean it occasionally during use. If you're hand sanding most regular cabinet woods (e.g., oak, walnut, mahogany), cleaning is as simple as slapping your sanding block against your leg occasionally to remove excess dust from the abrasive. However, slapping is not particularly useful for cleaning papers used for sanding resinous woods (e.g., pine, teak), panels with glue lines or excess glue, or finishes. Unfortunately, there's really no practial way to clean paper gummed up in these ways. Don't run the risk of marring or streaking the work by continuing to hand sand with gummed-up paper; change to fresh paper often, and use an abrasive with an anti-loading coating (see p. 30).

Using a cleaning stick I'm sure there isn't a belt-sander jockey out there who hasn't used a cleaning stick before. But in case you're a recent convert to power-tool woodworking, a cleaning stick is basically a stick of soft rubber that's pressed against a spinning belt, disc, or drum. This rubber is essentially the same kind that crepe soles for shoes are made of. (In fact, you can use the soles of old shoes for cleaning sandpaper; just take them off first.) The heat generated by pressing the rubber against the sandpaper causes dust particles to cling to bits of rubber abraded from the stick, which are then whisked away. In addition to removing gummy dust from resinous woods, cleaning sticks can do a pretty good job of removing deposits of glue or finish as well, if you use them frequently, before gunk builds up.

Cleaning sticks don't work as well on abrasives manufactured with phenolic-resin make and/or size coats. These abrasives actually have a greater affinity for glues and resins than abrasives manufactured with other glue systems (see pp. 29-30).

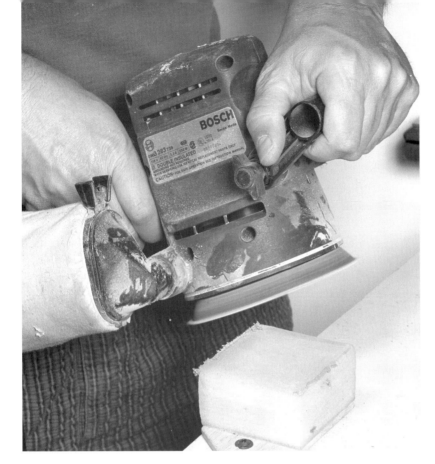

A bench-mounted rubber cleaning block is a safe, convenient way to clear swarf from the belts and discs of portable tools.

Keeping power-sanding abrasive paper clean not only allows the grit to cut better (and remove stock more quickly), but also keeps the abrasive running cooler, so its grains don't break down as quickly and the belt, disc, or drum will last longer. Just like voting, it's best to perform cleaning early and often; once the paper becomes thoroughly loaded, it's much harder to clean and only gets worse from that point on.

The technique of cleaning really isn't any more complicated than shoving the cleaning stick into the running abrasive. Moderate pressure seems to work best. Move the stick back and forth across the surface until the paper is clean (or isn't getting any cleaner). It can be a bit of a juggling act to hold the portable tool upside-down and feed the stick into it at the same time, so I prefer to use a bench-mounted cleaner (see the photo above). This is a block of soft rubber glued to a piece of wood that can be screwed to your benchtop. You can buy one of these, or glue the leftover butts of your cleaning sticks to wood scraps with contact cement. Never feed a too-short stick into a powerful, rapid running belt or disc; that can result in your fingers being suddenly pulled in and abraded to a pulp.

Running a portable sander against a scrap piece of medium-density fiberboard will help remove yellow or white woodworker's glue, which can quickly clog the abrasive grains of the belt.

Dealing with glue loading Some power-sanding jobs, such as flattening glued-up panels or woods heavy in resin or pitch content, can quickly load a belt, disc, or drum beyond the point where standard cleaning does any good. A little bit of loading makes the abrasive sand less efficiently; a lot of loading can glaze the surface of the paper to the point where the paper won't cut at all. The easiest way to remedy heavy loading or glazing is to change the paper; a quick cure, but one that isn't cheap. Here are a couple of methods that are likely to help you squeeze more life out of your overloaded abrasives.

You can coax a surprising amount of extra life out of partially loaded belts and drums by simply reversing their direction or rotation. You'll also usually get more aggressive cutting from a partially used abrasive, since you're using the reverse side of each abrasive grain. Except for unidirectional belts (see pp. 34-35), most belts and drums can be reversed by simply flipping them over and remounting (unfortunately, you can't do this with discs, unless your disc sander's motor is reversible). You'll find that cleaning reverse-running abrasives, using rubber sticks or by the method described in the next section, is very effective. Just clean them as thoroughly as you can right after remounting.

Sanding is certainly an expedient way to remove excess adhesive from a glued-up panel or assembly. Too bad the price for this convenience is shortened paper life; most glues bond with the resin coatings found on many belts and discs, and are very difficult to remove. Glue loading begets more glue loading, and pretty soon, you end up throwing out a belt that would otherwise have a lot of life left in it. Belt-cleaning sticks can help, but need to be used early and often to keep corns of glue at bay.

A somewhat effective method for removing yellow or white woodworking glues from a belt, disc, or drum is to run the loaded abrasive against a scrap piece of medium-density fiberboard (MDF). The MDF dust seems to stick to the glue and pull it off the abrasive. For use with a portable sander, nail or clamp the MDF block to your benchtop (see the photo above left). On a stationary machine, press the MDF scrap into the spinning abrasive. This works pretty well, as long as you don't let too much glue build up between cleanings. The only down side is the choking cloud of fine MDF dust (and glue used to manufacture MDF) that's produced. Squelch as much of this as possible by using proper dust collection (see pp. 151-155). A far better policy when sanding glued-up stock, such as boards glued edge to edge for a door panel or tabletop, is to reduce loading by simply scraping excess glue away before sanding.

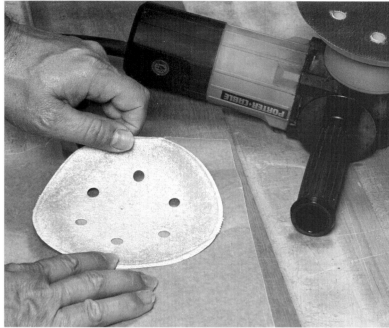

To remove resinous debris from a waterproof belt that has been sanding pitch-laden woods, such as pine, spray on a liquid belt cleaner, brush and rinse the belt, then let it dry.

To keep PSA discs clean and reusable, stick them onto a sheet of ordinary waxed paper immediately after removing them from the tool.

Removing resin One way to clean cloth belts or drum that have been gummed up with residue from sanding pitch-laden woods such as pine is to wash them: Immerse the belt or drum in a bucket filled with ¼ cup baking soda dissolved in a gallon of water. Use a plastic-bristle brush to scrub off the pitch, then let the belt or drum dry thoroughly before putting it back to work. Alternatively, you can use a liquid cleaner, such as ABC (see Sources of Supply, which begins on p. 209), a nontoxic product designed for this purpose (see the photo above left). Unfortunately, you can't use either cleaning method on belts loaded up with glue or finish.

Cleaning PSA discs If kept clean, a partially used PSA disc can be remounted many times; it's an economical way to get the most life out of partially spent discs. A clean sheet of waxed paper makes a good temporary backing material for partially used discs (see the photo above right). Just blow or vacuum excess dust off the sander and backup pad before peeling off the disc.

The Effect of Humidity on Sandpaper

Most abrasive backing materials (paper and cloth) are sensitive to changes in humidity. They exchange moisture with the air, just as wood products do. And just like a wood panel covered with plastic laminate on only one side, abrasive materials (which are coated with adhesives only on one side) will curl convex or concave as the humidity in your shop rises and falls. Unfortunately, it's nearly impossible to flatten sandpaper after it has curled. Ironing sometimes works, but don't try ironing sandpaper with anti-load coatings—they melt and come off!

High humidity, typical during moist summer weather, will soften water-soluble glues, such as hide glue, and affect abrasives made with an all-glue bond, glue bond and filler, or a resin-over-glue bond. Softening of the glue bond makes abrasive grains cut less effectively, allowing faster heat buildup, burning, and loading as well. Discs exposed to moisture can cup (abrasive side concave), making them hard or impossible to use. When excess moisture builds up, it can even dissolve the glue bonds to the point where the sandpaper will simply shed its abrasive grains.

At the other extreme, excessive dryness, common inside heated shops during winter weather, tends to make most abrasives less flexible and pliable. Paper-backed abrasive can even become brittle when exposed to dryness over a long period of time. Dry conditions also adversely affect the handling characteristics of sanding belts, making them cup (backing concave) and thus track poorly.

PROPER STORAGE

Sandpaper and coated abrasive products won't last long or perform at top efficiency unless they've been stored and handled properly. Because humidity affects the working property of sandpaper (see the sidebar above), sanding products should ideally be stored (and used) at between 60°F and 80°F, at or just below 50% relative humidity (humidity affects sandpaper more than temperature alone).

It's worth dedicating a clean drawer, cabinet, or shelf in a closet inside your shop to store abrasives. Never keep them outdoors or in an unheated (or uncooled) outbuilding. Even if your storage location is less than ideal, never store abrasives on a concrete floor or where they might be subject to dampness, such as under a sink or near a door where moisture can leak in. And don't keep abrasives on or near forced-air heaters, radiators, or heating ducts.

Smaller belts, sheets, and discs can be stored in the sealed box they came in until you're ready to use them. Larger belts need to be hung up on a large-diameter rod—a narrow hanger would cause them to crease (see the drawing on the facing page). Belts for wide-belt sanders should always be hung up or stored flat—never on edge. Laying such a wide belt on edge on a concrete floor, even for a few minutes between belt changes, can temporarily ruin its tracking characteristics (the bottom edge of the belt wicks up moisture and expands to make it slightly larger in diameter than the top edge).

Because high humidity can damage the paper backing of PSA discs, and high heat can adversely affect the pressure-sensitive adhesive, rolls of PSA-backed discs must be stored properly, both before and during use. Dust can easily contaminate unused discs—discs with holes for dust collection can even be ruined by dust while still on the roll. It's best to store PSA rolls in plastic bags and take them out only for disc changes. Never leave a roll out on the bench where it may be peppered by dust thrown up by your sander. (In some furniture and cabinet factories, workers stick handfuls of PSA discs onto their clean coveralls, where they're easy to grab when needed.)

Discs need to be removed from their backing discs or plates after use, lest they adhere to the backing and become difficult to remove (of the various types of backup discs I've tried, 3M's Silver backing discs seem to be the least susceptible to this problem). If

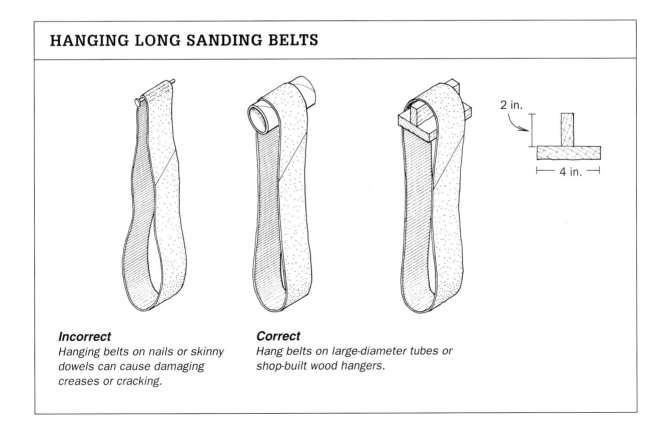

HANGING LONG SANDING BELTS

2 in.

4 in.

Incorrect
Hanging belts on nails or skinny dowels can cause damaging creases or cracking.

Correct
Hang belts on large-diameter tubes or shop-built wood hangers.

you forget (or just prefer to leave discs on) then simply heat the disc up by sanding on a scrap before attempting to remove it. Sometimes discs leave a trace of adhesive behind after they're pulled off (it looks like the trail left behind by a creeping garden snail or slug). To clean this slime away, wipe the backing pad with a clean rag dampened with a little naphtha or mineral spirits. If you find yourself changing grits often, you'll likely want to convert your PSA backup disc to use hook-and-loop style discs; see p 167.

Naturally, it's going to be tougher for you to maintain ideal sandpaper storage conditions if you live in Alaska or Florida, especially if your shop lacks heating or air conditioning. In such conditions, it's best to keep your sandpaper in a sealed plastic bag, stored inside the house if necessary. Take only what you need out to the shop when you sand. Better yet, insulate your shop and install heating or air conditioning and an air humidifier or dehumidifier as necessary. Not only will your sandpaper perform better, but you'll work a lot more comfortably as well.

KNOWING WHEN SANDPAPER IS SPENT

Although cleaning and proper storage can extend the life of any abrasive product, they do not confer immortality. Unfortunately, some woodworkers think they are saving money by using sandpaper until it is nearly bare. This practice will keep your yearly expenditures for sandpaper to a minimum, but it won't save you any work. Once the mineral grains are dull and not cutting up to par, you end up spending a lot more time and effort sanding than you should. At best, you'll spend twice as much time as if you'd changed to a fresh sheet. At worst, the dull abrasive minerals will burnish the wood instead of scratching it cleanly. Parts sanded with fresh paper end up staining and finishing differently than those sanded with dull paper, resulting in an uneven or blotchy appearance.

The useful working life of an abrasive product is determined by a great many things, such as the type of mineral, bond, backing, grit size, the kind of wood being sanded, and how the sanding is done (machine or hand). Since there's no practical formula that can account for all these factors, how can you know when a piece of sandpaper is spent? In a word: *experience*. An experienced user can actually feel how well a piece of sandpaper is cutting by sensing changes in resistance and cutting action as the abrasive dulls. In production shops, paper changes are often made on a per-part basis (e.g., after every four chair legs) or by a set period of time (e.g., every five minutes). Such rigid schedules may be wasteful, since paper is almost inevitably thrown out before its useful life is up. But they do buy a little insurance against potential sanding problems.

Burnishing with dull sandpaper Sandpaper with dull grains burnishes instead of cutting cleanly, which is usually a bad thing, but not always. Some woodworkers save used sandpaper and use it for the final stages of smooth sanding. Using dull paper to burnish the wood is like honing a final edge on a chisel by polishing it on a strop. Burnishing an already finely sanded wood surface can create a surface that's much smoother than the scratch pattern left by final sanding with a fresh sheet of very-fine-grit paper.

The trick to burnishing is that it must be done evenly. Burnishing effectively glazes a wood surface, making it less absorbent. Uneven burnishing leaves a surface that drinks up stain and finish to different degrees, leading to a blotchy appearance. Therefore, do your final burnish sanding as evenly as possible—a light hand sanding is the safest method (although, with care and practice, you can do it by machine as well). You might wish to wait until after raising the grain, and use the worn paper to dewhisker it (see pp. 65-68). The abrasive of choice for burnishing woodwork is used garnet paper (see p. 11). Its relatively soft grains round over more quickly than most artificial minerals, such as aluminum oxide.

Curing Sanding Problems

Just like all woodworking operations, sanding has predicaments that can perplex and frustrate a woodworker. Some, such as washboarding and woolly grain, can be remedied easily. Others, such as cross-grain scratching and veneer sand-through, can be prevented by slight alterations in work habits.

CROSS-GRAIN SCRATCHES

As discussed in Chapter 2, the job of leveling and smoothing a bare wood surface involves refining the pattern of scratches left by the previous, coarser grit. While sanding at an angle across the grain removes stock more quickly, your best chance of concealing the minute scratches left during final sanding is to sand with the grain of the wood. Scratches show more readily across wood's grain because they are slicing through fibers, rather than leaving grooves

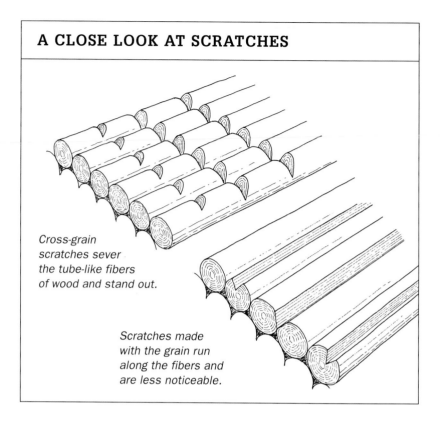

A CLOSE LOOK AT SCRATCHES

Cross-grain scratches sever the tube-like fibers of wood and stand out.

Scratches made with the grain run along the fibers and are less noticeable.

that are in line with them (see the drawing above). While coarse-grained woods tend to hide in-line scratches better, cross-grain scratches still tend to show, especially when the surface is stained and finished.

There are several ways to avoid cross-grain scratches in your sanded projects. One of the simplest is to sand all parts that will be joined cross grain (chair frames, table aprons, breadboarded tops) before assembly. You can hand-sand or power-sand these parts over their entire length, instead of worrying about inadvertently scratching cross grain where the parts connect. Joint surfaces must be left unsanded, and may need to be protected during sanding (see p. 59).

Parts that must be sanded level after assembly, such as cabinet face frames, require a different approach. Belt sanding is traditionally the quickest way of flushing up surfaces where stiles and rails join, but it demands the proper sequence and technique. These are described in detail in the sidebar on the facing page.

Steps for Belt-Sanding a Cabinet Face Frame

The cabinet face frame shown in the drawing at right can be leveled with a belt sander if you work in the proper sequence. With a light touch and a little practice, you can belt-sand a face frame in this manner quickly, and leave it with few or no cross-grain scratches, ready for further smooth sanding. Sand as follows:

The drawer-bank rails (labeled #1) are sanded first, leveling them to the stiles at both ends.

Next, the adjacent stiles are sanded, with the belt sander offset on stile #2 so that the belt sands only the stile.

The belt sander is offset also on stile #3, both to avoid sanding the #1 rails cross grain, and to level the joints where the #4 rails connect at the same time.

The #4 rails are sanded next, with the forward travel of the belt sander halted just shy of allowing the belt to cross stile #3.

At the other end, the belt is allowed to level the joint with stile #5.

Finally, stile #5 is sanded with the belt sander offset (see the photo at right) to avoid scratching the #4 rails.

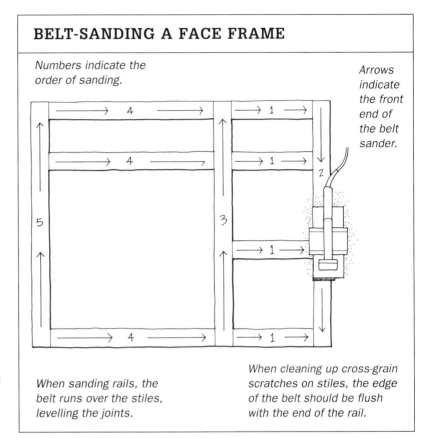

BELT-SANDING A FACE FRAME

Numbers indicate the order of sanding.

Arrows indicate the front end of the belt sander.

When sanding rails, the belt runs over the stiles, levelling the joints.

When cleaning up cross-grain scratches on stiles, the edge of the belt should be flush with the end of the rail.

You can prevent cross-grain scratches by belt-sanding the stiles and rails of a face frame in the right order. Here, a stile is sanded to remove scratches left after sanding the three rails.

Another popular way to thwart cross-grain scratches is to use a non-linear sander, such as an orbital or random-orbit sander. These machines sand with a circular rather than a back-and-forth motion, so remove stock both with the grain and across it simultaneously. While they don't leave obvious cross-grain marks where frame members meet, they may leave swirl marks (see pp. 108-109) unless used with finesse. If you sand in one place too long, random-orbit sanders can quickly create an undulating surface (in lieu of a flat one). Therefore, a light touch is called for. The narrower the frame member and the coarser the grit disc, the lighter the touch you need to use. Also, sharp corners can easily snag and rip thin paper discs.

WASHBOARD SURFACES

Like people, some woods develop more evenly than others. Most hardwoods are very homogenous and consistent in their surface hardness, but many softwoods, such as Douglas fir, hemlock, and cedar, have grain that's defined by alternating bands of soft and hard tissue. The so-called "earlywood" bands in such species are soft and wide, indicating that the tree grew rapidly during the sunlight-rich spring and summer. Harder, narrower (usually

WASHBOARD SURFACE

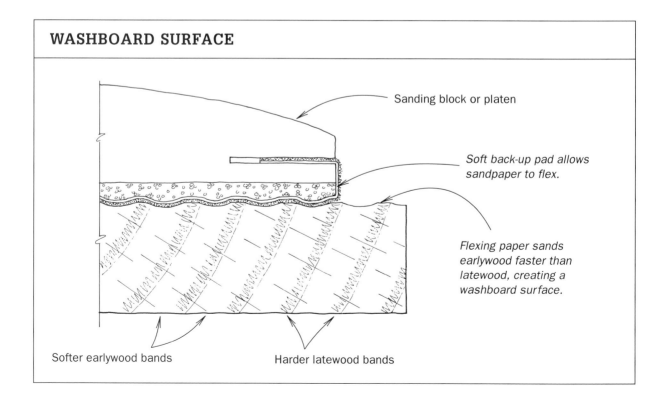

Sanding block or platen

Soft back-up pad allows sandpaper to flex.

Flexing paper sands earlywood faster than latewood, creating a washboard surface.

Softer earlywood bands

Harder latewood bands

darker) "latewood" bands reflect the tree's slower growth in the fall and winter. These undulating bands create pretty patterns in many woods, but they also make it difficult to sand their surfaces dead flat. The soft earlywood bands abrade away much more quickly than the hard latewood bands, resulting in a surface that's like an old-fashioned washboard (see the drawing on the facing page).

The best way to avoid washboarding when sanding uneven-grained woods is to sand at an angle across the grain for all but the last pass and support the sandpaper with a very firm back-up disc, block, or pad. Using paper with a heavier-weight backing can also help. A stiff backing firmly supports the paper so the abrasive grains are held in a flat plane, cutting both the latewood and earlywood evenly. In contrast, a softer backing allows sandpaper to deflect, so abrasive grains scrub out the softer earlywood valley, creating the dreaded washboard effect.

WOOLLY GRAIN

Sometimes you run into a few boards—or an area on a single board—that you just can't seem to sand smooth. These surfaces remain fibrous despite the fineness of the grit you scrub them with. Such fuzzy, woolly grain needs to be treated before sanding in order to get smooth results.

There are two ways to firm up woolly grain: Coat the surface with shellac, or paint it with a thin glue size. Both coatings work by soaking into the porous woolly grain and firming it up as they dry, so the fuzzy fibers can be sheared off more cleanly when sanded. Giving the wood a sealer coat of shellac is a good remedy for woolly grain if you plan to clear-coat it after fine sanding.

If you're going to stain the raw wood before applying a clear finish, coat the surface with a thin glue size instead. The size, created by mixing up a thin solution of hot hide glue, will take stain much in the same way the wood does. The glue is prepared just as you would regular hot hide glue, only the proportion of water is doubled. Synthetic glues—yellow or white aliphatic resins, epoxy, urea—are unsuitable for sizes because they will prevent proper stain absorption.

If you don't have hide glue (and foresee no other use for it), go to your local grocery store and buy a package of unflavored powdered gelatin, such as Knox gelatin (save the lime Jello for the kids). Gelatin, believe it or not, is a good hide-glue substitute that, when mixed 1 part powder to 3 parts water, makes a perfectly good glue size. Brush either mixture on the entire woolly-grained surface and let it dry completely before commencing with fine sanding and finishing. Even if the woolly grain is only on a section of the part, coat the entire surface to ensure an even-looking finish.

POWER-SANDING PROBLEMS

Sanding machines and tools make short work of many tedious sanding jobs, but their power and speed can cause problems. Powered abrasives may remove stock more easily, but they load up more quickly than when used by hand (for ways to clean them, see pp. 96-99). Power sanding generates a lot of heat and tends to burn the work. Even the speed with which powered abrasives can remove stock can be a liability, causing problems such as veneer sand-through. Each power sanding medium—disc, belt, and drum—also has its own special set of problems. A little know-how can help you quickly recover from these problems or prevent them from striking in the first place.

Swirl marks Because they sand both with the grain and across the grain at the same time (see the drawing below), orbital and random-orbit sanders tend to create little circular scratches called swirl marks. Three things—pressure, speed, and clinkers—can cause this problem, and consequently there are three things you can do to prevent it.

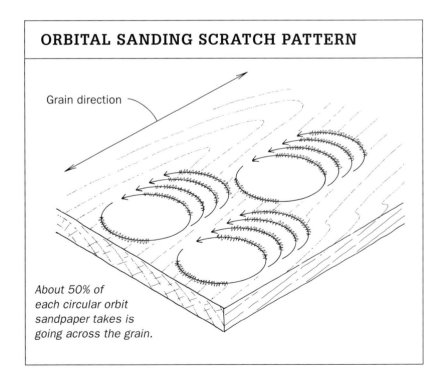

ORBITAL SANDING SCRATCH PATTERN

Grain direction

About 50% of each circular orbit sandpaper takes is going across the grain.

Abrasive paper used in a power sander requires no more pressure than the weight of the tool to cut at peak efficiency. More pressure actually decreases the rate at which the paper removes stock, and increases swirl marks and loading as well. The best remedy, as they say in stress-relief programs, is to lighten up.

In most power-sanding operations, moving too fast across a surface doesn't give the machine enough time to do its job, which is to refine the scratch pattern. For smooth sanding without swirl marks, the ideal speed for most orbital and random-orbit sanders is about 1 ft. every 10 seconds. This may feel excruciatingly slow, but it's not nearly as time-consuming as finding and sanding out swirl marks.

Cheaper, poorly graded sandpapers (e.g., "bargain" brand aluminum oxide) contain higher percentages of clinkers. These mineral particles may be considerably larger (or smaller) than the specified grit size and can leave major swirl marks. They defeat the whole point of sanding—refining the scratch pattern. Your best defense is to stick with higher-quality abrasive papers, especially when smoothing very-fine-grained hardwoods or leveling and polishing a finish. Many woodworkers prefer ultra-high-quality micron-graded papers for these tasks.

Burning Black marks on the end grain or scorch marks on the surface of a sanded workpiece indicate that the wood is actually being burned by the heat generated during power sanding. Burning is often just a surface condition, and the marks may be scraped or sanded away. It's an annoying problem that takes time to deal with and reduces the useful life of your abrasives.

There are a couple of ways to stop burning: Change the rate at which you sand, or use a different type of sandpaper. First, you can usually reduce burning by running the abrasive over the work (or feeding the workpiece into the running abrasive) more slowly. The slower cutting action produces less heat, and thus reduces the tendency for the wood to burn. On stationary belt, disc, and oscillating-spindle sanders, avoid burning by not pressing the work against the running abrasive as aggressively, especially when sanding end grain. On wide-belt and drum thicknessing sanders fitted with coarse-grain papers, decrease the feed rate and (more important) decrease the depth of cut to reduce burning. Ironically, slowing the rate of feed can actually increase burning when you are running finer-grit papers. If this happens, increase the speed slightly and set the tool for a very light cut.

Variable speed is a useful feature that can control the rate at which a power sander removes stock, to adapt it to fit different applications. Thumbwheel controls make speed changes fast and easy.

With portable sanders, you can usually reduce burning by slowing the rotational speed of the tool. Many modern power sanders have built-in variable speed selectors (see the photo above). Also—I hate to say this again, but it's really important—*avoid pressing down on the tool as you sand.*

Choosing a different type of sandpaper can eliminate, or at least reduce, problems with burning. Among the many choices of abrasive mineral, both garnet and ceramic are quite good at dissipating heat. Garnet dulls much more quickly than ceramic, but is also more affordable. More important, the paper you're using should be open coat, not closed coat (see p. 27). The extra free space on open-coat paper provides clearance for sanding swarf and so reduces heat buildup and burning. Also, a paper with an anti-loading coating (stearates) will have less swarf buildup and burning, especially when sanding resinous woods.

Streaking Streaking can occur on workpieces sanded on wide-belt, drum, or edge sanders that are running a damaged belt or drum. What usually happens is that the belt or drum has lost abrasive grains (or has been severely dulled) in a narrow stripe, from running over an exposed nail, screw, or other fastener (on rare occasions, an extra-dense knot can cause this problem). The narrow band of degraded abrasive naturally doesn't sand well, leaving streaks on the workpiece. There isn't much you can do about streaking except to replace the belt or drum, or save it for sanding workpieces narrow enough to be sanded with the undamaged portions.

Glazing—the loading of a sanding belt, disc, or drum in a narrow band —can be due to resinous wood, pitch pockets, or excessive feed rates.

Glazing Another kind of problem can occur when sanding panels on a wide-belt or drum thicknessing sander. A glue line, pitch pocket, or area of dense, gummy wood can load up the belt or drum, usually in a narrow band (see the photo above). The heavily loaded area doesn't sand well, leaving a shiny streak on the workpiece. Clean the abrasive (see pp. 96-99) to bring it back to tiptop shape.

Veneer sand-through Sanding through the face veneer on plywood is one of the nastiest problems a woodworker can encounter. The face veneers on modern hardwood plywoods are so thin that they invite disaster—I like to call them "breath of hardwood." Unless you take precautions, it takes a belt sander about a nanosecond to sand right through them, allowing the inside plies to show. Worse, such sand-throughs are nearly impossible to fix so that they're invisible; you either have to be an artist with touch-up paint or toning sprays, remake the part, or learn to live with the goof (for help on sand-through repair, see my book, *Fixing and Avoiding Woodworking Mistakes*, published by The Taunton Press in 1995).

There are three things you can do to prevent sand-through problems in the first place: Use the right abrasive mineral and grit, keep the sander moving, and use a sanding shield. Many of the new ceramic abrasives (or ceramic/aluminum-oxide hybrid products)

You can prevent veneer sand-though when flush-sanding face frames on plywood cabinets with a belt sander by clamping a long, thin piece of sheet metal over the plywood.

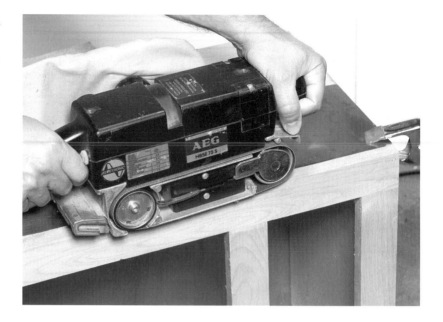

cut *very* aggressively. These are a poor choice for sanding hardwood plywoods, unless you have experience and a very light touch. To be on the safe side, fit a well-used (but not worn out) aluminum-oxide belt to your portable sander, preferably one or two grit steps finer than you'd normally use for sanding solid wood. Never use a belt that's fresh out of the box.

Even if you do have a helium-light touch, when belt-sanding plywood and veneers you must keep the sander moving constantly, lest you sand through. If you find manuevering a big belt sander to be too tiring, switch to a lighter and less aggressive type of machine, such an orbital sander, or sand by hand.

One case in which the veneer sand-through monster is most likely to rear its ugly head is when you are flush-trimming the solid-wood face frame on a hardwood plywood carcase. Even if you are using the right abrasive mineral, sanding with a light touch and keeping the sander moving, a little extra insurance never hurts. A sanding shield is a simple way to prevent trouble. A long, thin piece of sheet metal (stainless steel is best), the sanding shield can be clamped over the plywood to protect it while you sand the adjacent solid-wood part (see the photo above).

5

Hand Sanding

Most shops these days are so full of power tools that there's little need to do things like sawing or drilling by hand. But while we're usually glad to trade the tedium of sweating at a hand saw or brace and bit for the speed and convenience of a powered solution, there are still many wood shaping and smoothing jobs that aren't easily accomplished by powered sanders. Sometimes this is because you don't have—or can't afford—a power sander that will get the job done. Sometimes it's because crisp details demand the attention of hand sanding. And sometimes it's because you'd rather listen to Mozart's *Magic Flute* on the radio while you sand, rather than spending the afternoon in goggles, ear muffs, and a dust mask to protect yourself against the dusty, noisy assault of a power-sanding machine.

This chapter will present you with many helpful suggestions for getting the best results when hand-sanding flat surfaces, curved work, details, small parts, round parts, and turnings. You'll learn to handle all of these tasks with ease—and without paying the power company a penny.

Sanding Flat Surfaces

With hand planes, the straighter you want to make an edge or surface, the longer the plane body you should choose. A longer sole spans the little hills and valleys on an irregular edge or surface, allowing you to level the hills down to the height of the valleys to make an edge straight or a surface flat. The same principle holds true when sanding large surfaces flat: The larger the area of the sanding block, the more assuredly it will flatten a surface when leveling, or smooth a surface that's already been leveled without ruining its flatness. For really large surfaces, a sanding plane allows you to sand using large sheets of paper to cover more area with each stroke.

SANDING BLOCKS

Sanding blocks can be purchased or shop-built in many sizes to sand a wide variety of parts. Large blocks will support the paper and help you keep the surfaces you sand flatter. Small sanding blocks allow you to sand smaller parts more precisely, as well as to get into in areas where space is tight.

Most hardware stores and woodworking supply catalogs sell rubber or plastic sanding blocks. These are handy, as they all have some sort of clip or hold-down to keep the sandpaper in place. Such sanding blocks save hand fatigue that can develop from having to hold the paper in place. It does take time to release clips to change paper, but one production technique to get around this is to load the block with several sheets at once, then simply strip off the spent sheet when you want a fresh one.

You can easily make your own custom sanding blocks from scraps of solid wood and plywood, each sized to suit the job you have in mind. You'll generally get better sanding performance by adding a thin cushion to the working side of each block in the form of a layer of cork, rubber, or other resilient material. Cork is good because it helps the sandpaper conform to slight surface irregularities and prevents paper loading in localized areas. Cork is also durable and waterproof. One source for thin ($3/32$ in.) cork stock is Meisel Hardware (see Sources of Supply, which begins on p. 209); you just cut the size piece you want and glue it to your sanding block. For blocks not used for wet sanding, you can cover the underside with felt (Meisel also sells a sticky-back felt that's easy to mount) or with an iron-on fabric. Fabric and yardage stores sell iron-on denim patches that work well.

If you plan to use regular sheet sandpaper with your sanding block, its size should be big enough so that you can wrap a partial sheet around it. A good size for a general-purpose sanding block that uses a quarter-sheet of sandpaper is 5 in. long by 3 in. wide by 1½ in. thick. If you don't mind cutting sheets into odd-sized pieces, you can make blocks any size to suit your needs.

Your sanding blocks will be more versatile it they can work with PSA (adhesive-backed) paper. Instead of having to clip or hold paper on the block, simply stick the paper on. This saves you from having to hold the paper in place on the block as you sand. Also, you can cut the block to any shape—triangular, rounded, etc.—to sand into corners and crevices or deal with irregular surfaces (see the discussion of sanding sticks on pp. 126-127). You can use a cork cushion under PSA paper, but the adhesive sticks better to a thin layer of neoprene rubber, which is more durable than cork (see the photo at right). You can buy thin rubber (⅛ in. to ³⁄₁₆ in. thick) at many building supply stores, or cut up an inner tube from an old car or bicycle tire. Glue the rubber on with contact cement or spray craft adhesive. By the way, don't forget to remove the PSA paper from the block after you're done for the day; otherwise, it may get stuck (see pp. 101-102).

A thin piece of rubber glued to the bottom of a sanding block provides a mounting surface for PSA papers.

SANDING PLANES

You can make a sanding block big enough to hold an entire sheet of sandpaper, but you'll get hand cramps trying to grasp a block that large for a prolonged period of time. A better solution for sanding large panels and tabletops is to use a sanding plane (see the photo below). Like a bladed hand plane, a sanding plane has a flat sole

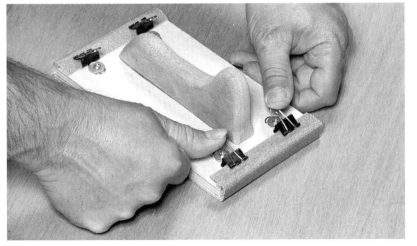

A shop-made sanding plane for smoothing panels and cabinet sides. Four notebook clips, attached to the plane with screws and fender washers, hold the sandpaper in place.

and one or two handles to allow you to put muscle into sanding without getting cramps. A good sanding plane should also have some built-in means for quickly attaching and detaching the coated abrasive, to save time on paper changes.

You can buy a ready-made sanding plane from an auto-body-repair equipment and supply store (see the sidebar on pp. 94-95) or make your own (see the drawing below). The biggest advantage to making your own sanding plane is that you can size it to fit any size of sandpaper you want, although it's probably most convenient to size the sole to take half-sheet or third-sheet sizes. Or you can size the sole to accept abrasives from cut-up old sanding belts. A plane can be almost any length; just keep in mind that pushing a really big piece of coarse-grit sandpaper around a large surface (such as the top of a harvest table) can be back-breaking work!

SHOP-MADE SANDING PLANE

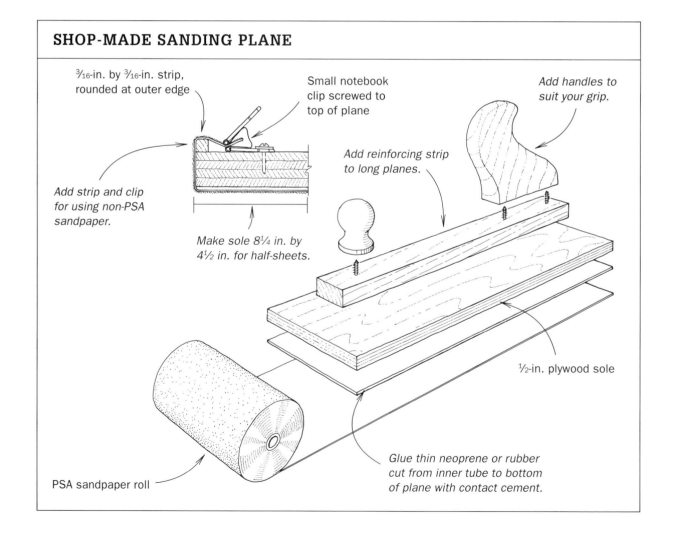

³⁄₁₆-in. by ³⁄₁₆-in. strip, rounded at outer edge

Small notebook clip screwed to top of plane

Add handles to suit your grip.

Add reinforcing strip to long planes.

Add strip and clip for using non-PSA sandpaper.

Make sole 8¼ in. by 4½ in. for half-sheets.

½-in. plywood sole

PSA sandpaper roll

Glue thin neoprene or rubber cut from inner tube to bottom of plane with contact cement.

A piece of ½-in. plywood makes a stable sole for your shop-built sanding plane that is sturdy and light. If the plane you make is longer than about 1 ft., add a reinforcing strip along the plane's centerline to keep the sole from flexing excessively. To cushion the paper, cover the underside of the sole with a thin layer of felt or, if you plan on using PSA paper, rubber (see p. 115).

If you build the plane to use regular (non-PSA) paper, you can make a simple paper-holding mechanism out of small- or medium-sized notebook clips. The clips, held to the top of the plane with pan-head screws driven through fender washers (see the detail in the drawing on the facing page), firmly hold the paper, which stretches over wood strips tacked to the front and back edges of the plane, in place. Size and shape the handles on your plane to suit the your grip, so you'll work more comfortably and raise fewer calluses.

Cleaning Up Curves

The flexibility of sandpaper makes it a good material for refining and smoothing curved shapes: a bowed cabinet side, the belly of a guitar back, or a curvilinear sculpture or carving. To smooth a regularly curved surface such as a cylinder or crown molding without distorting it (as sanding it freehand might do), you'll get the crispest results by supporting the paper with a curved sanding block—a constructed or molded block with a negative shape that matches the contour of the workpiece. For sanding irregularly curved parts, such as compound-curved surfaces and sculptural forms, you can refine and smooth with a sanding bow.

MAKING AND USING CURVED SANDING BLOCKS

A curved sanding block provides a fast, accurate way of smoothing any simple convex or concave surface, such as a bowed cabinet front or a circular pedestal ("simple" curved surfaces have a profile that bends only one way, like a cylinder—as opposed to compound curve shapes, which bend in all directions, like a ball or a doughnut). The block supports the paper in full contact with the part during sanding, for faster, more accurate stock removal.

The simplest curved blocks for sanding curved edges, such as a set of arched chair legs cut to a fixed radius, can be made by gluing sandpaper to edge of the concave or convex waste pieces left after rough-sawing parts to shape (see the photo below). Cut long waste pieces to a manageable length (4 in. to 6 in.) and glue sandpaper to the edge with a spray-on craft adhesive, or apply a strip of PSA-backed paper. If the edge of the waste piece is really rough, apply a layer of foam mounting tape first, then stick the sandpaper to it. The mounting tape adds a nice cushion beneath the abrasive paper to help keep the paper from tearing.

Concave curved surfaces, such as hollowed panels or coves, are sanded using a convex block. For small-radius curves, such on flutes and cove moldings, you can simply use dowels or tubes (for sanding more complex moldings, see pp. 123-126). Larger-radius convex blocks can be created using the simple technique of kerfing and bending. Start with a scrap block of ¾-in. plywood that's the size of the desired sanding block. Using a radial-arm saw or table saw, make a series of parallel, evenly spaced saw cuts across the block that go about two-thirds of the way through its thickness (see the drawing on the facing page). Space the cuts farther apart for a larger-radius curve, closer for a smaller-radius curve. Check the curve after cutting by applying clamping pressure to the edges parallel to the cuts (you may need to cut several profiles before you get the exact curve you need). When you're satisfied, partially fill

To make a curved sanding block for cleaning up the sawn edges of curved parts, mount sandpaper to the edge of a waste piece. White foam mounting tape allows you to use regular sandpaper and provides a soft layer beneath the paper that cushions the abrasive action.

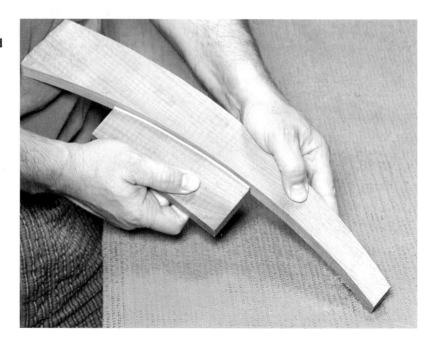

KERF-CUT CURVED SANDING BLOCK

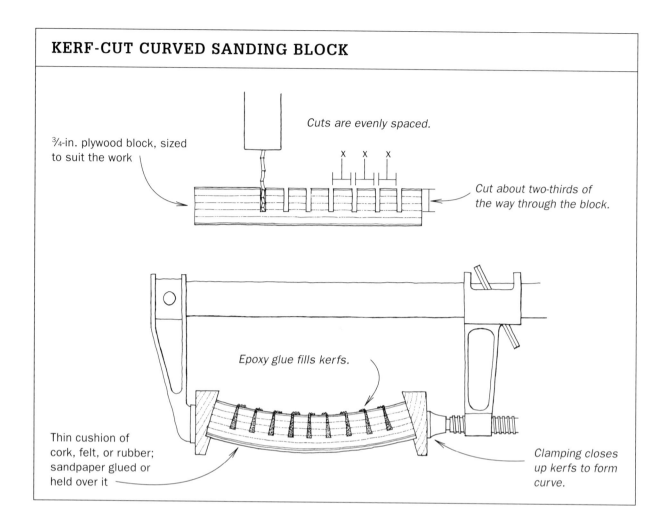

¾-in. plywood block, sized to suit the work

Cuts are evenly spaced.

x   x   x

Cut about two-thirds of the way through the block.

Epoxy glue fills kerfs.

Thin cushion of cork, felt, or rubber; sandpaper glued or held over it

Clamping closes up kerfs to form curve.

the kerfs with epoxy glue, and clamp to final shape. After the epoxy cures, cover the smooth, convex surface of the caul with a cushion of cork, felt, or rubber, as described on p. 115. Then glue on sandpaper, or hold it in place as you sand. You could also use PSA paper.

For sanding small- to medium-radius convex surfaces, such as a half-round molding or a coopered column, you can make a concave block with a radius that matches the panel's convex curve by cove-cutting on the table saw. Cove cutting is the process of passing a workpiece over the blade of the table saw at an acute angle relative to the normal line of cut (see the photo on p. 120). To set up for this, clamp an auxiliary rip fence (any straight board will do)

Cove cutting on the table saw is a great technique for making concave sanding blocks for sanding convex parts. Use a push block to keep your hands away from the blade.

to the saw table, angling it from your near left to your far right (an important detail, since this way, the blade tends to push the work tighter to the fence). The closer the angle of the fence is to the normal line of cut, the smaller the radius of the cove will be; the closer to perpendicular to the normal line of cut the auxiliary fence is, the larger the radius of the cove. When all is set up, the cove is cut a little at a time (after all, you're pushing the wood into the blade slightly sideways). Raise the blade only ⅛ in. above the saw table for the first cut, and no more than ¹⁄₁₆ in. to ⅛ in. for each subsequent pass until the desired depth of cut is reached. Cut a test piece or two, until you end up with a sanding block that matches the curvature of your workpiece fairly closely.

Once the block has been cut, glue or stick sandpaper to it (as described on p. 115). If the curved profile of the part was rough shaped by hand tools (drawknife, spokeshave), you'll want to use a relatively coarse grit to remove the tool marks and even up the curve. You can usually start sanding with finer-grit papers if the profile of the part was created by a shaper cutters or if the form was laminated. In any case, work the sanding block back and forth with the grain, keeping the block parallel to the edges of the surface—don't angle the block, as its corners and edges will dig in.

A sanding bow is convenient for smoothing or shaping a part with rounded contours, such as a chair leg, tool handle, or a ukulele neck.

SANDING BOWS

Though not as precise as a shape-specific sanding block, a sanding bow allows you to refine and smooth both regular and irregular convex curves with a surprising degree of control. A sanding bow takes a strip of sandpaper or a narrow sanding belt and stretches it between the two ends of a small bow, looking much like a violin bow. You can use a sanding bow to clean up hand-shaped parts, such as guitar necks and curvaceous furniture legs or sculpture, to knock off sharp edges on tops and panels, to smooth turned shapes, and more.

You can buy a nice ready-made metal sanding bow that uses special belts (see Sources of Supply, which begins on p. 209). As the abrasive is worked across the part, the bow flexes, allowing the belt to conform to the curvature of the work (see the photo above). When the abrasive wears out in one section, the sanding belt is rotated to access a fresh section of the belt.

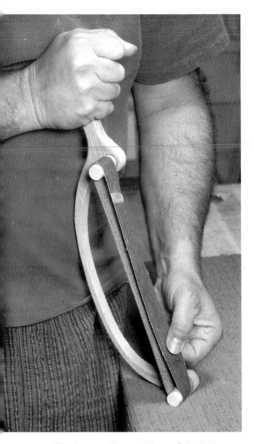

To change the position of the belt on this shop-made sanding bow, bend the bow by pressing its end against the benchtop.

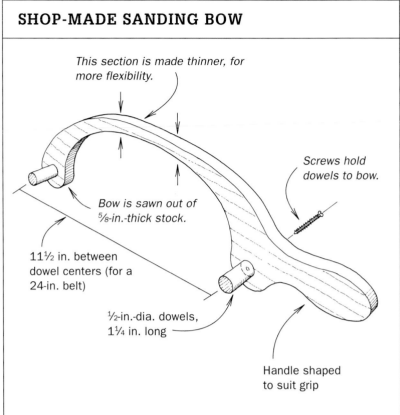

SHOP-MADE SANDING BOW

This section is made thinner, for more flexibility.

Bow is sawn out of ⅝-in.-thick stock.

Screws hold dowels to bow.

11½ in. between dowel centers (for a 24-in. belt)

½-in.-dia. dowels, 1¼ in. long

Handle shaped to suit grip

You can also make your own sanding bow, like the one shown in the drawing above. The sanding belt attaches to this bow by means of two short lengths of ½-in. dowel. The bow is sized to accept narrow belts torn from standard-sized 3x24 or 4x24 belts. The body of the bow can be sawn from any hardwood that has good natural flexibility. Ash, cherry, and yew are the best choices; avoid dense, brittle woods, such as ebony. I made my bow from ⅝-in. thick ash, but ¾-in. stock is fine too. Rough-cut the skinny part of the bow oversize, then test its flexibility. You can then increase the amount of flex by sanding away the inner and outer edges of the bow (I did this on a spindle sander). Remove only a little stock at a time. When you're satisfied with the bow's flex, glue and screw on the dowels and shape the handle to fit your grip comfortably. Before mounting or rotating the belt, flex the bow inward, as shown in the photo above left.

Sanding Moldings

Beyond simple curved forms, you can sand smooth all manner of complex profiles, shaped edges, and moldings quickly and easily by using profile sanding blocks. Like other sanding blocks, these are shaped to match the shape of the work, so that the profile of the work isn't distorted by sanding. Tadpole-brand rubber sanding blocks are great for this (see the photo at right). Made of medium firm rubber, these blocks come in sets of convex and concave shapes in a range of sizes. You simply pick the block that matches the shape of the section of molding you wish to sand, wrap a piece of sandpaper around the block, and go to work. If you need to sand a more complex profile, say a molding that's made up of coves, quarter-rounds and ogees, you may sand different sections of molding one at a time, using a separate profile block for each shape.

If you have a large quantity of the same pattern molding to sand, you may want to consider using a power-sanding alternative, such as a portable profile sander (see p. 169) or a stationary profile sander (see p. 188). In lieu of buying machinery though, you can do the job with a custom profile sanding block. This kind of sanding block accurately matches the entire profile of the workpiece, so you can sand the entire width of a complex molding—all the coves and ogees, all with a single swipe. There are several ways to do this. If you have a good selection of router bits or shaper cutters on hand, you might want to shape a profile into a single piece of wood. This typically requires you to cut and shape the wood in several stages, using a variety of different cutters and bits. Another approach is to assemble a profile block from separate pieces of molding, using short strips from an assortment of typical stock molding patterns—coves, radiuses, flat strips, and such. Hot glue is a quick, easy means of joining the individual molding strips into a single block; use the surface of the workpiece as a form for aligning the molding strips.

MOLDING A FOAM PROFILE BLOCK

Shaping or assembling a wood block, as just described, is usually time-consuming for more complex profiles, such as wide crown molding. A fairly quick method I came up with uses expanding foam sealant for making complex profile blocks, with a section of

Complex moldings, such as this crown mold, can be sanded a profile at a time by using a different rubber block for each cove, bead, and ogee.

MAKING A PROFILE SANDING BLOCK WITH EXPANDING FOAM

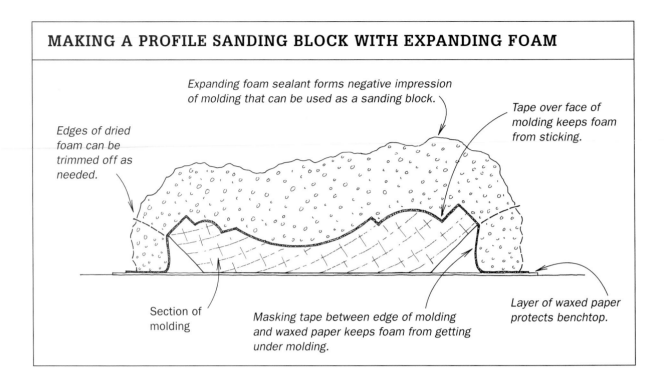

Expanding foam sealant forms negative impression of molding that can be used as a sanding block.

Tape over face of molding keeps foam from sticking.

Edges of dried foam can be trimmed off as needed.

Section of molding

Masking tape between edge of molding and waxed paper keeps foam from getting under molding.

Layer of waxed paper protects benchtop.

the workpiece serving as a mold (see the drawing above). The sealant, sold as a caulk for sealing a building's cracks and crevices, comes in cans and is available at home centers and hardware stores. (You can also use two-part urethane foam, but the stuff is expensive and has a limited shelf life.)

Start by covering a section of the workpiece, say a crown molding, with masking tape. It's best to apply two or more layers of tape to provide clearance for the sandpaper that will be glued onto the foam sanding block when it's done. Next, tape the molding section down to waxed paper or a scrap of cardboard laid out on the workbench. If the edges of the molding don't touch the paper or create a hollow space under the molding, use tape to create straight surfaces from the edges down to the waxed paper, as shown in the drawing. Eliminating any such "negative draft" (as moldmakers call it) will make it easier to lift the sanding block off after the foam hardens.

When you're ready, apply a thin layer of the expanding foam over the entire taped-over portion of the molding (follow the directions on the can for using the stuff). Lay down as many thin ribbons of the foam along the length of the molding section as it takes to cover it completely (see the photo at left on the facing page). Go easy on the foam—remember, the stuff expands about

You can make a custom sanding block for smoothing complex moldings by applying expanding foam sealant over a section of molding covered with masking tape.

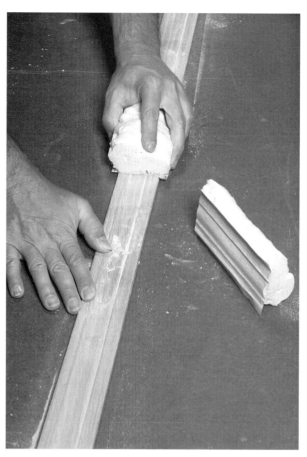

Expanded foam blocks are forgiving and apply sanding pressure more evenly than wood blocks. Each block here has a different grit of sandpaper—one coarse, one fine.

50% as it dries. The ribbons should be about ½ in. thick as they are laid down from the spout. Completely cover the molding at the edges as well; you'll trim off the excess later. Wear disposable gloves, and keep the wet foam off your skin and other surfaces—it's very sticky and hard to remove. Before setting the mold aside to dry, jiggle the foam-covered molding, tapping the underside as well, to get as many air bubbles out of it as possible.

Wait overnight before lifting the foam sanding block off the molding; if you can't wait that long, just to make sure the foam is completely cured all the way through. Try to leave a single layer of tape on the surface of the block. Carefully trim away any sections of the foam that prevent lift-off. You can then saw, sand, or cut away any parts of the block to trim it as needed. If you make a long piece, you can saw it into several individual sanding blocks, one for each grit (see the photo above right), or save some for extras.

If you've managed to leave a layer of tape on the block, you can use it to stick on any sandpaper with an A-weight paper backing. If the profile has any deep grooves or crevices, carefully precrease the paper as necessary to make it easier to conform to the block. Alternatively, you can glue or stick the sandpaper onto the foam surface of the sanding block (remove all bits of tape) using a spray craft adhesive (see p. 92). When the paper wears out, carefully peel it off and replace it with a fresh piece. You'll find these foam blocks are amazingly tough. If not abused, they will last through quite a few paper changes.

Sanding Details and Small Parts

Sometimes, the overall appearance of quality in a piece of fine woodwork comes down to the smallest details: the crispness of the edges of a box; the regularity of facets in a carved flower petal; the evenness of chamfers on a through dovetail; the flatness of small parts. Most woodworkers know enough to set aside their power tools when it's time to refine subtle details on their project, in preparation for final finishing. But even poor hand-sanding techniques can lead to mushy details, uneven edges, and rounded-over corners, spoiling the crispness and the look of quality we seek. This section contains a variety of tricks and techniques for handling the small stuff with aplomb: how to detail-sand using sticks and strips, how to sand small parts accurately, and how to break sharp edges and corners evenly and quickly, but with precision.

SANDING STICKS

Sanding sticks are like scaled-down versions of sanding blocks. You can use small sanding sticks on a wide variety of detail operations, such as sanding the edges of small parts or the inside of narrow enclosures, or touching up joinery. Commercially made spring-loaded sanding sticks (see the photo on the facing page) are fitted with tiny sanding belts, which can be rotated around to reveal fresh abrasive as the stick is used; the spring keeps the belt taut. The fine point on one end of the stick can get into very narrow slots and crevices. Sanding sticks are generally available commercially.

If you want to make your own sanding sticks, the range you can cobble up is limited only by your imagination. Sticks can be rectangular, square, triangular, round, or half-round—whatever shape you need to suit the shape of the part being sanded. Such sticks are great for sanding inside slots and holes to enlarge them, smooth them, or adjust the fit of moving parts in a mechanism, such as for a folding chair or an adjustable drafting table. You can glue sandpaper (or stick PSA paper) to only those sides of the stick that you want to do the sanding and leave the other sides smooth. The smooth surfaces guide the accurate movement of stick, but are "safe" (i.e., they don't do any sanding). Thus, a triangular stick with paper on only one surface may be used for touching up the base of the tail portion of a through dovetail joint without rounding over the sides of the tail.

Emery boards

A popsicle stick with sandpaper glued to it makes a neat little device for general detail sanding. An inexpensive alternative is to purchase emery boards (often called nail boards), sold at drug stores in the nail care section. At my local Walgreen's, I found an amazing assortment of nail boards, in many sizes and covered with different sorts of abrasive grits. The least expensive nail boards (ten for $1), were coated with a medium-grit garnet; they are good enough for light-duty chores. I find them really handy for touching up joinery surfaces or cleaning up hardware mortises. A few minutes is usually all it takes to refine a joint's fit, and I don't feel bad about throwing a 10¢ board away afterward (instead of keeping yet-another half-used piece of sandpaper around). "Better-quality" (at least more expensive) nail boards are covered with what appears to be aluminum-oxide or silicon-carbide minerals. These longer-lasting boards often come with coarser grit on one side and finer grit on the other, making them useful for refining and smoothing small details.

SANDING STRIPS

A simple strip of sandpaper can be a great device for cleaning up edges and corners, or (using coarser paper) for doing some aggressive shaping of more freeform parts. The idea is to work the strip over the part you want to sand using a shoeshine action. Sanding at an angle to the grain direction will yield maximum stock removal (see the sidebar on pp. 46-47), while sanding with the grain is best for removing (or hiding) finer sanding scratches. You can size the width of the sanding strip to suit the work. For narrow

Commercial sanding sticks are extremely handy for all kinds of detail sanding on small models as well as on full-size furniture. Each spring-loaded stick shown here has a small abrasive belt of a different grit.

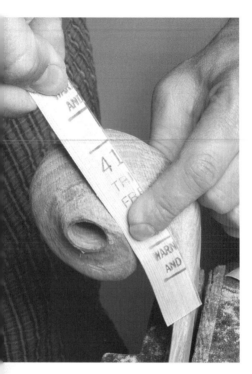

To sand a wood surface selectively, drape a strip of sandpaper over the area, put finger pressure on just the spot you wish to sand, and drag the strip through.

parts, you can rip sanding strips from old sanding belts. Regular lightweight paper-backed sandpaper can work well, but the strips will last longer if you reinforce their backs with strapping tape (regular masking tape will do in a pinch). Stick the tape onto the back of the sheet before cutting the strips with a razor blade or knife.

Strip-sanding small areas

Sometimes, you need to sand only a very small section of a part but not touch adjacent sections, say, when you want to clean up deep sanding scratches on the inside surface of a box lid without rounding over the edge of the lid. For jobs like this you can use a strip of sandpaper to sand in a special press-and-drag technique. Lay a strip of cloth-backed abrasive or a paper-backed strip reinforced with tape (see above) over the work. Press your finger directly over the section you want to sand, then grab one end of the strip and pull (see the photo at left). When working on fine details, apply pressure with your bare finger to the back of the paper. For more aggressive work (or when strip sanding for an extended time), you'll want to don canvas or leather gloves, as friction can burn your fingertips. The pressure concentrates the cutting action of the paper on just the spot you want to sand, while leaving adjacent areas untouched. With a little practice, you can do some remarkably precise work, such as smoothing the cheek on a carved face without blunting the nose (especially useful if you happen to be carving a statue of W. C. Fields or Jimmy Durante).

Softening sharp edges

Unless you use a router to round over the edges of your projects, straight 90° wood edges can be amazingly sharp. With a wide strip of sandpaper you can knock off sharp edges and soften sharp corners without ruining the crisp lines of a piece and blunting the definition that may be crucial to the effectiveness of your design. On a more practical level, people will be less likely to hurt themselves when using your project. (I once made a coffee table that had rather severe lines; I realized how severe when I was finishing it, and I cut my thumb open running my hand over the edge of the top!)

For tabletops, panels, and cabinets, work a sheet of sandpaper lightly over all the outer edges and corners, using it as you would a shoeshine cloth (see the photo at right). Work carefully to make sure that edges are softened to the same degree all around. I like to use used half-sheets left over from final sanding using my orbital sander. Used sandpaper cuts more slowly than a fresh sheet, so I'm less likely to overdo it accidentally.

SANDING REALLY SMALL PARTS

When parts get really small, such as pieces for wooden puzzles or models, it can become devilishly difficult to clamp or otherwise hold a part steady while sanding it. What's worse, it's tough to sand tiny parts without inadvertently rounding their surfaces (see the drawing below). In such cases, it's often better to keep the sandpaper stationary and move the part over the top of it. Clamp a sanding block upside-down in your bench vise, or stick some PSA paper down to a flat surface. Now work the part over the stationary paper. If your fingers are too large to hold the part, grasp it with a wooden handscrew or a pair of locking pliers. You can also use sandpaper stuck down on a large flat surface to level the top edges of boxes, lids, bowls, and other containers (see the sidebar on p 130).

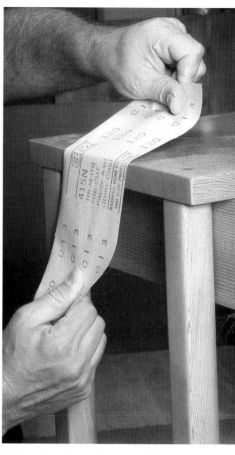

To break a sharp edge on a tabletop or cabinet carcase, lightly pull a sheet or strip of sandpaper over the edge like a shoeshine cloth.

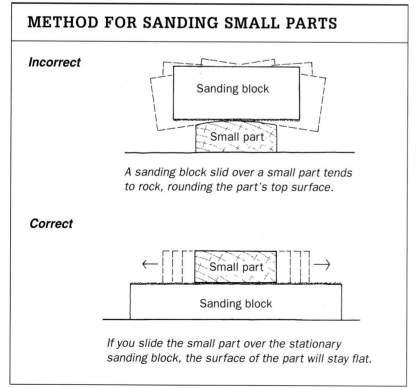

METHOD FOR SANDING SMALL PARTS

Incorrect

Sanding block

Small part

A sanding block slid over a small part tends to rock, rounding the part's top surface.

Correct

Small part

Sanding block

If you slide the small part over the stationary sanding block, the surface of the part will stay flat.

Leveling boxes, bowls, and lids

A handy method for straightening up and leveling the rim of a box, bowl, or lid is to invert it over sandpaper that's been glued down to a flat reference surface, such as a machine table or benchtop (see the photo at right). You can stick down regular sandpaper with double-stick tape or a light coating of a general-purpose craft adhesive. More conveniently, tear off a couple of strips from a PSA-backed paper roll and stick them side by side to make a sanding surface the width you need.

Set the box or bowl open side down on top of the paper and carefully move it around in a slight circular motion. If the box or bowl has a top, level the edge of the top as well. In addition to leveling the rim, this process also removes saw marks (on boxes that have had their lids

sawn off on the table saw or bandsaw) and creates a tight, clean fit between a container and its lid. You can even employ

this method for leveling and smoothing the top or bottom edges of an apron for a small table or chair-seat frame.

To smooth and level the top edge and lid of a small box, stick sandpaper down to a machine table and move the part over it in a circular motion.

Sanding Round Parts and Turnings

Sanding spindles and other lathe-produced turnings isn't that different from sanding flat or curved parts. You just need to pay attention to a few details to get the best results. Sanding straight or tapered cylindrical forms, such as dowels and cones, is straightforward: Paper can be wrapped around the piece and then worked back and forth. When sanding a rough-surface part using coarse grits, work the sandpaper around the diameter with a back-and-forth action, shoeshine fashion. Sand at an angle across the grain to remove stock quickly. When smooth-sanding with finer grits, move the sandpaper up and down, with the grain, to remove cross-grain scratches prior to finishing. You can also use concave sanding blocks, as described on pp. 117-120.

Not surprisingly, sanding more elaborate curved forms, such as spindles for chair parts or banisters, finials, or curvaceous vessels, is more difficult than sanding round parts. The problem is getting them smooth without blunting their delicate shapes and fine details. These parts are usually fashioned on a lathe, and the lathe can also be employed to sand them smooth, using both regular sandpaper and special sanding cords and tapes.

SANDING ON THE LATHE

Generally, if you turn parts on a lathe using conventional methods (with gouges, scrapers, parting tools, and so on), then it's best to smooth those parts as they rotate on the lathe. You could argue that this is really power sanding, unless the lathe is run by a treadle. But, since the sandpaper is hand held, I'm calling it a hand-sanding operation. Techniques for power sanding lathe-turned parts using portable tools are discussed on p. 177.

Many turned shapes, such as spheres, bowls, and non-intricate spindles (without fine details) are usually best sanded freehand, using a folded pad of sandpaper (see the sidebar on pp. 134-135). A folded pad not only provides you with several surfaces of fresh paper at your disposal, but the added thickness also lends a little protection from the heat that builds up very quickly when sanding a spinning turning. You can use the flat surfaces of the pad to sand convex forms, such as the bulging sides of a vase, and the edges and corners of the folded sanding pad to smooth coves, beads, fillets, and V-grooves. Coves can also be sanded by wrapping the paper around a dowel, a wine cork, or the shank of a turning tool of appropriate diameter, and pressing the paper against the turned form, as shown in the photo on pp. 132. Just don't accidentally round over the crisp edges that define the transition between turned elements. Sharp details are the hallmark of a good turning, whereas mushy, rounded-over details are a hallmark of sloppy work. If elements are too narrow or fine to sand with a hand-held pad, switch to a narrow strip of sandpaper or an abrasive cord or tape, as described on p. 133.

As to choice of grits, it's crucial when sanding a turning not to choose a paper that's any coarser than absolutely necessary to remove tearouts, tool marks, and scratches. Remember that you're sanding a spinning turning across the grain the majority of the time. Deep, coarse scratches become rings that, if not sanded out,

To smooth coves on a turned bowl or spindle on the lathe, wrap a piece of sandpaper around a dowel that's padded with a piece of felt or rubber to cushion the sanding action.

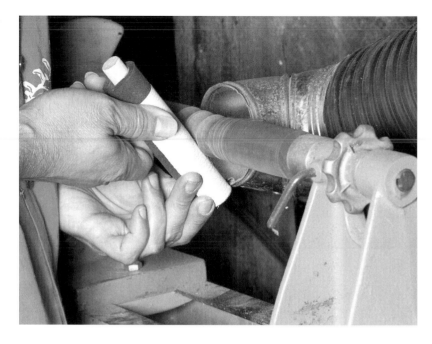

become highly visible—especially if a pigmented stain is applied, which tends to highlight deep scratches. If you're reasonably adept at turning, you shouldn't need paper coarser than about 100 grit for faceplate work and 150 grit on spindles and other between-center turnings. Plan on sanding down to at least 220 grit on coarse-grained woods, such as oak and ash. On finer-grained wood, such as maple and cherry, sand to at least 320 grit to 400 grit to ensure a smooth, clean final appearance.

When sanding on a power lathe, you must work very cautiously to prevent accidents. First, remove the lathe's tool rest and set the speed 25% to 35% slower than when doing regular turning. The slower speed helps the sandpaper to cut best and also reduces the amount of heat produced by sanding friction. Always keep the paper on the lower section of the turning, as shown in the drawing on the facing page. This way, if the sandpaper snags on the work, it will be thrown down and away from you. More important, never wrap strips of sandpaper, or lengths of sanding cloth or tape around your hands or fingers! If they should suddenly snag, the lathe could pull your hand into the spinning work, with disastrous consequences. Instead, pinch the ends of strips and cords between your thumb and index finger. If a snag occurs, the strip will simply be pulled out of your hand. The very safest way to sand on a powered lathe is to use a lathe that's has been fitted with a foot-

HAND-SANDING TURNINGS ON THE LATHE

Direction of rotation

Apply sandpaper to spinning turning only in the indicated zone.

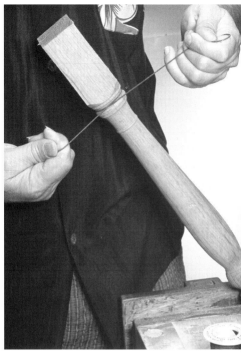

Small grooves, coves, and fillets can be effectively sanded with abrasive cord or tape. Wrap a length once around the part and pull it back and forth gently until the detail is smooth.

operated clutch (see *Fine Woodworking* #79, p. 72). If something goes wrong, you can quickly stop the workpiece from spinning by releasing the clutch.

For lathe-turned work, short lengths of abrasive cord or tape (see p. 39) can be hand held and pressed against the spinning work. Cords and tapes can also be used on stationary work, with the part held in a vise or clamp: Simply wrap a goodly length around the part and work it back and forth, as shown in the photo above right. You can take just a partial wrap around the turning, or go one or two times around it to sand a larger area at one time. Since you are sanding across the grain, don't use a cord or tape that's of a grit any coarser than necessary to get the job done.

Hand sanding sans block

Supporting a piece of sandpaper with a sanding block or plane is great for sanding most flat parts. But touch-sanding surfaces, breaking sharp edges, or smoothing gently curved or irregularly shaped parts is often best handled by using the sandpaper freehand, without a rigid backing block. Using paper freehand is also sometimes necessary when sanding in restricted spaces, such as inside pigeonholes or cubbies in a cabinet or desk.

Folded sandpaper pads

Instead of just tearing off a small piece of sandpaper and going to town, you'll get the best use from regular-size (9-in. by 11-in.) sheets by folding them into hand-sanding pads. Pads are easier to hold, and the added thickness protects your fingers from getting burned (the friction generated from hand sanding can create plenty of heat fast!).

The drawing at right shows an efficient (and traditional) way to fold a standard sheet: After the paper is flexed (see p. 91), the sheet is folded in half the long way, then into thirds across the shorter dimension. This leaves

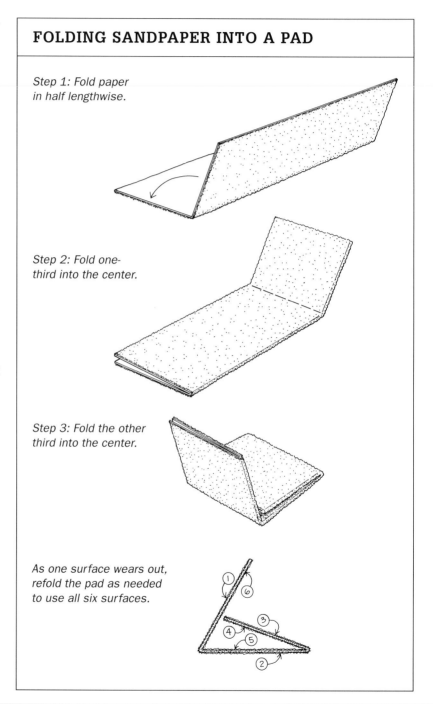

FOLDING SANDPAPER INTO A PAD

Step 1: Fold paper in half lengthwise.

Step 2: Fold one-third into the center.

Step 3: Fold the other third into the center.

As one surface wears out, refold the pad as needed to use all six surfaces.

you with a pad that's one-sixth the size of the full sheet with abrasive grit on both sides.

If you'd rather work with a slightly smaller pad, you could also fold the sheet into eighths, or you could start with a smaller piece of sandpaper in the first place. This would be desirable for sanding inside of small boxes or turnings, the latter done while they are spinning on the lathe (see pp. 131-133). However you initially fold a pad, the paper can be refolded as the abrasive wears to expose a fresh surface until the whole sheet is used up.

PSA disc sanding pads

Another dandy way to sand freehand is to use a PSA disc stuck to a rubber hand-sanding pad (see the photo at right). The foam-rubber disc is durable and provides good protection from heat and splinters, and the fabric strap on the back of the pad holds it to your palm, making it less fatiguing to use for long periods of time than a folded pad, which must be grasped. The PSA discs are the same kind used on random-orbit sanders. You can buy discs without dust-collection holes (see Sources of Supply, which begins on p. 209) but discs with

A PSA disc stuck on a foam-rubber hand sanding pad is a comfortable way to sand parts freehand. The pads use standard-diameter PSA discs made for random-orbit sanders.

holes will also work. As with other PSA papers, the PSA disc should be removed from the rubber pad after you're done

sanding (see pp. 101-102 for information on how to remove a stuck PSA pad).

6

Power Sanding

Most power sanders work in much the same way that we do when sanding by hand, but power sanders do the work much faster. But if you've ever ruined a plywood carcase with a belt sander or had a small part torn out of your hands by a flap wheel or sanded a tabletop too thin with a wide-belt sander, you know that harnessing the quickness and power of these sanding machines can be a real challenge—and a skill in its own right.

With the proper techniques, tempered with careful workmanship, power-sanding tools and machines can make short work of many tedious tasks, such as leveling and smoothing large panels. Some sanding machines, such as wide-belt sanders and drum sanders, can expand the traditional role of sanding in the woodshop to include thicknessing and surfacing rough lumber. This chapter offers advice and instruction for getting the most efficient performance from power sanders and also explains how to use both portable and stationary tools safely. Power sanders generate copious amounts of fine dust, so at the end of the chapter there is a discussion of basic dust collection, as well as advice on choosing the right mask or respirator for personal protection.

Steps to Efficient Power Sanding

Power sanders do most jobs without a lot of sweat and muscle power from the operator. But you can still end up with beads of perspiration from ruined work or frustrating problems if you don't use these tools correctly. Whether you use only portable tools or a combination of portable and stationary sanders, you must pay attention to the running speed of the tool, the feed rate, and the sanding pressure. These factors, combined with the type of abrasive paper and backing pad you use, will have a profound effect on performance and your satisfaction with the result of your efforts.

RUNNING THE TOOL AT THE RIGHT SPEED

The speed at which a belt, disc, drum, flap wheel, or other power-sanding device runs is extremely important. The proper rotational speed will result in faster stock removal with less loading of the abrasive and less burning of the stock. Excessive speed can cause premature dulling of the abrasive and shorten its life. Worse, larger-diameter sanding wheels can even self-destruct when run at excessively high speeds.

Many power portables manufactured in the last 10 years feature variable-speed controls (see the photo on p. 110). Some of the newer stationary tools also have speed controls, particularly those powered by universal motors. These controls allow you to dial in the best speed for the task you have at hand. While each tool is designed to allow speed selection within a useful range, there are really no hard-and-fast rules as to what speed is best for a particular task. It would be nice to have a chart that showed exactly what speed to use for each tool under every circumstance of use. But, even if such an ideal chart existed, it would be exceedingly tough to use. Most variable-speed tools have dials calibrated with numbers that are different from tool to tool. They usually don't correspond to standard measures of speed, such as sfpm (surface feet per minute, for sanding belts) and rpm (rotations per minute, for discs, drums, and wheels). However, there are clear guidelines to help you know when to increase or decrease the speed of the sanding machine you're using.

The faster the belt, disc, or drum rotates, the faster it will remove stock. Hence, you'll want to choose higher speed settings for jobs such as abrasive shaping or thicknessing and leveling rough stock, which require hogging away lots of material rapidly, if the tool's motor has enough power for the job. Conversely, slower speeds allow you to remove stock more slowly, and are a generally good choice for jobs that require some finesse, such as flush-sanding face frames on plywood carcases. Burning of the wood and excessive loading of the abrasive are indications that the speed of the sander might be set too high.

On some stationary machines, such as disc and drum sanders, speed changes aren't possible. These tools are often direct drive, so you couldn't change the speed if you wanted to. But you can change speeds on stationary sanders that are belt driven. Rotational speed is raised or lowered by changing the belt position on multi-step pulleys. For a slower speed, choose a smaller motor pulley and a larger arbor pulley; for a faster speed, do the opposite. On machines with single-step pulleys, changing the motor and/or arbor pulleys can reduce or increase speed.

If you're mounting a sanding disc or flap wheel to an arbor, make sure to heed the maximum recommended rpm, which is usually printed right on the hub. Exceeding the maximum rpm is dangerous, and sanding performance is also likely to suffer—the abrasive will wear out more quickly. By the way, there's no real minimum rpm. You just don't get the kind of sanding action out of an abrasive running really slowly that you would if it ran closer to the speed recommended by the tool manufacturer.

CONTROLLING THE FEED RATE

When it comes to getting a job done, we often have to trade off getting it done quickly for getting it done right. It's the same thing when choosing the right feed rate—the speed with which a workpiece is fed into a stationary sanding machine. The rate at which the work is fed into the belt, drum, or disc greatly affects sanding performance and the final smoothness of the surface left by the abrasive. This is true whether you are hand feeding the workpiece or using a machine that has a variable-speed conveyor-type belt feed, such as a wide-belt sander. Once again, there are no rules, only some guidelines.

The heavier the cut, the slower the feed rate should be. It takes a lot of work (and power) for the machine to abrade away a goodly layer of solid wood. Slowing the feed rate keeps both the sandpaper and the motor driving it running cooler, thereby preventing overloading and tripped circuit breakers. If your sander stalls, slow down the feed rate and/or reduce the depth of cut.

The finer the finish you want, the slower the feed rate—up to a point. Just as with a planer, you'll get a smoother final surface if you run the stock through a sander at a slower feed rate. Too fast, and you're likely to get chatter marks, signs that the abrasive is skipping across the surface (not unlike planer marks). Chatter marks can be quite subtle and hard to see until the stain and finish are applied, when they may become quite prominent. Examine the surface carefully if you're inching up feed rates to try to get the job done more quickly. How slow is too slow? Scorching and burn marks on the work may be one indication of too slow a feed rate. Excessive contact by the abrasive with the same area on the stock builds up heat, which will often scorch the surface and dull the abrasive prematurely. Running a dull or too-fine abrasive can also cause burning; see pp. 109-110.

Rate of feed for portables When using portable power sanders, feed rate translates into the speed with which the tool moves over the stationary workpiece. Just as with stationary machines, sanding at a rate that's too fast or too slow can cause problems. One of the chief problems that woodworkers encounter when using orbital and random-orbit sanders is swirl marks, which are formed by moving the tool too quickly across the surface of the work (see pp. 108-109). Problems with portable belt sanders usually only come about when you move them too slowly, in which case they remove stock unevenly, leading to unleveled surfaces and, on plywood panels, veneer sand-through.

AVOIDING EXCESS PRESSURE

There is little advantage to using heavy pressure when power sanding. With portable power sanders, the weight of the sander alone is adequate for good stock removal. Excessive pressure tends to cause swirl marks with orbital or random-orbit sanders and surface gouging and veneer sand-through with belt sanders.

On stationary sanders, pressing work too aggressively into the disc, belt, or drum causes burning of the workpiece and tends to dull the abrasive prematurely. Heavy pressure when sanding gummy woods or finished surfaces also causes the paper to load more quickly. On drum and wide-belt sanders, pressure is regulated primarily by the depth of cut. A deep cut puts more pressure on the sanding drum or contact roll/platen. In most cases, the best cut is achieved by bringing the abrasive in light contact with the workpiece (if the stock thickness varies, set depth of cut relative to the thickest part). Aggressive sanding on the lighter-duty kinds of machines found in small and medium-size shops is likely to stall the spinning abrasive. Thicker passes can be taken with heavier-duty industrial sanders, because they have the horsepower to handle the extra load. But these machines can cook belts and scorch work too, if work pressure and feed rate aren't set judiciously.

DISTRIBUTING THE WORK LOAD

If you did all your sanding on the same portion of a sanding drum, disc, or belt, that part would load up (glaze) and wear out before the rest. In an extreme case, such use could cause the abrasive to be worn off entirely, a condition called stripping. An unfortunate consequence of localized wear is that if you then need to use the entire surface of the abrasive for sanding a large or wide part, the worn or glazed portion doesn't do its job, leaving a band or a streak on the workpiece (see pp. 110-111). This can be a particularly nasty problem on wide-belt and drum sanders, where replacement of the unevenly worn abrasive can be a costly proposition.

The best way to avoid uneven wear is to distribute the workload across the entire surface of the abrasive whenever possible. Run narrow stock through wide-belt and drum sanders at an angle for all but the final smoothing pass (see the photo below). In addition to using a wider portion of the sanding belt or drum, angling the grain direction also results in more efficient stock removal (see the sidebar on pp. 46-47).

On a horizontal edge sander, you can also distribute the work load by tilting the machine's table (see the drawing on the facing page). Tilting not only uses a larger section of belt when sanding thin workpieces, but also generates downward pressure that helps to keep thin stock and small workpieces flat on the table during

Running narrow workpieces through a stationary wide-belt sander or drum sander at an angle distributes the work load across the abrasive and results in the fastest stock removal.

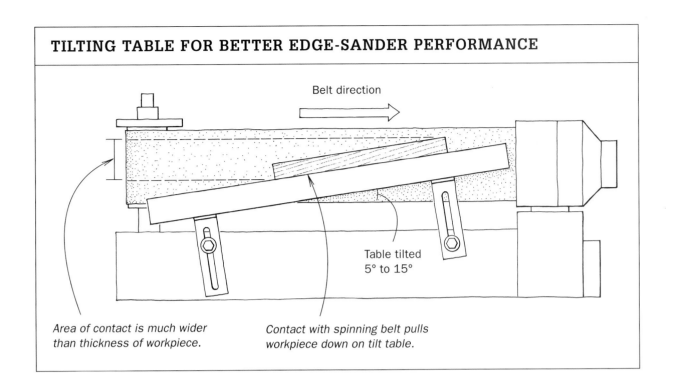

TILTING TABLE FOR BETTER EDGE-SANDER PERFORMANCE

Belt direction

Table tilted
5° to 15°

*Area of contact is much wider
than thickness of workpiece.*

*Contact with spinning belt pulls
workpiece down on tilt table.*

sanding. Further, if the wood has resinous streaks, pitch pockets, or areas of extra hard grain, these will be distributed in a wider area across the belt or drum, rather than being deposited in a single streak (see the photo on p.111).

CHOOSING THE RIGHT ABRASIVES

Because power sanders create lots of heat during use, the choice of abrasives is more crucial than when performing hand-sanding chores. Unfortunately, few of the many abrasive minerals and products developed in industry have trickled down to the small-shop (or even the cabinet-shop) woodworker. By default, aluminum oxide has for many years been the abrasive of choice for power sanding—it was just about the only mineral used for power-sanding abrasive products (it's still hard to find anything other than aluminum-oxide discs for random-orbit sanders). In recent years, aluminum oxide has been supplemented by several other abrasive minerals, including silicon carbide, ceramics, and aluminum-oxide/ceramic hybrids. These materials offer power-tool woodworkers more choices—and better performance for more demanding sanding applications.

Artificially made ceramic minerals are remarkably sharp, tough and long-lasting; the particles renew sharp cutting edges as they fracture, a trait known as friability (see the sidebar on p. 13). These qualities make ceramic abrasive products, such as 3M's Regal, terrific for really heavy-duty uses, such as abrasive thickening and grinding tasks. All-ceramic abrasives are still difficult for consumers to find (see the sidebar on pp. 94-95), and they are considerably more expensive than garden-variety aluminum-oxide products.

Fortunately, you can take advantage of ceramic's properties at more affordable prices by buying abrasives coated with a combination of aluminum oxide or alumina zirconia mixed with ceramic minerals. For example, sanding belts coated with a ceramic/aluminum-oxide mix, such as 3M's Regalite or Norton's SG, can last up to 10 times longer than a standard aluminum-oxide belt. This, in my opinion, makes them more than worth their added cost. Mounted on either portable or stationary belt sanders, these two-mineral belts are a great choice for heavy- and medium-duty sanding tasks. And because of their aggressive sanding characteristics, you can get a coarser-grit performance from a finer-grit belt: A 50-grit two-mineral belt compares favorably to a 36-grit aluminum-oxide belt, but leaves its finer (50 grit) scratch pattern.

If you have a project that requires power sanding of medium-density fiberboard (MDF), particleboard, hardboards (such as Masonite), or high-pressure laminate materials (such as Formica), silicon-carbide abrasives are a good choice. Silicon carbide has the right combination of hardness and mineral shape to handle these dense, difficult-to-sand materials well. Silicon-carbide abrasives are available primarily in sheets, for orbital and in-line sanders, and in discs for random-orbit sanders (for the latter, usually in grits finer than 220).

Choose the right grit The biggest mistake woodworkers make when selecting abrasives for power-sanding chores is choosing too fine a grit. Sanding with a grit that is too fine requires more time to remove a given amount of stock. Hence, with a portable sander, you're inclined to speed things up by applying more pressure than necessary. The weight of the tool is usually adequate pressure; more pressure only creates more heat, which can damage the surface and ruin the abrasive or, at the very least, shorten its life dramatically.

For heavy-duty tasks, such as abrasive shaping and thickening stock with either your portable or stationary sander, don't choose abrasives that are finer than 36 grit to 60 grit for the first pass. For more assistance in selecting the right coarse grit, see pp. 48-50.

Choose the right backing and belt splice If you have ever done heavy sanding using an orbital sander fitted with A-weight paper, you already realize that backing weight in an important consideration in power sanding. A-weight papers tend to tear easily when power-sanding bare wood, especially when sanding near or over sharp edges and corners. Choose A-weight papers only when using a sander fitted with a soft backing pad (see p. 144). C-weight backings are a much better choice when power-sanding with paper sheets and discs. D-weight paper backings are appropriate for even heavier work, say when running coarse-grit discs in an angle grinder. For more on backing materials and weights, see pp. 22-26.

When it comes to cloth abrasive belts, using too stiff a backing can actually become a problem: Y-weight cloth belts are too stiff to roll around the small-diameter rollers found on light-duty machines and are likely to track poorly and crack the coatings. X-weight cloth belts are just right for most small-shop sanding on stationary and portable machines, which is why they're the most common belt backings on the market. Lighter-weight backings, such as J-weight cloth, are preferable for jobs such as profile sanding, since they allow the backing to flex easily to conform to the shape of the workpiece.

Choosing the right belt splice (see pp. 33-35) is important for good power-sanding performance. Avoid top-skived splices, which may leave objectionable marks on the workpiece. For general work, butt-spliced belts are best for the 8-in.-wide and narrower belts found in most small shops.

Change sandpaper often Even if you choose the best abrasive mineral and grit for the task at hand, it won't do you any good if you continue to sand with that abrasive once it is dull. Dull abrasive grains not only tend to burnish the wood, which can lead to a blotchy finish (see p. 57), but also require more energy to remove stock. A drum sander that can easily remove $\frac{1}{32}$ in. of stock with sharp paper might bog down or even stall (at least overload the motor) while taking the same cut with dull paper. You can tell easily enough when the paper is dulling in your power sander: Coarser papers take much longer to remove material, and the motor typically slows down and sounds like it's under more load (if your sander is fitted with an ammeter, it'll register a higher load). Dull fine-grit abrasives also take longer to cut and tend to leave a shiny surface on the work. On woods with harder and softer grain areas, dull sandpaper will also tend to create a washboard surface (see pp. 106-107).

BACKING PADS, HARD OR SOFT?

The backing pad or contact roll that supports the sandpaper on a power sander has a profound impact on the tool's sanding performance. A harder pad keeps the paper flatter, so the abrasive grains cut more aggressively and leave a flatter, truer surface. A softer pad (used in conjunction with an abrasive with lightweight backing) allows the paper to flex more, so it can more easily mold to contoured surfaces. Therefore, a stiff backing pad or disc is a good choice for a task such as grinding away stock quickly with an angle grinder or disc sander. A hard backing pad gives the abrasive a lot more support and less resilience. This quality is desirable when you're trying to sand a flat panel or top—and keep it flat. Hard backing pads are especially desirable for avoiding washboarding when sanding woods with hard latewood and soft earlywood (see pp. 106-107).

Conversely, an orbital or random-orbit sander fitted with a softer backing pad is better suited for sanding curved or irregular surfaces cleanly without gouges from the edge of the disc digging in. A soft pad also makes the angle of the paper to the work surface less critical: you won't leave swirl marks if you tip the tool slightly (see the photo at left). When sanding a finish, the softer pad softens the scratch pattern of the abrasive grit, making it cut less aggressively. Hence, you reduce the likelihood of sanding through the finish, as well as reducing swirl marks. You can make a soft pad somewhat more stiff by using abrasives with a heavier-weight backing.

Graphite platen pads Sanding belts can generate amazing amounts of heat, as anyone who has touched the platen (the thing that keeps the working part of the belt flat) on a hard-working sander has already experienced. Commercial-duty stationary machines sometimes have air- or water-cooled platens, but these are far too costly for small-shop woodworkers. One lower-tech solution for reducing belt heat is a simple graphite pad that covers the platen, a feature now standard (or available as an option) on many stationary and portable sanders. The pad is a graphite-impregnated canvas-like material that may be glued or mechanically fastened to a metal platen (see the photo on the facing page). Just as graphite powder can act as a dry lubricant on

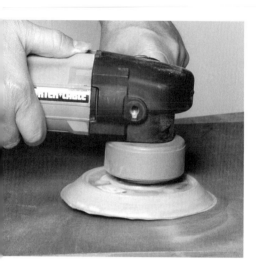

Fitting a random-orbit sander with a soft backing pad makes the sanding action less aggressive, so tipping the tool is less likely to result in swirl marks.

Covering a belt sander's metal platen with graphite-impregnated canvas reduces belt friction, effectively increasing the sanding power of the tool.

hinges, a graphite pad significantly cuts friction between the belt backing and the platen that supports it. The pad reduces heat buildup, and the reduced friction allows the motor to use less power to run the belt under load. About the only drawback to using a graphite platen pad is that it tends to coat the inside surface of the belt with shiny black graphite, making it difficult or impossible to read the imprinted information. If you're using uni-directional belts, be sure to note their correct rotation direction when removing the belt from the machine; I stick on a piece of tape with an arrow.

If your belt sander lacks a graphite pad, don't feel slighted. You can retrofit most machines with a pad made from graphite-impregnated canvas material you can buy by the yard (see Sources of Supply, which begins on p. 209). If you can't or don't want to fit a graphite pad, an alternative for reducing friction is to treat the back of your belts with a graphite stick (also see Sources of Supply). Wiping the stick over a belt's backing quickly deposits a layer of friction-robbing graphite.

Working Safely

Compared to flesh-eating tools like shapers and saws, sanding machines may seem rather harmless. But a power sander fitted with a coarse-grit belt can do plenty of damage if things get out of control and your hand ends up in harm's way. What's worse, a fingertip severed by a sharp blade usually can be reattached. If you sand off that fingertip, there's nothing to reattach—it's gone for good. Even relatively tame tools such as random-orbit sanders can inflict painful injuries, like deep cuts from accidentally coming in contact with the edge of the rapidly spinning disc. When working with power sanders, it pays to be as careful as when you operate bladed power tools, and institute many of the same precautions.

KEEPING CORDS AND HOSES CLEAR

Just as with any portable power tool, a sander's electrical cord, vacuum hose, or air hose (for air tools) can get in your way as you work, and sanders fitted with coarse belts or disc can chew through cords and hoses with hair-raising rapidity. A belt sander can be especially troublesome because it tends not only to sand through its cord, but also to suck the cord up between the belt and the body casting, where it's tough to pull out. (If this happens to you, be sure to disconnect the plug before attempting to pull the cord out; hand-turning the belt in reverse will help.)

About the best way to keep your portables' cords and hoses clear is to hang them from a tether during use. A simple tether, used as shown in the photo at left, supports the cord much like the tethers built into snazzier ironing boards. You can make a tether by bending a wire coat hanger to shape, with a tight loop at the bottom (for a screw that will anchor it to your benchtop), and a short, loose spiral at the top to hold the cord or hose. Alternatively, you can suspend hoses and cords using a bungee cord hooked to a ceiling joist or rafter in your shop.

STARTING AND STOPPING THE TOOL

Portable power sanders can generate a surprising amount of force. Setting down a running tool onto a workpiece can cause the tool to grab and jump out of your hands. At the least, the tool is likely to leave heavy scratches, gouge the wood, or, with random-orbit sanders, deposit unsightly swirl marks. Unless the sander has a variable-speed trigger, allowing you to ramp up power slowly with the tool resting on the work surface, it's wiser to bring the tool up to full speed while holding it above or in light contact with the wood, then set it to work gently and gradually. When using rotary

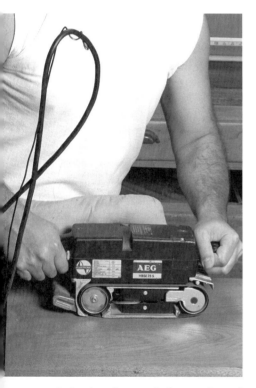

A simple tether, made from a piece of coat hanger wire screwed at one end to the workbench, will keep the cord out of your way when sanding with portable power tools.

discs (in a disc sander or random-orbit sander, or chucked in a portable drill), take care when working at or near sharp edges of panels, where the forward-spinning part of the disc may catch the edge and gouge it.

Setting a power tool down before the moving parts have stopped spinning also presents its share of surprises. Anyone who has absentmindedly laid down an idling belt sander and had it abruptly lurch from the benchtop knows just what I mean. (Years ago, after observing this phenomenon, I realized that belt sanders can be raced, and started a belt-sander drag-race event for woodworkers in my home town.)

SANDING PARTS ON STATIONARY TOOLS

Shaping or smoothing small parts on a stationary abrasive sander is fast and efficient. But feeding them into a spinning belt, drum, or disc can be tricky. One slip or incorrect movement and the sander can easily grab the part out of your hand and hurl it against the wall or floor (or your foot) with a frightening amount of force.

You can stay clear of problems when working on stationary machines by following a few handling tips. First, always keep the sharp edges on workpieces being sanded pointing "downstream," that is, toward the direction the abrasive is rotating in (see the photo above right). Edges are what usually jam or catch against a spinning belt, disc, drum, or flap wheel. If you must sand a portion of the part at or near a sharp edge—and can't position the part with the edge pointing downstream—change to a finer-grit paper and reduce the machine's rotational speed (on discs, sand closer to the center of the disc). Don't try this with flap wheels, though, which grab parts eagerly.

It's easier and safer to sand corners or curved sections of parts on a disc sander or a vertically running belt sander. If you use a horizontal belt sander, it's helpful to clamp a starting pin to the machine's table (see the photo at right). A half-round starting pin, cut from a large-diameter dowel or a scrap of 4/4 hardwood, works the same way as the starting pin on a router table or shaper: It keeps the rotational force of the tool from grabbing the workpiece. The flat side of the starting pin should be positioned about ⅛ in. from the belt surface, to prevent small parts from getting pulled in between the disc and the belt. To use the pin, bear the workpiece against it before feeding it into the running abrasive. When sanding curves, feed the part into the belt or disc in the same direction that the paper is traveling in, using the force of travel to help rotate the part. This maneuver can be tricky to master, but results in smoothly sanded curves.

A spinning flap wheel can easily grab a part out of your hands and hurl it across the shop. Therefore, work with caution and always introduce edges, corners, and ends of workpieces pointed in the direction of rotation, down and away from you.

A short, half-round piece of wood clamped to the table of an edge sander acts as a starting pin, making it easier to sand curves and sharp ends with safety and better control.

Vibration from the long-term use of orbital sanders can cause hand injuries. Avoid problems by wearing anti-vibration gloves.

REDUCING VIBRATION PROBLEMS

Certain portable power tools can subject your hands to a lot of vibration. Short periods of exposure can cause an annoying tingling in your hands and wrists; prolonged exposure can actually cause (or exacerbate) carpal-tunnel syndrome. The orbital sander, designed to produce sanding action via the oscillation of an eccentric weight just above the pad, is one of the most common culprits for vibration-related user discomfort and injury.

You can reduce hand fatigue as well as your risk of developing carpal-tunnel problems by wearing vibration-reducing gloves. Special gloves designed for woodworkers (see Sources of Supply, which begins on p. 209) have palms padded with a vibration-absorbing gel. To make them less cumbersome to wear, most models have cut-off fingers (as shown in the photo at left), just like touring gloves for bicycle riders. (As a matter of fact, many bike gloves also are padded with vibration-reducing gel, and cost less than the special woodworking gloves.) You can wear just one glove, on the hand you hold the power tool with, or wear gloves on both hands, if you often hold the workpiece you're sanding.

Personal Protection against Dust

Even if you reduce the risk of injury by handling power-sanding tools as safely as possible, you must still contend with the unpleasant fact that sandpaper produces very fine dust. At best, fine dust is a nuisance. At worst, prolonged breathing of dust can cause all manner of respiratory ailments, including bronchitis, emphysema, and nasal cancer.

Power sanding is the biggest culprit in the production of fine dust, but even hand sanding can create enough dust to be an annoyance and a health concern. Primary collection, via a shop vacuum, portable collector, or central collection system, is the best means of controlling the abundant amount of dust produced by power sanders (see pp. 151-155). But even if you do mostly hand sanding and use power sanders only occasionally, you should at least protect yourself from airborne sanding dust by wearing a dust mask or an air helmet. These devices can provide protection that's portable and easy to use, both in the shop and at the job site.

DUST MASKS

Wearing a disposable dust mask is one of the easiest things woodworkers can do to protect their respiratory health. Technically known as "disposable respirators," basic dust masks are

To get good respiratory protection with a disposable dust mask, you must choose one with two straps and a tight-fitting nosepiece. The mask at top center is designed for "nuisance dust" only and is inappropriate for serious power sanding.

inexpensive and lightweight. If used properly, can they provide you with first-rate protection against sanding dust particles between 1 and 10 microns (the size most likely to cause serious respiratory problems). For maximum protection, there are three simple requirements:

First, you must choose the right mask. Select one that is designated by NIOSH (National Institute of Occupational Safety and Health) as acceptable for protection against fine particulates. As of this writing, the standard is "TC-21-C rated." Masks with this rating are designed to protect you against airborne dusts and mists (but not from vapors, such as from paints and thinners). Do not purchase and wear "comfort masks," which are designed for short periods of wear and protection against "nuisance dust." Masks are easily distinguished by their straps (see the photo above). A comfort mask has a single strap. A TC-21-C mask has two straps, as well as a thicker shell.

Second, the mask must fit your face correctly. It doesn't matter how well a mask filters out fine particles if dust is sneaking into your nose around the edges of the mask. No mask seals properly to a bearded or stubbly face; an air helmet (see the bottom photo on p. 150) is the best choice. Even clean-shaven wearers often have problems with the mask's nosepiece; better-quality masks have molded nosepieces and/or nosepiece cushions that help seal the mask to the face. These not only prevent dust infiltration, but also improve comfort and help keep moisture from traveling up around the nosepiece and fogging up your eyeglasses or safety glasses.

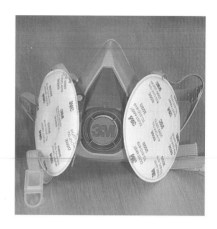

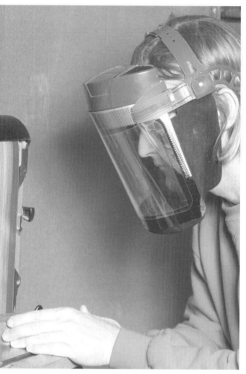

Cartridge respirators, top, and air helmets, above, are excellent defenses against fine dust.

Third, you should wear the mask both during and after sanding. The fine particles spewed out in huge quantities during heavy sanding are so light that they stay airborne for hours after sanding. Especially if you're not using dust collection at the tool, you'll need to wear your mask in the shop to gain continued protection (air-cleaning devices, described on p. 155, can help reduce this problem).

Cartridge respirators

While disposable masks are convenient and inexpensive, respirators with replaceable cartridges (see the photo above left) are more economical in the long run than disposables: You just change the filter cartridge when it's worn out. If you buy different cartridges, you can use the same mask facepiece for either dust protection (using a TC-21-C cartridge) or when spraying a solvent-based finish (using a TC-23-C rated cartridge). On the down side, respirators are heavier than disposables and require more maintenance, as they should be disassembled and cleaned after each use.

Air helmets

Known in the industry as PAPRs (powered air-purifying respirators), air helmets are pretty much the ultimate device for personal protection against fine dust. A typical model contains a battery-powered fan that pulls air through a filter and blows clean air to the user's face. A plastic safety shield and a fabric or rubber collar completely surround the user's face, containing the clean air and providing eye protection along with lung protection. Despite the name, not all air helmets have a helmet; some enclose the top of the user's head with a fabric hat. Some units incorporate the fan, battery, and filters into a helmet or visor worn on the users' head (see the photo at left), while other models locate these components in a separate belt pack, which supplies clean air through a flexible hose.

Such thorough protection does come at a cost: Be prepared to pay anywhere from $125 to $350 or more for an air helmet. Also, air helmets can be cumbersome: you'll have to get used to taking the helmet off to answer the phone or drink your morning coffee. Air helmets are probably of greatest value to bearded woodworkers, who really can't get adequate personal protection any other way. And if you are extremely allergic to various wood dusts, an air helmet may provide the only practical protection to allow you to continue woodworking.

Power-Tool Dust Collection

Dust masks, respirators, and air helmets will protect your lungs from fine sanding dust, but they are only a secondary means of control—they deal with dust after it's been blown around the shop. Dust collection, on the other hand, is a primary control measure; the idea is to trap and gather wood chips and fine sanding dust before they end up on the bench and floor, where you must sweep them up, and in the air, where they are harder to deal with.

Fortunately, most portable and stationary power tools built in the last decade include some provision for dust collection. Portables often include a collection bag or a port for connecting a hose to a shop vacuum. Stationary tools have hoods to contain dust and ports for hoses that connect the tool to a large shop vacuum or a portable or central collection system.

Delving into all the ins and outs of setting up a full-blown dust-collection system can occupy an entire book (one which, incidentally, I've already written: *Woodshop Dust Control*, published by The Taunton Press in 1996). Here, I'd like to present some ideas on how to hook up both portable and stationary sanding tools to a collection system, as well as other methods for capturing sanding dust churned out by sanders, before it messes up your shop (and your health).

BAGS AND HOSES (PORTABLES)

The removable canvas bags and filter cartridges found on most portable sanders are a great convenience. Using just the power of the fan built into the tool, they are moderately successful at collecting a reasonable amount of dust (see the photo on p. 152). Emptying most bags is, unfortunately, a dusty task—and one for which you should definitely don a mask. At least one manufacturer (Bosch) has solved this problem by offering disposable paper dust bags for its random-orbit sanders.

While using a portable sander's dust bag is better than not using it, you'll definitely breathe easier if you connect the tool to a shop vacuum or other collection system instead. On most portable sanders, you can remove the bag and connect a small-diameter (1-in. to 1½-in.) vacuum hose directly to the port. Some tool companies offer accessories that will adapt the ports on their tools to fit other standard-size hoses. Besides saving you the trouble of emptying the bag, the suction through the hose catches a lot of particles that would otherwise escape and become airborne. To prevent the vacuum hose from getting in the way, attach it (along with the tool's power cord) to a tether, as described on p. 146.

A portable power tool's built-in dust collector can capture at least some of the fine dust at the source. Dust is collected in a plastic canister (left) or a canvas bag (right).

Some of the newer models of shop vacuums, such as the Porter-Cable 7810, come with a built-in automatic switch that turns the shop vacuum on and off in concert with the power tool. The sander plugs into a special outlet on the vacuum with a circuit that senses the tool's operation.

Dust tables

Another convenient way to collect the dust churned out by portable sanding machines is to sand parts on top of a downdraft-style dust table with a slatted or perforated top. As you sand, suction pulls dust down through the openings in the table and away from the operator. Dust tables work best with fairly small workpieces; they aren't that good for sanding large panels, as dust that collects in the center isn't much affected by the downdrafting air. You can buy a dust table, which is basically just a slat-topped box with a port for connection to your portable or central dust-collection system. You can also make your own benchtop dust table, as shown in the drawing on the facing page. This table is made from ½-in. plywood or MDF, covered on top with a grid of thin wood slats. Cut these slats from pine, alder, or other soft wood, so that parts sanded atop them won't be marred. Make the slat grid removable to allow the box to be cleaned out occasionally (some dust inevitably settles to the bottom). To help curtail the dust slung out horizontally by disc, belt, and random-orbit sanders, add a three-sided baffle to the top of the dust table.

A SHOP-MADE DUST-COLLECTING SANDING TABLE

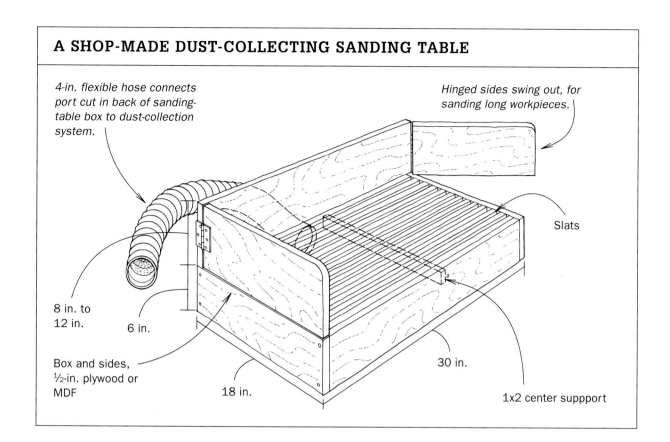

4-in. flexible hose connects port cut in back of sanding-table box to dust-collection system.

Hinged sides swing out, for sanding long workpieces.

Slats

8 in. to 12 in.

6 in.

Box and sides, ½-in. plywood or MDF

18 in.

30 in.

1x2 center suppport

Portable dust hoods

Dust tables aren't much help when using tools that really spew dust, such as right-angle grinders and die grinders. Nor are they good for collecting dust from parts and assemblies too large or cumbersome to set on top of them. In such cases, you'll get much better results—and cleaner shop air—by grinding or sanding in front of a portable dust hood. A portable hood can be mounted on a stand (see the photo on p. 154) or set on the benchtop. The idea is to set the opening of the hood in the path of the dust plume thrown out by the tool. Suction is provided by connecting the hood to a portable or central collection system (once again, shop vacuums are too wimpy for this application).

For the most efficient collection, it's important to position a portable hood as close to the dust source as possible. As it gets farther away, the ability of the collector's suction to capture and entrain the fine dust is reduced tremendously.

For portable tools that don't have built-in dust collection, such as this right-angle grinder, set up a portable dust hood where it will capture the lion's share of chips and fine dust.

DUST HOODS FOR STATIONARY SANDERS

Any stationary sander will operate more cleanly with dust collection, and many machines, such as wide-belt sanders and drum sanders, must be connected to efficient dust collection to operate properly. Without adequate collection, dust builds up on the belt or drum, causing poor abrasive performance. Eventually, the accumulating dust fouls the motor and workings of the machine.

To collect fine sanding dust from a stationary machine, a hood is used to enclose a portion of the belt, disc, or drum. The hood prevents dust from being thrown out, and it concentrates the suction of the collection system in one area, so dust may be entrained more efficiently. Most stationary machines come with a built-in hood of some kind or offer one as an optional accessory. The hood has one or more ports that allow the connection of a flexible hose or rigid ductwork. Most home-shop tools, such as small disc and combination sanders, have a 2¼-in.-dia. port, designed for connection to a regular shop-vacuum hose. This size is more of a convenience than an optimum dimension for the port. You'll get far better performance in some cases by enlarging the port and fitting a larger-diameter (at least 3 in., but 4 in. is better) hose and connecting the machine to a portable chip collector or central collection system.

Of course, you can't collect dust if you can't get it off the surface of the abrasive in the first place. The problem is that some stationary machines—stroke sanders in particular—develop a static electric charge that makes dust cling to the abrasive and resist removal. New belts with anti-static backings can help (see p. 32). You can also fit the machine with a stripper jet, a device that uses compressed air to blow dust off the belt. For instructions on building your own stripper jet, see *Woodshop Dust Control* (The Taunton Press, 1996).

AIR-CLEANING DEVICES

Even if you install and use an expensive dust-collection system, some fine dust will always elude capture. Dust masks can protect us from this dust, but air cleaners can actually remove a good portion of fine airborne dust particles from the air. Used for many years in a variety of industries, air-cleaning devices help circulate and filter particles from the air inside any enclosed workspace. Installed in a woodworking shop (see the photo at right), an air cleaner can provide an unobtrusive means of reducing the amount of respirable fine sanding dust that assaults shop users. A basic air cleaner is simply a fan and a set of filters enclosed in an airtight cabinet. The fan pulls dusty air through the filters, where a pre-filter (usually an inexpensive, replaceable furnace type) removes coarser dust; then the more expensive main filter (rated for its efficiency at removing fine dust) removes many of the respirable dust particles before the clean air is blown back into the shop.

Air cleaners are sold in different sizes, and rated to move a certain volume of air (in cfm). Ideally, all the air in your shop should pass through an air cleaner six to eight times every hour. What size cleaner does your shop need? That depends on how big it is. Calculate volume in the usual way (length × width × height) unless your ceilings are extremely high; in that case, use 12 ft. as the height. Then multiply the volume of your shop (in cubic feet) by 6 (or 8) and divide by 60. The result should equal the cfm capacity of the air cleaner (large shops need multiple cleaners). In my experience, the cfm ratings of many air cleaners are rather optimistic. To be safe, buy a unit with a cfm rating at least half again as high as your calculations say you need.

Once you have your air cleaner, install it properly. Locate a single unit on one of the long walls of the shop, with its exhaust side one-third of the way from the closest end wall. Locate multiple units on opposite walls, with their exhausts oriented to help generate a circular air movement pattern around the shop. Since very fine dust can stay aloft for hours, you should run an air cleaner both during sanding and for up to two or three hours after sanding is done.

A fan-powered air-cleaning device hanging in the shop can filter much of the very fine dust created by sanding, which otherwise would linger in the air for hours. Vacuuming the pre-filter on the front of the unit helps maintain good air flow and cleaning efficiency.

7

Portable Power Sanders

There are few woodworking shops that don't have a couple of portable power tools on hand to speed up the tedious task of sanding. But while most small shops have at least a belt sander and an orbital sander, there are lots of other portable sanding tools and devices to choose from. Some of these tools, such as profile sanders and narrow-belt sanders, have specialized purposes. Others, such as random-orbit sanders and flap wheels or foam-backed sanding discs, are versatile enough to perform many different types of sanding duties.

Portable power sanders are used primarily for smoothing wood, but they perform a great variety of other woodworking tasks as well. They can remove tool marks and refine forms; they can level rough or irregular wood surfaces, shape parts from rough-cut billets, and scuff-sand, level, and polish finished surfaces. Portable power sanders not only speed up sanding, but in many cases they also improve the quality of results over hand sanding. And, because they're portable, you can take power sanders where the work is: atop a tall armoire or stereo cabinet, or inside assembled casework. They can also do sanding at job sites away from home.

In this chapter, we'll examine a wide range of portable sanders one at a time. I'll try to point out each tool's strong suit as well its shortcomings, and offer tips for getting the most out of the tool. Occasionally, I suggest modifications you can make to enhance a tool's performance or adapt it for special functions. Accessories can further expand the capabilities of sanding tools, so these are mentioned where applicable. The chapter ends with a discussion of pneumatic sanders, with information on setting up a basic compressor system and making good use of these handy tools.

Portable Belt Sanders

One of the most popular tools in workshops of all sizes, belt sanders are truly one of the most versatile of woodworking tools. They are the portable tool of choice for leveling rough or uneven surfaces and for trimming parts flush, such as the pins and tails on the sides of a dovetailed box or drawer, or a cabinet face frame flush with its carcase.

Belt sanders commonly come in three sizes, which are described by the width and length of the belt: 3x21, 3x24, and 4x24. In addition to having a wider belt that covers more territory (and hence sands a larger area of stock at a time), 4x24 machines tend to be heavier and more powerful than machines with 3-in.-wide belts. While the 4x24 models are best for flattening large panels, they can also be quite heavy and difficult for some woodworkers to handle. Manufacturers are making improvements though; Bosch recently revamped its rugged 4x24 models, making their frames from weight-saving magnesium. For general tasks, you'll appreciate the lighter and more maneuverable 3x21 and 3x24 models. With a little practice, you can even put one of these to work sanding an edge or end of a panel freehand, although it's a bit of a balancing act.

In terms of design, many early portable belt sanders had their motors mounted perpendicular to the belt and offset to one side (like my old Sears 4x24 cast-metal dinosaur). Sanders designed this way are more difficult to keep flat—an essential task whenever working on a panel, since tipping the sander can cause the edge of the belt to gouge the surface. Many modern models, such as the current 3x21 sanders from AEG, Bosch, and Ryobi, have the motor located in line with the belt and directly above it, for better balance and ease of control.

When buying a new sander, make sure that the belt is easy to change; the levers on some models can require a surprising amount of force to operate. Some models offer important features, such as a graphite platen, which reduces friction (see pp. 144-145). Other accessories, such as sanding frames and accessory stands (discussed on pp. 158-160), can significantly enhance and expand the precision and usefulness of a portable belt sander. Be sure to check which options a manufacturer offers before buying a particular model.

Tuning Up a Portable Belt Sander

A portable belt sander (known as a "take-about" in industry) can be one of the most wonderful and versatile machines in the shop. Here are a few procedures that will help you tune up this machine and maintain it in top working condition. Some of these tips apply to stationary belt sanders as well, especially the section on belt tension.

Clean the rollers

When changing a belt or after you've run the same belt for a long time, it really pays to take the time to clean the sander's drive and idle rollers. A large buildup of dust on the rollers can cause dust to accumulate on the back side of the belt in little clumps. In addition to shortening belt life, these can telegraph through the backing and cause marring and scoring of the workpiece. A stiff brush is usually all that's needed to whisk clumps of dust and debris away. If your sander has a graphite platen pad (see pp. 144-145), belt slippage may be caused by a buildup of graphite on the drive roller, transferred from the platen by the belt backing. Wipe the graphite off with a mineral-spirits dampened rag.

Adjust the tracking

Good sanding performance from a take-about depends on the belt's tracking well. Poor tracking—the belt refusing to stay centered on the rollers, or oscillating back and forth—can be due to many causes. The belt itself may be defective, or it may have been improperly stored or left in contact with a cement floor (see pp. 100-102). Moisture from the floor can cause one side of the belt to swell to a slightly larger dimension than the other side, which is dry. Problems can also arise from belt tension being too low or too high, as discussed at the end of this sidebar.

Dust accumulating between the belt and rollers can cause poor or erratic tracking, so rollers should be kept clean. More serious tracking problems may be due to wear on the sander's drive and/or idle rollers. Excessive wear of the idle roller in the middle (where its crown helps keep the belt tracking in the center) will cause the belt to track erratically. Replacing the worn rollers should fix the problem.

The way in which you handle a sander can also affect belt tracking. Using uneven sanding pressure or pressing down too hard can cause erratic tracking in a portable belt sander. The solution is simple: Lighten up your touch. On stationary wide-belt sanders, variations in work thickness will throw belt tracking off, since the belt will creep away from the side that's removing more stock.

Regardless of brand or model, the trick to making any belt sander a good performer is to tune it and maintain it correctly. The sidebar above explains a few procedures that will help you get your portable belt sander into top shape.

SANDING FRAMES AND ACCESSORY STANDS

When trying to keep a large surface flat while sanding it level, stability is the name of the game. A sanding frame is like the stabilizing skirt around a hovercraft; it helps to keep the sander's

To check the flatness of a belt sander's platen, apply marker pen to a sheet of thick glass and rub the platen on it. High spots, which must be ground off, are revealed by the presence of the ink.

True up the platen

You'll have a hard time sanding surfaces flat with a belt sander if the tool's platen isn't flat to begin with. (The platen is the part that supports the back side of the belt in the area where sanding is done.) Platens can warp, due to heat, or wear down over time from friction (see pp. 144-145). You can check the flatness of your platen by applying ink from a wide marker pen or some paint on a sheet of glass, then setting the sander atop the glass (remove the thin metal backing plate or graphite pad first, if necessary). The ink or paint will show up on only the high areas, indicating where the platen needs to be ground down (see the photo at left).

To flatten the platen (it rhymes!), stick sandpaper—silicon-carbide paper, preferably—down to a flat machine table. Then work the platen over it until the ink/paint test shows an even coat on the entire platen surface.

Set the belt tension

Belt tension is usually preset on power portables, but generally requires user adjustment on stationary machines. Too low a tension can lead to belt slippage, flutter, and tracking problems, while excess tension can cause the belt to break. There's a simple test you can perform to check belt tension. After disconnecting the tool from its power source, grab the edge of the stationary belt with your fingers, then lightly pull it toward you from somewhere near the middle of the platen area. If the tension is right, the edge of the belt should pull away no more than ¼ in. Adjust the belt tension as necessary. Next, plug in and start the tool and adjust the tracking. Once the belt is tracking evenly and has run for a minute or so, check the tension again by feeding a thick section of hardwood end grain into the abrasive quite aggressively. You shouldn't be able to stall the belt with anything short of jamming the workpiece into the belt with gorilla-like force. (Naturally, the motor strength of the unit must be considered; you can stall a small fractional-horsepower motor before the belt will spin.) If the belt stalls with medium or medium-heavy pressure, crank up the tension a notch further.

platen dead level with the surrounding surface, and it also helps to regulate the belt's depth of cut. A sanding frame also eliminates the possibility of gouges due to tipping. Available as an accessory for quite a number of different models (AEG, Bosch, and DeWalt all offer them), the sanding frame is adjustable up and down relative to the working surface of the belt, so the sander's depth of cut can be adjusted. Even if you're fairly adept at handling a belt sander, a sanding frame (see the photo at right on p. 160) is a great asset when leveling a large expanse of wood, such as a tabletop.

Like a stabilizing skirt on a hovercraft, a sanding frame acts to keep a belt sander level and to control its cut. This is a great help when flattening large surfaces, such as tabletops.

A portable belt sander becomes a benchtop stationary tool with the addition of a stand and guide fence. This setup is ideal for precisely shaping or smoothing the edges and surfaces of small parts.

Another handy accessory is a work stand that transforms the portable belt sander into a small benchtop tool. The DeWalt DW 431 has a detachable inversion stand that supports the sander in a vertical position (see the photo above left). An adjustable fence on the stand allows you to sand accurate miters and beveled edges. This kind of stand makes it easy to use a belt sander to shape or smooth small parts for toys or models as well as drawer pulls, tenon wedges, and trim for full-sized furniture pieces. I find it much more comfortable to sand such parts on a small sander, rather than a huge stationary model. For a shop-built setup to transform your portable belt sander into a stationary edge sander, see the drawing on p. 189.

PORTABLE NARROW-BELT SANDERS

Also called power files, narrow-belt sanders typically sport a belt that's ⅜ in., ½ in., or ¾ in. wide and 12 in. to 24 in. long. Most models are pneumatic, requiring a relatively small volume of air; Black & Decker has an electric-powered unit currently on the market. Narrow-belt sanders are terrific for curvaceous shaping and smoothing, especially where access space is limited. You can easily work in tight places, such as the bottom of grooves and notches, deep recesses in carvings or sculpture, and dentil moldings (see the photo on the facing page).

A portable narrow-belt sander is an extremely handy tool for doing work in places that are hard to get to, such as the recesses on a dentil molding.

A pneumatic narrow-belt sander has a handle, which houses the mechanism that drives the belt, and a narrow head, which can be adjusted to various angles, to make the work position more comfortable. Some models have interchangeable heads, so a shorter or longer head can be fitted as need prescribes. A longer head (hence, a longer belt) offers more abrasive surface area and a longer platen to sand thicker work or reach into deeper cavities. A shorter head is more maneuverable and easier to control, though the shorter belts wear out more quickly when used for heavy-duty stock removal. I generally use my narrow-belt machine with the longer head, but have fitted a small, removable handle near the end of the head for better control. I simply tapped a hole into the head bar about 1 in. from the idler roll and fitted a plastic handle.

Most work with a narrow-belt sander is done by pressing the long side of the belt, which is supported by a narrow, flat platen, against the work. You can, however, use the end of the belt (where it runs around the idler roll) for creating or smoothing small dimples or hollows. One woodworker friend of mine even uses his narrow-belt portable sander to create large mortises, though not for refined joinery.

Because narrow belt sanders were originally developed for metal-grinding duties, such as deburring and removing casting marks from metal parts and fabricated metal assemblies, you can get belts in a wide variety of minerals and range of grits. You can also fit these sanders with non-woven plastic abrasive belts for finishing and polishing purposes.

Orbital Sanders

Orbital sanders were among the first portable electric sanders to be used in the woodshop. Also called pad sanders, orbital sanders have square or rectangular backing pads sized to take partial sheets of sandpaper. The most common sizes are quarter- and half-sheets, but there are also third-sheet and eighth-sheet units on the market. They come in both electric and pneumatic versions; the latter sometimes are called "jitterbugs."

Orbital sanders differ from random-orbit sanders (see pp. 166-168) in the way the pad is moved. An orbital sander moves the pad in an orbit without rotating it. Hence, it removes stock more slowly than a random-orbit sander. However, an orbital sander is much easier to keep flat on a work surface or edge, so it's still the tool of choice for many woodworkers for smoothing panels. I like to switch to an orbital sander for the final one or two passes when finishing up the smoothing of a panel; for large surfaces, my favorite is the powerful Milwaukee 6014 half-sheet orbital (see the photo below). For getting into tight spots, I like to use the Ryobi S-500A, with its 2¾-in. by 4-in. pad.

When smoothing a large cabinet side or panel, the large footprint of a half-sheet orbital sander helps you cover a lot of surface area quickly.

Instead of having to change paper each time it wears out, loading an orbital sander with several sheets at a time allows you to rip off the worn sheet and keep working.

On orbital sanders, a clamp holds the sandpaper to the pad. Some sanders, like the Porter-Cable model 330 Speed Bloc, require a small lever tool or screwdriver to lift the paper clamp; others, like the Makita BO4510 or Black & Decker 4011, have built-in levers that allow the paper to be changed without tools. I prefer the built-ins, as I hate to waste time searching for the lever tool, which is easily misplaced. Regardless of the lever style, sandpaper may be mounted a sheet at a time, or you can fit several sheets in place at once. The latter is a time-saving production technique that allows you simply to rip off the worn paper and reveal a new sheet, rather than removing and replacing used paper a sheet at a time (see the photo above). Alternatively, you can retrofit many popular models with a special rubber pad that's designed to take PSA paper (see p. 90), making sandpaper mounting via standard paper clamps unnecessary.

Just as when sanding by hand, the hardness or softness of the backing that's supporting the sandpaper affects the performance of the abrasive. Because they're designed primarily for smoothing, rather than shaping or leveling, the backing pads on orbital sanders are generally thick felt or soft rubber. They conform easily to non-flat surfaces and edges and generate a soft scratch pattern. However, soft backing pads are more likely to round over crisp details or cause washboarding when sanding certain woods (see pp. 106-107). Backing pads designed to take PSA paper are generally stiffer than felt pads, and they tend to make the tool sand more aggressively and create a flatter surface.

Because orbital sanders generate a considerable amount of vibration, it's also a good idea to wear padded gloves (see p. 148) to avoid carpal-tunnel syndrome and other nerve-related problems. You'll also want to set loose panels and parts on top of a soft surface before sanding, as vibration tends to emboss any debris or little bumps present atop the workbench (such as loose grit or hardened glue drips) into the underside of the work. I like to work on a piece of carpet or sound board (a soft composition material also called beaver board, which is available at home centers and lumberyards). You can also cover the bench with an old towel, foam, or a plastic routing mat.

DETAIL SANDERS

Using an oscillating pad, like an orbital sander, detail sanders have small, triangular heads that allow sanding into tight inside corners and grooves. They are also handy for sanding sections of a piece that should have been sanded before assembly, such as the inside of a chair leg between the stretchers, or the sides of a pigeonhole compartment in a secretarial desk. Used for such tasks, a detail sander allows machine sanding to be done where only hand sanding would suffice otherwise.

Many models have standard or optional extension accessories that allow you to sand into thin slots and tight spaces between parts, such as in between the slats on a louvered door (see the photo on the facing page). If you're loathe to buy another sanding tool, Woodworker's Supply sells an accessory for detail-sanding duties that mounts to the edge of a quarter-sheet orbital sander; see Sources of Supply, which begins on p. 209.

Like random-orbit sanders, detail sanders come with either PSA or hook-and-loop type backing pads. I find the hook-and-loop particularly useful for this type of tool, since you're apt to use it more often for small touch-ups and localized sanding where you need to change grits before wearing out a triangle. To get the most wear out of a pad, remove and rotate the three-sided pad as the forward-facing tip starts to dull. Hook-and-loop backing pads also allow you to mount non-woven abrasive pads, which stick naturally to them. These are handy for scuff-sanding or evening up a finish in hard-to-reach corners or surfaces and in the recesses of a cabinet or furniture piece.

The low-profile head of a detail sander can reach into tight spaces where no other sander will work, such as between the slats of an assembled louvered door.

As is true with all orbital-type sanders, it's best to switch a detail sander on and let the motor come up to full speed before bringing it in contact with the surface of the work. Switch the tool off only after removing it from the work surface. In addition to preventing deep scratches and swirl marks, manufacturers say non-load starting and stopping also prolongs the life of the tool's motor. And, again, as with all portable sanders, you shouldn't apply undue pressure as you sand. A light touch allows the tool pad to oscillate at full speed, so the sandpaper will cut better, with less risk of leaving swirl marks.

If you're using a detail sander in conjunction with other sanders, say for the inside corners of a drawer or recessed panel, use the detail sander in the corners first. Then come back and sand the middle parts of the work, feathering out the sanding near the corners where the detail sander has been used. If you must use the tool to cover a larger surface area, use a slight circular motion, or move the tool in parallel passes, each overlapping the previous pass by at least half.

Small, pistol-grip random-orbit sanders are light and easy to heft single-handed or to use overhead or on vertical surfaces. If you remove the front handle, as shown here, you can sand well into inside corners.

Random-Orbit Sanders

The random-orbit sander is a hybrid that combines the eccentric movement of an orbital sander with the rotation of a disc sander (see pp. 170-173). The simultaneous spinning and oscillation produce a unique and supremely useful sanding action. Because the eccentric orbit changes the path of the abrasive particles as the disc spins, it evens up the sanding pattern without creating hordes of swirl marks. And because the sandpaper disc runs across the grain as much as it runs with the grain, stock is removed very fast.

These days, the random-orbit sander is probably second only to the router or belt sander as the most popular tool in the woodshop. This fast-sanding tool came to woodworking via the auto-body shop, where pneumatic random-orbit sanders have been used for decades to sand body putty and smooth primers and paints. There, they are known as "DAs," which stands for dual-action. Pneumatic random-orbit sanders are popular in woodworking production shops (or any shop with a powerful enough compressed-air system to drive them). Air-powered sanders are small yet maneuverable. They are mechanically simple (see the sidebar on pp. 181-183) and lack electric motors that can clog with dust and burn out over time.

For woodworking purposes, random-orbit sanders come in three distinctly different styles: palm grip, pistol grip, and barrel grip. The palm-grip models, like the Porter-Cable model #333 and DeWalt DW421, and pistol-grip models (the Bosch 3283DVS and Ryobi RS-115) are generally more compact and maneuverable than their barrel-grip cousins. I prefer palm and pistol-grip models for general-duty sanding because they can be held with only one hand, which is convenient when sanding overhead, or reaching into tight quarters, or for when you have to hold the work with the other hand. Pistol-grip models have an extra handle in front, which provides better control when you need to use both hands. The front handle is often removable, to allow sanding into a tight corner (see the photo above left).

Barrel-grip random-orbit sanders, such as the Porter-Cable 97355 and 97366 and the Bosch 1370DEVS, strongly resemble right-angle grinders. In fact, you can buy a special attachment, made by Wolfcraft (see Sources of Supply, which begins on p. 209), that mounts directly to a small right-angle grinder and transforms it into a random-orbit sander. A barrel-grip sander has a side-grip handle (see the photo on the facing page) and requires two hands to operate with any degree of control. While less compact than pistol-grip or palm-grip random-orbit sanders, barrel-grip models usually have a more powerful motor, enabling them to hog off stock using coarse grit discs without stalling.

Although they require two hands to operate, barrel-grip random-orbit sanders are powerful enough to make short work of tough jobs, such as sanding the finish off a cabinet door panel.

Most random-orbit sanders sport either a 5-in. or 6-in. disc, the only nonconformist being the Ryobi RS-115, which uses a 4½-in. disc. The advantage to a larger disc is, of course, more abrasive area, and the ability to sand larger surfaces faster. Larger-disc machines also tend to be easier to keep flat. Conversely, smaller sanders are handier for sanding small parts or for working in cramped quarters.

The backing pads on random-orbit sanders are designed to accept either PSA or hook-and-loop sanding discs. Palm-grip and pistol-grip models, which are more consumer oriented, tend to come with hook-and-loop backing pads, while barrel-grip machines, which are more production-shop oriented, usually take PSA discs. If your sander takes PSA discs but you'd rather use hook-and-loop, simply add a conversion disc: a hook-and-loop disc with PSA on the back that sticks onto a standard PSA backing disc. If you're keen on using PSA discs on a hook-and-loop pad, simply switch backing pads (see Sources of Supply, which begins on p. 209). You can also switch to harder or softer backing pads to adapt the sanding action to your task (see p. 144).

Most sanders use backing pads with holes in them for dust collection. Drawing air through the holes in the pad does a pretty good job of cutting down on fine dust, especially if the sander is fitted with a rubber or plastic skirt that surrounds the disc. But the system won't work at all if the hole pattern on the discs doesn't match the hole pattern on the pad. Discs on various models have different numbers and patterns of holes in them—5, 6, 8, or even 16 holes. If you have sanders with several different hole configurations, you can always buy discs without holes and punch them to suit each disc (the hole punches sold by hobby stores for leatherworking work very well for this purpose).

Random-orbit sanders have a couple of limitations. They aren't the best tools to use for leveling operations (a belt sander is much better). Random-orbit sanders runs best on larger, flatter surfaces; on small parts, the paper tends to round over the edges or to hang up on sharp edges and corners. However, with a little practice, you'll find that a random-orbit sander is excellent at removing stock quickly on end grain, allowing you to sand below tool marks or deep scratches.

Straight-line sanders

Another portable tool that comes to woodworking via the auto-body shop is the straight-line sander, sometimes called a powered body file (see the photo on p. 181). The tool operates with a reciprocating back-and-forth action, resulting in a stroke of about ½ in., overall. This makes for a very smooth sanding action and a tool that's easy to control. You can use the basic reciprocating sanding action two ways: To remove stock more quickly, you can run a straight-line sander at an angle off the grain direction (see pp. 46-47). For final smoothing and maximum scratch-hiding, run the sander with the grain. Used with coarse-grit papers, straight-line sanders do a terrific job of leveling large panels while maintaining flatness. And by mounting very fine abrasive papers or non-woven plastic abrasives to the tool's pad, a straight-line sander becomes an effective and easy-to-use tool for leveling or polishing a finish (see the bottom photo on p. 80). The narrowness and controllability of the straight-line sander make it my tool of choice for edge sanding, especially on large panels and tabletops.

Currently available only as pneumatic tools, straight-line sanders have a 12-in.-long, 2¾-in.-wide pad that's usually made of dense rubber. The tool has paper clamps, like the ones on most orbital sanders, but you must buy special 17-in.-long strips (available from auto-body-repair equipment and supply shops) or cut strips from sandpaper rolls. Another option is to cut strips from PSA-backed roll paper (which comes in 2¾-in. wide rolls for this purpose) and stick them directly to the dense rubber backing. With PSA strips, paper changes are quicker and more convenient than with regular paper and the paper clamps.

For even more accurate leveling work, replace the sander's stock rubber pad with a 15-in. by 2¾-in. piece of ½-in. plywood (use a high-grade plywood, such as Baltic birch). Glue a piece of thin rubber (a segment of an old auto-tire inner tube will do) to the bottom of the replacement pad to make a good mounting surface for the PSA paper. I don't know any other way of sanding wood with a portable power tool that will yield a smoother, flatter surface.

PROFILE SANDERS

Like the straight-line sander, the profile sander works with a reciprocating back-and-forth motion. Among the models of this relatively new breed of sander currently on the market are the Dremel 6000 and the Porter-Cable model 444 (see the photo below). The 444 has a set of interchangeable rubber inserts in a variety of angled, convex, and concave profiles that are ideal for smooth-sanding shaped edges and complex moldings. Each insert fits into a holder that snaps onto the bottom of the tool. A small piece of PSA paper, cut from a roll, is stuck onto the working surface of the profile. Changing sandpaper is relatively effortless.

A special holder included with the profile sander holds two rubber inserts at once. Although sanding is done with only one at a time, having two profiles available makes it much quicker to sand complex forms, such as shaped edges and moldings. By reorienting the head of the sander, you can use, say, a ½-in.-radius cove profile to smooth a convex portion of a crown molding, then switch to a ¼-in.-radius bead to sand a cove. The Porter-Cable 444 also comes with a diamond-shaped sanding pad that snaps on, allowing the tool to be used as a detail sander (see pp. 164-165).

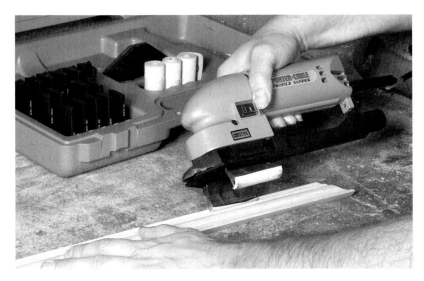

An electric profile sander provides a way of power-sanding moldings and shaped edges. This model is fitted with two convex rubber inserts that match the large and small coves on the molding.

Rotary Sanding Tools

One of the simplest ways to turn a piece of sandpaper into a power sanding tool is to cut it into a disc and spin it around. Rotary sanding using a sanding disc backed by a flexible pad can be done with any number of portable power tools, such as electric drills, right-angle grinders and polishing machines. For work on a smaller scale, there's a profusion of small-diameter wheels, discs and drums that can be used on die grinders, Dremel tools, and flexible-shaft tools.

A rapidly spinning disc fitted with a coarse abrasive can remove stock quickly, although it usually leaves deep scratches when it does. Swirl marks are also part of the bargain; they are a product of the basic motion of the disc, and it takes a very light touch and good control to keep scratches and swirl marks to a minimum.

Unlike a random-orbit sander, you never place a spinning sanding disc flat on the work surface. Instead, you angle the tool so that only a portion of the disc makes contact; the back-up disc flexes so that about one-third of the disc can make contact at a time. To sand a larger area, the tool is drawn across the surface while maintaining that third-of-the-disc contact.

ELECTRIC DRILLS

You don't need to buy a special machine in order to do disc sanding: Simply chuck the shaft of a rubber or plastic backing pad into a portable powered drill. Most electric drills are suitable, either battery or AC powered, as are pneumatic drills, such as the Northern straight-line ⅜-in. drill (model #11284-C112). Most electric and pneumatic drills rotate a 4-in. to 6-in. disc fast enough (1,500 rpm to 2,500 rpm) to be effective portable sanding tools. It helps to use a drill that has a side handle, mounted close to the chuck. This offers superior control, which is especially important if you're using coarse-grit discs to hog away lots of stock for a power-shaping operation. As with other types of sanders, different backing pads are available, and these can significantly change the way the disc performs. Stiff pads let you sand aggressively; soft pads are better for sanding contours with minimal distortion and a softer scratch pattern.

For heavy-duty shaping work, such as scooping out a solid-wood chair seat, few tools fit the task as well as a right-angle grinder fitted with a coarse sanding disc or an abrasive flap disc, as shown here.

RIGHT-ANGLE GRINDERS

Normally a tool for welders and auto-body shops cleaning up metal parts and surfaces, a right-angle grinder employed as a disc sander is a useful tool for the woodshop. It's perfect for removing stock quickly when rough-shaping parts for curvilinear furniture parts or sculpture (see pp. 41-43). It's also one of the best tools for scooping out the waste on a solid-wood chair seat (see the photo above).

The right-angle grinder is usually fitted with a coarse (24-grit to 36-grit) sanding disc (with heavy-weight paper or fiber backing) mounted to a stiff rubber or plastic backing pad. Such a coarse disc can be used for removing old paint or a thick coat of finish as well as for heavy stock removal. For shaping workpieces, fit the tool with an abrasive flap disc or a carbide grinder wheel (see pp. 173-174).

DIE GRINDERS

Pneumatic die grinders are compact, inexpensive machines that are capable of handling many smaller-diameter sanding discs. However, you must be very careful not to exceed the maximum rpm of the wheel or disc (which is usually printed right on it. Most die grinders run at upwards of 20,000 rpm, a speed that is much too fast for many sanding wheels. Small-diameter wheels won't create quite the havoc that large-diameter grinding wheels do when they explode, but they can still cause serious harm.

With an electronic speed-reduction unit, the speed of an electric die grinder can be decreased so that it is safe to use with many small sanding wheels, such as the flap wheel with alternating strips of non-woven plastic abrasive and sandpaper shown here.

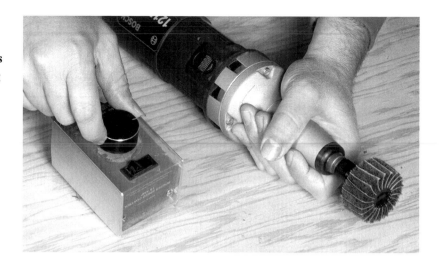

To run small wheels safely, you can buy a special pneumatic hand piece, such as the FlexaBrade sander (available from Klingspor; see Sources of Supply, which begins on p. 209), which is designed to run at only 4,000 rpm. Some die grinders, such as the Jet ¼-in. die grinder have a variable-speed feature, so you can reduce the speed of the tool to between 2,500 and 4,000 rpm, which is in the range of safe operation for most small wheels. Small-diameter wheels can be run in a Dremel tool or flexible shaft tool (discussed below).

Alternatively, you can reduce the speed of a regular pneumatic die grinder by lowering the air pressure feeding it; however, power will drop substantially. Electric die grinders, such as the Bosch 1215 (which normally run at 25,000 rpm), can be slowed down by powering them from an electronic speed-control unit that's adjusted for a lower rpm, as shown in the photo above. The main problem with slowing down these tools is that you can't easily verify the exact rpm. Therefore, be very careful and err to the side of running wheels too slowly, rather than taking the chance of running them too fast.

DREMEL TOOLS

A Dremel tool is basically a small die grinder. It's the perfect device for running small sanding wheels that have a spindle or arbor that's ⅛ in. (or smaller) in diameter. These pint-sized sanders can handle a plethora of small rotary-sanding tasks that don't require a lot of power. You'll find them handy for cleaning up carved surfaces, refining flutes, reeds, coves, beads, and other details on furniture, and sanding the inside of cutouts, holes, and slots.

There are literally hundreds of different sanding and cutting accessories that can be chucked into a Dremel tool, including tiny sanding discs, drums, flap wheels (see the photo at right), and cartridge rolls. For shaping operations, there are also endless varieties of vitrified abrasive grinding points and high-speed-steel and carbide burrs.

FLEXIBLE-SHAFT TOOLS

A flexible shaft is another way of running small discs, drums, and wheels. Like the tools used by dentists to drill out cavities and perform other excruciating therapies, a flexible tool consists of a handpiece that has a collet, or chuck, for holding the spindle of a rotary sanding wheel. A flexible shaft, sheathed on the outside by a non-rotating housing, connects the handpiece to an electric motor that powers the tool. Most flexible-shaft tools have a variable-speed control regulating the motor, so that the rpms can be adjusted to suit the diameter of the tool being run, as well as its application. Slower speeds are better for larger-diameter wheels or when delicate work is being done, and you want to remove stock less quickly. Conversely, faster speeds suit smaller-diameter tools, and are good for more aggressive stock removal.

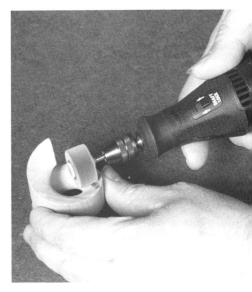

Like a diminutive die grinder, a Dremel tool can be outfitted with any number of little sanding drums and wheels to refine details or smooth small parts.

Discs, Wheels, Drums, Spindles, and Rolls

Drills, die grinders, and the other rotary power tools discussed in the previous section wouldn't be very versatile or effective without a variety of sanding discs, wheels, drums, spindles, and rolls to use with them. These "whirling dervishes" come in a staggering array of sizes and configurations and are coated with an equally extensive range of abrasive minerals and grits. Let's examine each one to learn more about what rotary tool it works with, and what sanding jobs it is best designed to tackle.

ABRASIVE FLAP DISCS

The abrasive flap disc, normally used by metalworkers for removing scale and slag after welding, has many uses in the woodshop. Flap discs (also called SMT discs) have a series of small overlapping sheets of cloth-backed abrasive mounted to a stiff composite-material backing wheel. The angle of the sheets provides aggressive cutting and minimizes loading during heavy shaping operations. Flap discs come in several diameters, from 7 in. down to about 2½ in. Used on a right-angle grinder with a very stiff backing (see the photo on p. 171), abrasive flap discs are great for roughing out all manner of concave surfaces and edges, for furniture or boat parts, and for large carvings and sculptures.

STRUCTURED CARBIDE DISCS

Another fabulous tool for hogging wood away quickly with a right-angle grinder, carbide wood grinder discs are metal wheels with hundreds of conically shaped needle-like carbide teeth welded to the surface. This construction, referred to as "structured carbide" is also available on grinding burrs that are used in die grinders and Dremel tools. A structured carbide wheel has a surface that, like metal-backed abrasive plates (see p. 39) may be cleaned off with a brass-bristled brush and reused indefinitely. These wheels cut very aggressively, so they're primarily for power-shaping work. Because of the depth of the carbide needles, the wheels work well on both dried and green hardwoods and even on resinous softwoods, such as pine.

FLAP WHEELS

Smaller versions of the wheels used for sanding contours on an arbor (see pp. 206-208), flap wheels, also called PG wheels and "sanding stars," consist of small strips of sandpaper permanently anchored to a central hub. The hub has either a hole to allow arbor mounting or a spindle that inserts directly into a chuck or collet on a drill, die grinder, or Dremel tool. The sandpaper strips may be thin and narrow, making a "mop" style wheel (see p. 207), or wider strips that are slashed (scored along their length) so that they'll feather at the working end, allowing them to conform better to a shaped surface. Flap wheels may also be made of non-woven plastic abrasive or alternating strips of sandpaper and non-woven abrasive (see the photo on p. 172). The latter provides a nice balance of fast cutting with a scratch pattern that's softer than that left by abrasive paper alone.

FLUTTER-SHEET WHEEL

The flutter-sheet wheel consists of 4-in.- to 6-in.-long strips of sandpaper, slashed at both ends and assembled onto a mandrel. The strips are mounted in back-to-back pairs (see the drawing on the facing page) that are staggered around the mandrel to form a basically round wheel. The mandrel may be chucked into a die grinder or a hand-held drill, or used with a drill press. Before use, the flutter sheets should be broken in by running the wheel against a hardwood scrap, which softens the edges of the sheets so they will conform more easily to the contours of the work surface. The paper strips are changed as they wear out.

SETTING UP A FLUTTER-SHEET WHEEL

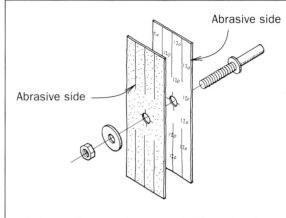

Abrasive side

Abrasive side

1. Mount flutter strips to mandrel in back-to-back pairs.

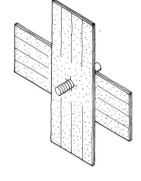

2. Place second pair of strips at 90° to first pair.

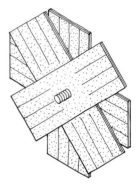

3. Mount subsequent pairs at 45° to first two pairs. Continue in this fashion, stacking 16 to 48 sheets on mandrel.

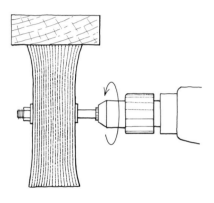

4. Before using, run wheel against edge of scrap hardwood block to soften the ends of the strips.

SNAP-LOCKING DISCS

An extremely handy sanding system, snap-locking discs consist of a 2-in.-dia. plastic backup pad with a spindle to chuck in a drill or die grinder. The sandpaper discs themselves have a small threaded stud that twist-locks into a socket on the pad, just as a bayonet-style lens mounts on a camera (see the photo on p. 176). This way, discs mount very securely to their backup pads, but can be removed and changed in an instant. 3M and Merit Abrasives both manufacture similar snap-locking systems.

Snap-locking discs chucked in a drill or die grinder are terrific for small shaping jobs, as well as for power sanding on the lathe. A small threaded stud on the back allows discs to be changed easily.

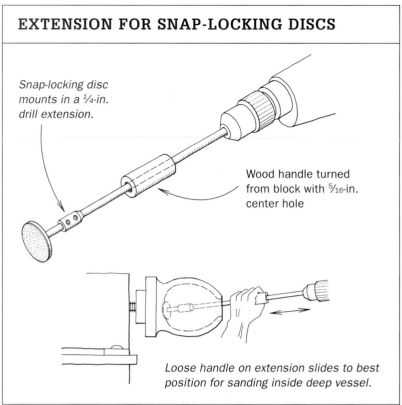

EXTENSION FOR SNAP-LOCKING DISCS

Snap-locking disc mounts in a ¼-in. drill extension.

Wood handle turned from block with ⁵⁄₁₆-in. center hole

Loose handle on extension slides to best position for sanding inside deep vessel.

Snap-locking discs are the tool of choice for many wood turners who like to shape bowls and other vessels by power sanding on the lathe (see the sidebar on the facing page). The stiff backup pad allows you to use a coarse (36-grit to 60-grit) sandpaper disc to cut very aggressively and remove stock quickly, yet without tearing out delicate figured or weak punky grain. The discs are also handy for other shaping operations, such as for making sculptural boxes and freeform creations.

To allow you to sand safely into deeper bowls and recesses within vessels, you can mount a snap-locking disc on the end of a drill extension (available at hardware stores). To give you more control of the sanding disc, add a sliding handle to the shank of the drill extension (see the drawing above). You can make one by turning a handle from a 4-in.-long by 1-in.-square block that's been drilled out lengthwise. Use a drill that's slightly larger than the shank diameter of the extension.

Power Sanding on the Lathe

Using a portable power tool fitted with a sanding disc or wheel to sand a spinning turning is an effective way to shape or refine turned vessels. But if you've never done power sanding before, it may seem foolhardy to use two power tools at once. The operation can be performed safely, however, if you work conscientiously and take a few simple precautions.

First, remove the lathe's tool-rest assembly and remove the tailstock or slide it well out of the way (unless it's being used, of course). Because power sanding generates lots of dust, position your portable dust hood where it will be out of the way, but close enough to capture dust effectively. Naturally, you should don a protective visor, as you would for any woodturning operation. Don't wear a shirt or coat with long, loose sleeves that can get caught in the turning or the portable tool's wheel or disc. (I once had a small sanding disc "roll up" my sleeve while power sanding; it was a very frightening experience I wouldn't want anyone to share.)

When you're ready to begin sanding, start the lathe, bring the portable tool up to speed, and slowly bring the disc or wheel into contact with the work (don't exceed the maximum rpm of the disc or wheel). For the most aggressive cut, run the wheel or disc so that it counter-rotates against the surface of work. Sanding against the rotation of the work gives you the fastest stock removal, but it can be the hardest to control and can also generate lots of heat (enough to melt the hook-and-loop material on a small-diameter disc back). For a gentler cut, run the section of the disc that contacts the turning in the same direction that the turning is spinning.

Many wood turners like to use foam-backed discs to smooth the surface of their work because the soft foam backing pad allows the paper to conform to convex or concave profiles (see the photo at left). This allows the user to smooth-sand the outside or inside of a bowl, platter, or other vessel to clean up torn grain or deep scratches left from turning without changing the shape excessively. When using foam-backed discs, keep in mind that sanding this way can generate enough heat to melt the hook-and-loop backings! Therefore, take it easy, and check the temperature of the disc once in a while to avoid meltdowns.

The soft, thick pad on a foam-backed sanding disc makes it ideal for removing tearouts and deep scratches on a turned bowl or spindle. Here, the rim of a small walnut vessel is smoothed while it spins on the lathe.

Using the rotational force generated by contact with the spinning turning, a non-powered sander (a foam-backed disc in an arbor mounted on a plastic handle) smoothes the outside of a small vessel.

NON-POWERED POWER SANDING

If you're uncomfortable power sanding, you can still sand parts while they are turning on the lathe by using a clever tool called a "non-powered sander" as shown in the photo above. The tool, which is essentially an arbor with a foam-backed disc mounted on a plastic handle, uses the rotational force of the spinning turning to sand (the disc turns with the direction of the turning). You can also sand on the lathe using a variety of hand-sanding techniques, as described on pp. 131-133.

SANDING DRUMS

A sanding drum is a rubber drum mounted on a spindle and covered with a cylindrical sandpaper sleeve. Sanding drums come in a multitude of diameters and lengths to suit a wide range of jobs. Small drums are useful for cleaning up inside radiuses of holes, mortises, cutouts, and other recesses. Larger drums are good for smoothing concave edges, cleaning up beveled or chamfered edges, and similar tasks. Having the drum mounted on a portable tool is best for situations where the workpiece is too large or cumbersome to be brought to a stationary drum sander.

While most sanding drums use abrasive sleeves (the mineral is often bonded to a fiber or cloth backing material), you can also buy sleeveless sanding drums. These take sheet sandpaper, which is cut and wrapped around the drum. A locking mechanism holds the sheet in place on the drum and keeps it from coming loose during sanding. Pneumatic drums, normally used on stationary tools (these are described on pp. 197-198) are also available for use with portable tools (Industrial Abrasive Co. sells these; see Sources of Supply, which begins on p. 209). These pneumatic drums have a shaft that chucks into the tool, just like other sanding drums, but they also have a handle at the other end of the drum. This handle provides the user with greater control of the sanding operation.

SANDING SPINDLES

Invented by my ingenious colleague Roger Heitzman, sanding spindles, are terrific for sanding all types of tight inside radiuses and coves (see the photo at right). The spindles consist of a ¼-in.-dia. brass or steel rod that is 4 in. to 12 in. long with one threaded end (see the drawing below). At the threaded end, two small ball bearings are held in place by a pair of lock nuts. The other end of the spindle is left smooth, and chucks into the drill, die grinder, or other rotary sanding tool. Sandpaper is then wound around the spindle as many turns as necessary for the desired diameter.

In use, the ball bearings act as a handle, allowing you to hold the outboard end of the spindle for better control. You can work the

Sanding spindles are handy for cleaning up corners and curved transitions in shapely furniture. A pair of ball bearings at the tip allows you to grip the end, for better control.

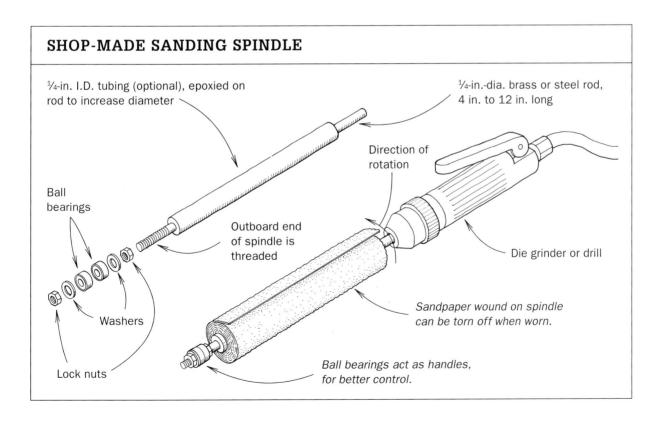

SHOP-MADE SANDING SPINDLE

¼-in. I.D. tubing (optional), epoxied on rod to increase diameter

¼-in.-dia. brass or steel rod, 4 in. to 12 in. long

Direction of rotation

Ball bearings

Outboard end of spindle is threaded

Die grinder or drill

Washers

Sandpaper wound on spindle can be torn off when worn.

Lock nuts

Ball bearings act as handles, for better control.

spindle down into tight corner fillets or to use it to clean up holes. If you wrap the spindle with enough sandpaper so that its diameter is at least as big as the outer diameter of the bearings, you can even sand down flush with a surface.

CARTRIDGE ROLLS

A strip of sandpaper wrapped around a mandrel, a cartridge roll is both a small-diameter sanding drum and a grinding point. In other words, you can sand with the shank of the tool to smooth rounded forms or with the tip of the roll to sand down into recesses.

A sanding roll (see the drawing below) is a simple variation of a cartridge roll, and you can make one by taking a wood dowel or metal rod and cutting a centered lengthwise slot into one end (the dowel may be long or short, thick or thin, to suit the application). The rod holds a strip of sandpaper cut as wide as the length of the slot and long enough to wrap around the dowel (you can use paper- or cloth-backed paper). To make the sanding roll thicker, use a longer strip of sandpaper. Chuck the dowel into a drill or die grinder and run it up to speed, while pressing the slotted area flat against a scrap of wood. This will wind the strip around the shank. You can't use the end of your shop-made sanding roll like a regular cartridge roll, but it's easy to make and very handy for reaming and smoothing the inside surfaces of holes and slots.

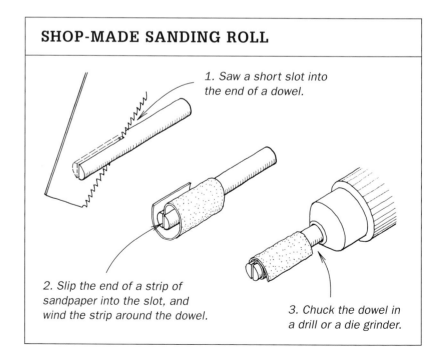

SHOP-MADE SANDING ROLL

1. Saw a short slot into the end of a dowel.

2. Slip the end of a strip of sandpaper into the slot, and wind the strip around the dowel.

3. Chuck the dowel in a drill or a die grinder.

Pneumatic Sanders

More and more small-shop woodworkers are replacing their electrically powered portable sanders with air-powered equivalents. The standard for many decades in auto shops around the world, pneumatic sanders pack a surprising amount of power in a tool that's usually smaller and lighter than its electric counterpart. And air tools are also mechanically very simple, an important advantage for sanders, which are subjected to tons of fine dust. They're also safe to use outdoors, or in wet conditions, without fear of electric shock.

Although most auto-shop models are expensive tools designed for professionals, a newer breed of inexpensive imported pneumatic sanders is now available to the small-shop woodworker. Random-orbit sanders, straight-line sanders, die and angle grinders, narrow belt sanders (see the photo at left), and other air tools provide amateur woodworkers with a lot of bang for the buck. In addition to a compressor fitted with a moisture trap and filter, all you need to run an air-powered sander is a hose and fittings to connect it. If you work in a cold climate, you'll also need warm work gloves; the air passing though the tool has a significant cooling effect, which can make these metal-bodied tools uncomfortable to hold during extended periods of use.

Air requirements

Unfortunately, pneumatic sanders tend to gobble up a tremendous volume of air. For example, an air random-orbit sander typically requires between 9 and 12 cfm, and up to 18 cfm at around 90 psi. This means you'd need a 3-hp to 7½-hp compressor to operate the tool continuously. Not all air tools are this hungry though; see the chart on p. 182 for typical psi and cfm requirements for different types of tools.

Fortunately, a big compressor is extremely useful in a woodshop—so useful, in fact, that I can't imagine living without one. In addition to powering air tools, blowing dust off work, running a spray gun, and inflating the occasional bike or car tire, compressed air can be used with a venturi valve to generate vacuum for air clamping or vacuum veneering. Compressed air is also useful for other sanding-related duties: the belt-tracking mechanisms in most wide-belt sanders require air pressure to run them. And a compressed-air-powered stripper jet (see p. 155) can make dust collection from many stationary sanders more efficient.

If you lack the space (or the budget) for a large compressor, you don't necessarily have to do

Inexpensive imported pneumatic portable sanders deliver a lot of performance for the money. Shown here (back to front) are a straight-line sander, a narrow-belt sander, a random-orbit sander, and a die grinder.

(continued on page 182)

Pneumatic Sanders (continued)

Compressed-Air Requirements for Various Pneumatic Sanders

Tool	Approximate air volume for continuous operation (cfm)	Recommended working air pressure (psi)
Random-orbit sander (6-in. disc)	9 - 18	90
Orbital sander (half-sheet)	6 - 7	80 - 100
Straight-line sander (2¾-in. by 17½-in. paper)	5 - 7	80 - 90
Twin-pad in-line sander	6 - 11	90 - 100
Disc sander (4-in. or 6-in. disc), single/dual action	4 - 5	60 - 90
Narrow-belt sander	3 - 5	70 - 90
Die grinder	2 - 5	80 - 100
Right-angle grinder (4-in. disc)	6	90

without the more air-hungry pneumatic sanders. Even the smallest portable compressor can create enough pressure for powering an air tool; most small-storage-tank units just don't produce enough air volume to operate tools continuously. If you can live with running the tool in short bursts (and waiting for the compressor to recharge in between), you can operate many pneumatic sanders on 1- or 2-hp units with a 10- or 20-gal. tank. There are ways to gain air volume —and longer running times. You

can refit the compressor with a larger storage tank, or connect it to an auxiliary air-storage tank (solution #1 in the drawing on the facing page). On non-portable systems, you can augment the compressor's air capacity by installing a manifold: A length of 1½-in. to 3-in. pipe works fine (solution #2). The longer and larger diameter the pipe, the more air capacity the compressor will have. Beware of condensation problems; don't run the manifold pipe outside if your shop is in a harsh climate.

Lubrication

Unlike electrical power tools, air tools require constant lubrication to keep them running smoothly. Basic lubrication can be accomplished by putting a few drops of special air-tool oil into the air inlet of the tool each time you use it. To oil your air tools automatically, fit each one with an in-line oiler (see the photo on the facing page). This device screws into the tool's air inlet and has a small refillable reservoir that you top up occasionally with air-tool oil. Air

ADDING AIR-VOLUME CAPACITY TO A SMALL COMPRESSOR SYSTEM

Regulator on compressor set to 100 psi to 120 psi

Solution #2: Pipe manifold, 1½ in. to 3 in. in diameter

Bell end fittings

Regulators set for working pressure of tool

Solution #1: ASHRAE-approved air-storage tank

Air filter/ moisture trap

Either solution will extend the operation time for air-volume hungry pneumatic tools.

Pneumatic sander

pressure causes a small amount of lubricating oil to be misted into the tool during use. You should never use the same air line that you use with air tools for blowing off bare wood surfaces or for spray finishing, as the line is probably contaminated by oil. If you have lots of air tools and a dedicated air line feeding them, you can fit a single line-mounted oiler that will service any tool connected to the line. Line-mounted oilers are available from Harbor Freight; see Sources of Supply, which begins on p. 209.

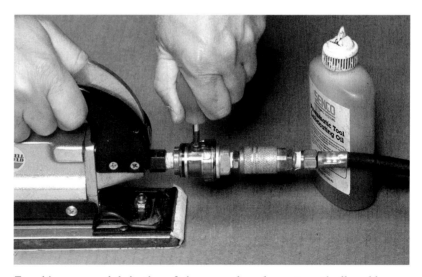

To achieve proper lubrication of air-powered sanders automatically, add an in-line oiler to the tool's air inlet. A small fill screw is removed to allow the oil to be topped up.

8

Stationary Sanding Machines

Hefty cast-iron sanding machines have always been a mainstay of large production shops and factories. Over the past decade, the Taiwanese tool revolution has taken many of these behemoths and resized them to fit the capacity and budget requirements of small woodshops, resulting in affordable horizontal edge sanders and drum thicknessing sanders. Another major impact on the home shop comes as a result of the do-it-yourself craze. As homeowners endeavor to improve and remodel their homes, machinery manufacturers have designed smaller "benchtop" sanding machines that are sized and priced for the single- or two-car-garage-sized woodshop. These include dozens of different oscillating spindle sander and combination (disc and belt) sander models.

Though not as compact and stowable as portable power sanders, benchtop and freestanding sanding machines more than justify the amount of valuable space they occupy in a small shop. They'll perform jobs that are really tough to do without them, like smoothing and thicknessing a beautifully figured board that would tear out horribly if run past the knives of a standard thickness planer, or evening up the edges of a box or face frame, which is much easier to do on an edge sander than with a hand plane or portable belt sander. Other sanding machines make daily sanding chores so much easier that it's hard to imagine how you ever got along without them. I used to clean up concave edges on curved wood parts with a sanding drum chucked in my drill press. Now I use an oscillating spindle sander that produces a smoother surface in less time (and, since it has built-in dust collection, with less lung-choking wood dust as well!).

Although all sanding machines perform the same basic woodworking task—abrading wood—each one is designed differently for a particular range of application. Hence, unless you have the space (and the budget) to install one of everything, it's important to acquire the machines that best serve your purposes. This chapter will provide you with guidance in choosing the right machines to suit your needs and style of work. There are also some strategies and accessories for doing sanding tasks on woodworking machines you may already have, such as disc sanding on the table saw or narrow-belt sanding on the bandsaw.

As wonderful as stationary sanders may be, getting the most out of any machine takes more than just setting it up and plugging it in. Therefore, we'll explore a number of ways of enhancing the performance of stationary sanding machines by using both store-bought and shop-made accessories. I'll also share a number of jigs you can build to expand the capabilities of your sanding machines farther than you might have considered possible, including a simple jig that lets you create smooth wood balls!

Edge Sanders

One of the first stationary sanding machines that many woodworkers go out and buy is an edge sander. As their name implies, these stationary belt sanders are designed primarily for shaping or smoothing the edges of parts and assemblies. They're extremely useful for cleaning up tearout on the edges or ends of a tabletop, as well as flush-sanding the ends of frame and panel cabinet doors or face frames (see the photo on p. 186). You can also flush-sand the sides of assemblies that aren't too deep, such as dovetails or finger joints on drawers or small boxes.

Edge sanders comes in a wide variety of sizes, from small benchtop units that take a 4x24 belt, such as the Woodtek oscillating belt sander, to large commercial machines, such as the Delta 31-390, which takes a 6-in. by 132-in. belt. The longer and wider the belt, the bigger the sander's primary platen is, and hence the larger the surface that can be sanded at one time. Just as having longer tables on a jointer makes it easier to plane a straight edge on a long board, a longer platen allows a long edge, such as a door frame, to be sanded straight.

An edge sander fitted with a coarse-grit or medium-grit belt makes fast work of cleaning up the edges of a frame, in this case trimming the ends of the stiles flush with the rails at the same time.

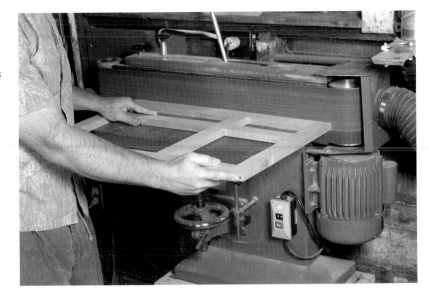

Most edge sanders come with a single table that runs the length of the platen. Some have large wood or cast-metal tables that make it easier to support big panels or cumbersome frames during sanding. Many tables feature a bolt-on miter gauge that attaches near the drive-roll end of the table. The miter gauge serves as both a stop and a guide, so the ends of workpieces can be sanded square or to an accurate angle. Rounded ends of parts and panels can be more easily (and safely) sanded by clamping a starting pin to the end of the table, as described on p. 147.

To make more efficient use of the belt when sanding thin workpieces, edge-sander tables often tilt lengthwise. Know as "bias tilting," the right side of the table (nearest the drive roll) is set higher than the left side. This way the workpiece is still kept square to the belt surface, but a wider portion of the belt is used. The belt wears more evenly, and loading or burning a narrow band of the belt is prevented (see pp. 140-141 ch6). The Grizzly G1173, as well as the benchtop Woodtek machine, oscillates the belt—moving it up and down—at the same time it is rotating. This feature further distributes sanding load and prevents stripping.

Many edge sanders have tables that can be tilted laterally to 45° or more for accurate sanding of beveled or chamfered edges and surfaces. On some machines, the entire motor/belt-drive assembly tilts laterally, so the belt runs horizontally (see p. 195). A small auxiliary table is sometimes fitted around the belt's drive or idler roller to allow sanding of concave parts. For more versatility when

DOWEL-POINTING JIG FOR EDGE SANDER

1. Drill a hole slightly larger than the dowel through the block.

2. Cut off a corner of the block at the desired angle.

3. Clamp the block to the edge-sander table; feed the dowel through the hole, and rotate to sand.

sanding contours, the Delta 31-390 allows different-diameter sanding drums to be mounted atop the drive roller (the table is raised up for this operation).

In addition to handling flat stock, you can also use your edge sander on convex surfaces, cylindrical forms, or dowels. With the simple jig shown in the drawing above, you can accurately chamfer or point the end of a dowel or other rounded part. The jig is simply a chamfered block with a hole bored through it that is clamped to the edge sander's table so that the dowel will protrude at the same angle (relative to the belt) that you wish to sand. You can mount the block to the sander's dust hood, up and out of the way of normal work. This jig makes needle-sharp points in a flash—you can even use it to sharpen pencils.

PROFILE SANDING WITH AN EDGE SANDER

Dedicated profile sanders are industrial machines that have little place in small woodshops. However, some edge sanders provide the capability of rounding over edges to a preset radius or smooth-sanding shaped edges, such as raised panels, and moldings that aren't too complex. These machines usually feature two tables, one on either long side of the belt. On one side, the belt has a standard platen for sanding flat and convex parts. On the other side, behind the belt, is an adjustable bracket, to which a form platen (the negative image of the profile of the workpiece) mounts (see the drawing below). As the workpiece, say a simple cove molding, is pressed against the section of the belt running in front of the form platen, the flexible cloth belt (which should be a light-weight cloth), conforms to the shape of the form platen, so it accurately sands the work without significantly changing its shape.

PROFILE-SANDING SETUP FOR EDGE SANDER

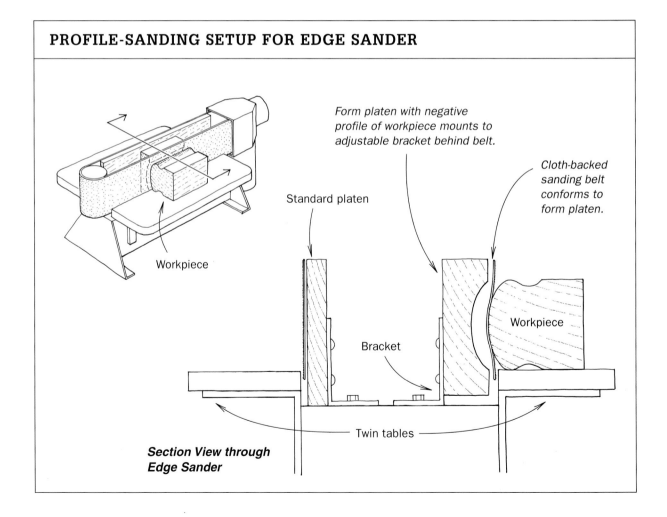

Form platen with negative profile of workpiece mounts to adjustable bracket behind belt.

Cloth-backed sanding belt conforms to form platen.

Standard platen

Workpiece

Workpiece

Bracket

Twin tables

Section View through Edge Sander

In many cases, you can make your own profile blocks by first rough-cutting the negative profile and mounting the block to the sander. Next, turn the sanding belt inside out, so the abrasive side faces the platen, and press a section of the workpiece over the area of the profile block, which is sanded to final shape (edge sanders with a graphite straight platen must be fitted with a thin sheet-metal protector, lest the reverse-run belt abrade away the graphite).

AN EDGE-SANDING SETUP FOR THE PORTABLE BELT SANDER

If your shop is small and you need an edge sander to handle small parts, you can make a handy jig that transforms your portable belt sander into an edge sander. As shown in the drawing below, the

---

EDGE-SANDING JIG FOR PORTABLE BELT SANDER

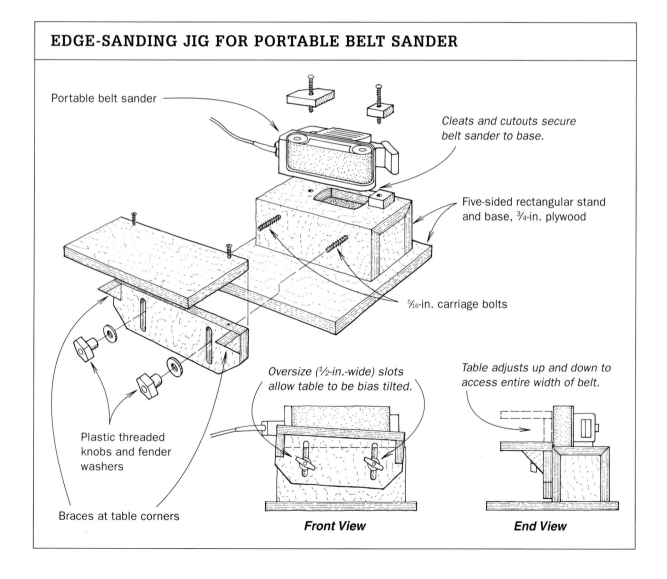

Portable belt sander

Cleats and cutouts secure belt sander to base.

Five-sided rectangular stand and base, ³⁄₄-in. plywood

⁵⁄₁₆-in. carriage bolts

Plastic threaded knobs and fender washers

Braces at table corners

Oversize (¹⁄₂-in.-wide) slots allow table to be bias tilted.

Front View

Table adjusts up and down to access entire width of belt.

End View

table stand and base for the jig are made of ¾-in. plywood, glued and screwed together. Two carriage bolts attach the table through slots that allow the table to adjusted up and down and bias tilted (see p. 186). Cleats and cutouts sized and shaped to suit your sander's body and handles hold the tool firmly in the jig, yet allow it to be removed quickly, so it can return to portable duty as needed.

Benchtop Narrow-Belt Sanders

Stationary narrow-belt sanders designed for small-shop use are compact machines that offer a lot of versatility for the amount of space they occupy. The narrow belt is usually combined with a small disc in a benchtop unit such as the Delta 31-340, which has a 1-in. by 42-in. belt and an 8-in. disc.

Benchtop narrow-belt sanders can be used to sand both straight and curved edges, but they really shine when sanding slots, notches, and cutouts (see the photo below) or convoluted curves on small parts, such as for children's toys, puzzle parts, or Victorian gingerbread decorations. Because the narrow belt is supported by a thin metal platen, there is clearance behind it, which allows you to sand inside forms and concavities. To lend even greater flexibility, the platen can be removed for cleaner sanding on curved or odd-

Stationary narrow-belt sanders have a thin, close-fitting platen and belt for sanding into notches and cutouts. The tilt table and miter gauge allow accurate sanding of angled or beveled work.

shaped work. You can also remove the guard from the top idle roller and sand concave shapes. On most units, the tables have a miter-gauge slot and tilt as well, to allow the shaping and smoothing of angled or beveled surfaces. You can sand compound angles using the tilted table and miter gauge in combination.

With a silicon-carbide or ceramic-mineral belt, a narrow-belt sander can quickly create or restore the beveled edge of a plane blade or chisel. It's good too for deburring or cleaning up the edges of bolts and metal parts for jigs or tools you may be building. You can also fit these machines with belts made from non-woven plastic abrasive or felt and use them for finish-sanding or polishing.

NARROW-BELT SANDING WITH A BANDSAW

If you wish to reap the benefits of a stationary narrow-belt sander but don't have the space or budget for a dedicated machine, you can fit your bandsaw with a narrow sanding belt (see the photo below). Abrasives suppliers, such as Econ-Abrasive and Industrial Abrasive Co., will gladly make up $\frac{1}{2}$-in.- to 1-in.-wide belts to fit your bandsaw (see Sources of Supply, which begins on p. 209). Industrial Abrasive Co. also stocks $\frac{1}{2}$-in.-wide sanding belts sized to fit the popular Delta 14-in. bandsaws.

To set up a narrow sanding belt on the bandsaw, first reposition the saw's guide blocks so that the block facing the working side of

You can transform a regular bandsaw into a narrow-belt sander by replacing its blade with a $\frac{1}{2}$-in. to 1-in.-wide sanding belt. The band deflects enough to allow you to sand gentle curves.

the abrasive belt is entirely out of the way. Now install and track the narrow belt as you would a blade, adjusting the tension so that the belt doesn't flap excessively. Don't set the tension so high that the belt is as taut as a bow string; it's liable to break. To support the belt so it won't deflect as you sand, clamp a platen to the table directly behind the belt. You can buy such a platen as an attachment for the Delta 14-in. bandsaw from Industrial Abrasive Co. (see Sources of Supply, which begins on p. 209), or you can clamp a narrow hardwood block to the table behind the belt to support it.

Stationary Disc Sanders

Available as stand-alone units or combined with either a narrow belt (see pp. 190-191) or a vertical/horizontal belt (see p. 195), a stationary disc sander can sand flat or convex edges, ends and surfaces of parts very accurately. Depending on the size and the power of the unit, the diameter of the disc can be anywhere from 8 in. (small hobby machines) to 24 in. (big industrial machines). The disc may be attached directly to the end of the motor shaft, or mounted to an arbor and driven by a V-belt from a motor pulley.

To keep the workpiece flat on the sander's table during sanding, you must work on the half of the disc that's traveling down toward the table (on most machines, the disc rotates counterclockwise). You can use the full width of the disc for sanding wider, thicker workpieces, but you'll have to hold the work firmly and work carefully to keep the upward-spinning portion of the disc from lifting the work.

Some industrial-type disc sanders have a reversing switch that allows you to choose the disc's direction of rotation. This is convenient, since you can choose which side of the table you wish to work on. Reversing rotation also allows you to get more service out of every disc: As the abrasive wears down, you can reverse the rotation to use the other cutting face of the abrasive grains.

The table on a disc sander is designed to tilt, allowing you to sand mitered and beveled workpieces. A miter slot in the table, running parallel to the surface of the disc, allows use of a standard miter gauge, for precise sanding of miters or, with the table tilted, compound angles. The part is held securely against the face of the miter gauge, and the gauge is slid past the disc. When using coarse grits, gently feed the part into the disc while moving it back and forth slightly; this prevents the abrasive from creating deep, straight scratches across the surface of the work. With a little practice, you'll be able to sand miters that are smooth and true enough for final assembly.

In addition to a standard miter-gauge slot, some disc sander tables include a special slot in the table designed expressly for shaping and smoothing the edges of circular discs. The slot runs perpendicular to the face of the disc, and is located so it intersects the downward-spinning face of the sanding disc.

If your disc sander lacks this feature, you can easily build a jig to do the job, as shown in the drawing below. The workpiece is first sawn slightly oversize (about 1/16 in. over the desired diameter), and its center point is pressed down onto a pin that protrudes from a sliding block. The block is then placed in the circle-jig groove and the work is slid towards the spinning sanding disc. The work is rotated by hand, to sand it all the way around. A stop block is screwed into the groove to limit the travel of the sliding block, so sanding is stopped when the desired disc diameter is reached. You can use this jig to sand the edge of a round (or half-round) tabletop, or to make wheels for toy cars, trains, or wagons.

On most machines, the abrasive disc mounts directly to the surface of the metal plate. There's no soft backing pad, so the abrasive cuts very aggressively, and produce surfaces that are surprisingly flat and accurate (patternmakers love to use stationary

CIRCLE-SANDING JIG FOR DISC SANDER

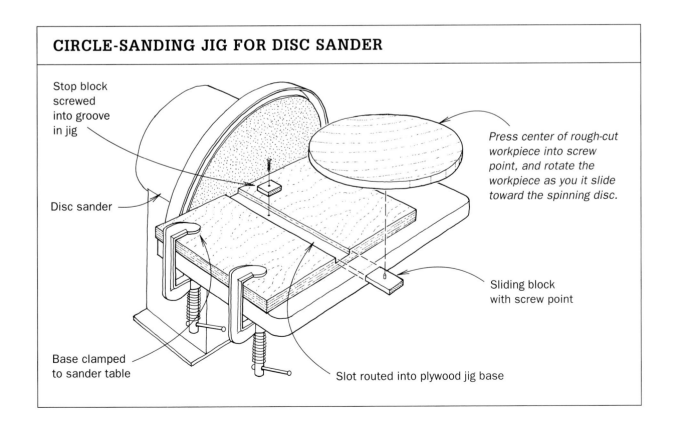

Stop block screwed into groove in jig

Disc sander

Base clamped to sander table

Press center of rough-cut workpiece into screw point, and rotate the workpiece as you it slide toward the spinning disc.

Sliding block with screw point

Slot routed into plywood jig base

disc sanders for creating accurately sized parts). PSA discs are most convenient to use, since they are already coated with adhesive; you simply peel the backing off the disc and stick it in place. To make it easier to remove discs cleanly, first heat up the PSA adhesive by sanding a piece of scrap stock aggressively. To mount a non-PSA sanding disc, you must use a special disc-mount adhesive (see Sources of Supply, which begins on p. 209).

If you'd prefer to use hook-and-loop type discs (they are more convenient to use if you change discs often), you can stick on a PSA hook-and-loop adapter: a disc with a standard PSA backing, but with hook material on the face side. However, using an adapter has some disadvantages. Remember that mounting the disc directly to the metal plate is what allows you to sand very flat, true surfaces. The adapter layer adds padding that allows the disc to deflect somewhat. During heavy sanding, it's also possible to generate enough heat to melt the plastic hooks on the adapter.

DISC SANDING ON THE TABLE SAW

If you don't have the space for a dedicated disc sander, you can still do disc sanding by installing a special sanding disc on the arbor of your table saw (see the photo below). The precision-machined metal disc is like a sawblade without teeth, and takes a PSA-backed sandpaper disc that has a hole in the center. These metal sanding discs and PSA discs are available from Hartville Tool; see Sources of Supply, which begins on p. 209.

Like a sawblade without teeth, a machined metal disc with PSA paper on it can turn your table saw into a stationary disc sander.

Combination Belt/Disc Sanders

Stationary sanders often combine two (or more) types of sanding in one machine; a narrow belt and a disc, or a belt and a drum. Of these, combination belt/disc sanders are perhaps the most useful. They team up two of the most versatile stationary sanding tools in a compact package. Available in benchtop or floor models, a combination sander typically sports a 6-in.-wide, 48-in.-long belt and a disc that's anywhere from 9 in. to 12 in. in diameter. The belt and disc are powered by the same motor, either by direct or V-belt drive. Some combination sanders, such as the Delta 31-280 Sanding Center (shown in the photo at right), have accessories that allow the unit to be fitted with a pneumatic drum or a sanding drum, flap wheel, or flexible shaft. These add even more working flexibility to an already versatile machine.

Most combination sanders feature a belt sander with a rigid platen (on most machines, the belt runs directly against a ground cast-iron platen), allowing you to do extremely accurate belt sanding. I've even used my sander (with an 80- or 100-grit aluminum-oxide belt) to flatten the surface on my Japanese waterstones! On most machines, the sanding belt may be set to run either vertically or horizontally. This adapts it to a wider of variety of sanding tasks. For example, using the belt in the horizontal position might be more convenient for sanding the bottom edges of a box or drawer, while the vertical position is preferable for sanding the end of a long workpiece. (The horizontal position is also used for shaping spheres on a sander, using the jig described in the sidebar on p. 196). Some machines allow the belt assembly to be tilted to any angle between vertical and horizontal. I find this particularly useful for sanding a bevel or chamfer on a large or bulky workpiece. I tilt both the belt and table, so the workpiece remains level.

The disc portion of a combination sander has its own tilting table and works in much the same way as it does on a dedicated disc sander (see pp. 192-194). Most combination machines give you a separate, tilting table (with miter-gauge slot) for the belt sander, while others supply a simpler backstop to support the work during sanding. If you lack a drum sander, you might use the idle-roll end of the belt (with its protective cover removed) to sand inside curves, although some manufacturers advise against this.

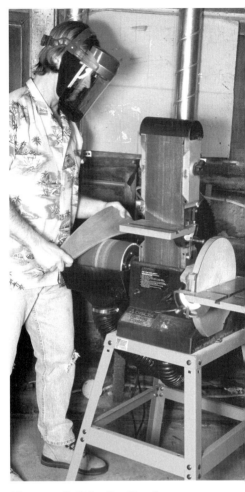

The versatile Delta Sanding Center couples stationary disc and belt sanders with a power shaft that can be used to run sanding wheels, flexible shaft tools, or a pneumatic drum, as shown here.

Sanding Squares into Balls

Most sanding of wood is done to make rough surfaces flat and flat surfaces smooth. But not all. Here's a clever little jig that you can build and use to turn small wood squares into near-perfect round balls. The jig (see the drawing below) can be used with a horizontally positioned medium-coarse belt on a combination sander or edge sander. You could also build a smaller version and use it with a portable belt sander inverted in a stand (see pp. 189-190).

The jig is a four-sided plywood box with a plastic lid that is clamped to the table or backstop and positioned just above the sanding belt (leave only enough clearance so the belt doesn't sand the bottom edge of the frame). Small wooden cubes are put in the box and the lid is screwed shut or fastened with tape. When the sander is switched on, the cubes are tumble sanded, a process that knocks off sharp corners until the cubes are entirely rounded over into small spheres. Making the lid out of clear plastic, such as $3/16$-in. thick polycarbonate, allows you to monitor the progress of the operation without having to switch the sander off and lift up the lid.

BOX JIG FOR MAKING WOOD BALLS ON HORIZONTAL BELT SANDER

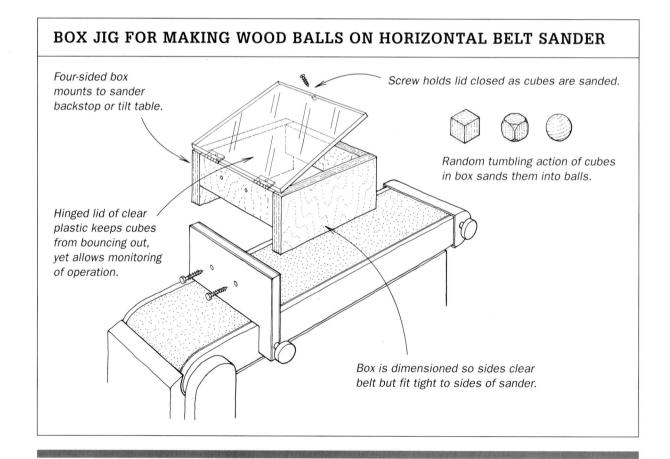

Four-sided box mounts to sander backstop or tilt table.

Screw holds lid closed as cubes are sanded.

Random tumbling action of cubes in box sands them into balls.

Hinged lid of clear plastic keeps cubes from bouncing out, yet allows monitoring of operation.

Box is dimensioned so sides clear belt but fit tight to sides of sander.

Drum Sanders

Sanding drums of one type or another are used on quite a few different machines for shaping and smoothing concave and irregular edges and surfaces of parts. For a basic drum sander, you can chuck a shaft-mounted drum into a drill press. For more rigorous drum sanding, you can buy a dedicated machine, like the oscillating spindle sander. You can also fit sanding drums as accessories to combination sanders, or adapt a non-sanding machine, such as a lathe or drill press, for drum-sanding duties.

PATTERN-SANDING DRUM

An interesting variation on the basic sanding drum is the Robo Sander, a simple device that allows you to sand the edge of a shaped workpiece smooth without changing its profile (see the photo at right). This technique, called pattern sanding, is accomplished by temporarily fastening a template to the bottom of the workpiece. The template, which may be ¼-in. plywood or MDF, or ½-in. Masonite, is cut to the exact size and profile of the desired part. The workpiece is first cut slightly oversized (no more than ¹⁄₁₆ in. all around) and then attached to the top of the template with small brads, double-stick tape (such as carpet tape), or adhesive transfer tape. The Robo Sander is chucked in the drill press, and its guide bearing set to contact the template. The bearing rides on the template as the work is sanded to contour.

PNEUMATIC DRUM

Imagine replacing the stiff rubber sleeve in a sanding drum with an inflatable bag and you have the concept of the pneumatic sanding drum. The sanding sleeve, made with a thin fabric backing, fits over a cotton-fabric-covered rubber bladder that's permanently bonded to a metal hub. A standard Schrader valve (the same kind as on an automobile tire) allows you to inflate the bladder. The hub can be mounted over an arbor on a pedestal grinder or fitted to a shaft and used on a combination sander, such as the Delta Sanding Center (see the photo on p. 195). You can even buy kits that allow you to mount a pneumatic drum on your drill press or between the centers of a wood lathe, as shown in the photo on p. 198. These kits are available from Woodcraft; see Sources of Supply, which begins on p. 209.

Pneumatic drums are great for cleaning up tool marks and smoothing shapely furniture parts, such as cabriole legs, or rounded forms, such as gunstocks or handles for axes, hammers,

Parts can be pattern sanded to exact size and shape with a special sanding drum called the Robo Sander. A free-spinning guide bushing on the bottom of the drum follows a template, temporarily mounted to the bottom of the rough-cut part.

Softening or rounding over the edges of curved parts is easy on a pneumatic sanding drum. If you lack a bench arbor, you can mount the drum between the centers of a wood lathe with a special kit and set up a portable hood to remove most of the dust.

and other tools. The cushioned backing allows the drum to flex much more than a standard rubber drum. To make the backing stiffer, for more aggressive stock removal, simply inflate the drum to higher pressure (not exceeding 20 psi to 25 psi). You can use your compressed-air hose or a small bicycle pump. To soften the drum and allow its surface to conform to more rounded or irregular surfaces, deflate the drum. You can also soften the drum's sanding action by fitting an additional soft cotton sleeve under the abrasive (available from Klingspor; see Sources of Supply, which begins on p. 209).

Oscillating Spindle Sanders

You can do a pretty good job of sanding the concave edges of a curvaceous chair leg or a table apron or the wavy-shaped rail of a wine rack using a basic sanding drum chucked into a drill press (see p. 197). But an oscillating spindle sander will do a much better job. The reason is that this machine takes a long sanding drum (the spindle) and in addition to rotating it, moves it up and down at the same time (the motion can be anywhere from ½ in. to 1 in., depending upon the unit). The oscillating action serves two purposes. First, it distributes the contact over a greater portion of the spindle. Hence, you don't wear out a narrow band on the spindle when sanding a thin workpiece. Second, and more important, the dual motion of the spindle tends to soften the scratch pattern and not leave grooves on the edge of the work, as a plain drum sander does.

Once available only as large, industrial-duty machines, oscillating spindle sanders sized for smaller shops are currently made by quite a few manufacturers. Some of these machines are benchtop models, such as the Ryobi OSS450, the Clayton machine, and the Delta B.O.S.S. (Benchtop Oscillating Spindle Sander), shown in the photo below. Delta also manufactures an accessory that transforms a drill press into an oscillating spindle sander.

To suit the sanding of curves of different radii, each machine has its own set of interchangeable spindles; you can choose the diameter that you need. The most common spindle diameters are ½ in., ¾ in., 1 in., 1½ in., 2 in., and 3 in. A sandpaper sleeve fits over the spindle, which has a steel shaft and a rubber body. To change the sleeve, you usually have to loosen a nut atop the spindle and slide it off. You slide on a fresh sleeve, tighten the nut (which expands the rubber body, holding the sleeve in place), and resume sanding.

Like table saws, oscillating spindle sanders have a removable throat plate. Always use a throat plate that has a hole in it that's just slightly larger than the diameter of the spindle, to provide support for the workpiece close to the spindle and prevent chatter. You'll also eliminate the possibility of really small parts getting wedged down between the spindle and the throat plate.

You'll get the smoothest finish when power-sanding concave surfaces by using an oscillating spindle sander. The drum moves up and down while it spins, virtually eliminating the concentric scratches that drums tend to deposit.

The spindle on an oscillating spindle sander is almost always longer (4½ in. to 9 in.) than the thickness of the stock being sanded, Therefore, to get the full use out of a sleeve, you need to remove it when the lower section is worn out and reinstall it upside-down (this also gets better use from the abrasive grains on the worn portion). Alternatively, you can distribute wear over different sections of the sleeve if you raise the level of the workpiece by placing one, two, or more layers of plywood or MDF atop the sander's table.

While the tables on most small oscillating spindle sanders are fixed at 90° to the spindle, a few models, such as the Powermatic Artisan, have tilting tables. These allow you sand beveled or chamfered curves, such as you might find on the edge of an oval coffee table or a freeform wood base for a bronze sculpture. You can adapt a fixed-base model for sanding beveled parts by building

ADJUSTABLE TILT TABLE FOR OSCILLATING SPINDLE SANDER

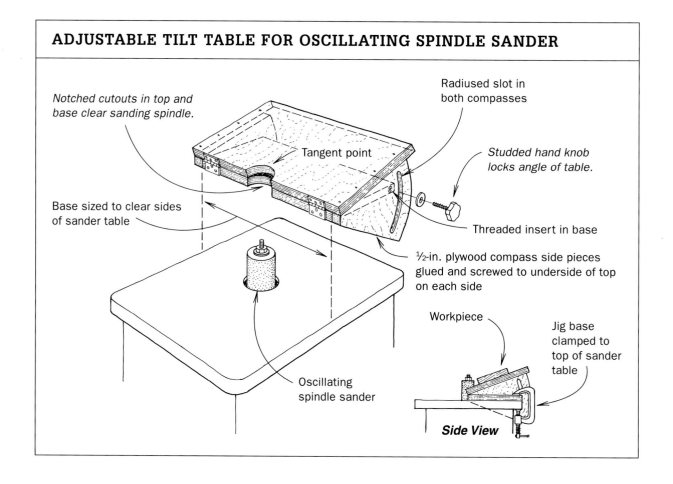

Notched cutouts in top and base clear sanding spindle.

Radiused slot in both compasses

Tangent point

Studded hand knob locks angle of table.

Base sized to clear sides of sander table

Threaded insert in base

½-in. plywood compass side pieces glued and screwed to underside of top on each side

Oscillating spindle sander

Workpiece

Jig base clamped to top of sander table

Side View

a simple adjustable tilting table and clamping it atop the tool's table, as shown in the drawing on the facing page. Note that to sand at the precise angle, the part must only contact the spindle on a single tangent point (marked on the drawing). Also, the steeper the angle of the table, the less of the spindle that will extend above it. This limits the thickness of the work you can sand.

Thicknessing Sanders

Abrasive thicknessers, once the domain of large cabinet shops and factories, have now "trickled down" to the small-shop woodworker. Feature-laden, affordable models now abound, and while these lighter-duty machines might not have the horsepower to take thick passes on wide panels, small-shop models come in sizes comparable to smaller thicknessing planers. There are several models with belts that are 13 in. to 15 in. wide. Drum sanders offer even greater capacities; up to 37 in. in a single pass! And many models have a cantilever design, so that one end of the drum or belt is open. This allows you to sand the full width of a wide panel, such as a table top, if you are sanding one-half at a time (see the photo at right).

A thickness sander fitted with a coarse-grit abrasive can smooth and dimension a rough board, just as a planer would. However, the advantage of abrasive planing is that you don't have to worry about grain direction or tearout in areas of irregular or figured grain—the sandpaper abrades the wood away instead of slicing it with rotary knives. You can also thickness-sand parts across the grain (an operation not recommended with a regular thickness planer), so an entire cabinet face frame can be leveled in a single pass. Cross-grain scratches on the stiles or rails are touched up later, using a portable belt sander.

Instead of having a cast table, as a planer does, thickness sanders have a conveyor belt (either a rubberized fabric or coated abrasive) below the belt or drum that moves the workpiece past the abrasive during sanding. This feature allows you to thickness-sand short, irregular parts, such as toys and parts for small production items, as well as long, wide boards. If you build a carriage jig (see the drawing on p. 202), you can even sand parts that aren't flat on both sides.

Some thicknessing sanders have one end open, allowing you to sand a panel that is up to twice as wide as the belt or drum.

CARRIAGE JIG FOR THICKNESS SANDER

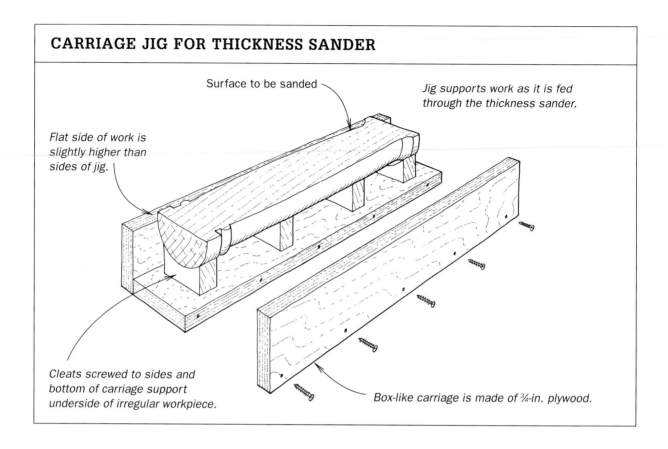

Surface to be sanded

Jig supports work as it is fed through the thickness sander.

Flat side of work is slightly higher than sides of jig.

Cleats screwed to sides and bottom of carriage support underside of irregular workpiece.

Box-like carriage is made of ¾-in. plywood.

WIDE-BELT SANDERS

A wide-belt sander is a cross between a basic belt sander and a thickness planer. The belt runs vertically on rollers above a conveyor belt, which adjusts up and down to set the depth of cut and handle stock of various thicknesses (see the photo on the facing page). The lower roll is a rubber-covered drive roll, which is where the belt actually contacts the work. Large industrial machines may have two or more belt assemblies (heads) in a row, one after the other. By fitting these with successively finer belts, you can take the surface of a board from rough to smooth in a single pass. Multiple-head machines usually have a platen installed between heads. The platen is basically a flat steel plate that is adjustable up and down. In the down position, it provides for a wider surface of contact between the abrasive belt and the work, resulting in a flatter, truer surface. It's run in the down position on finishing passes with finer-grit papers and left up when using coarser belts for thicknessing, where more surface contact with the belt is unnecessary.

Just as with a backup pad on a portable sander, the hardness or softness of a wide-belt sander's contact roll affects performance. A harder roll leaves a flatter surface, with little round-over at the edges, but tends to leave a harsher scratch pattern. A softer roll leaves a softer scratch pattern, but tends to round over the edges of frames and panels slightly. A soft roll is also more forgiving when sanding workpieces that vary in thickness.

To keep a wide belt moving smoothly on its rolls, some wide-belt sanders incorporate an air-powered automatic tracking mechanism that moves the top (idler) roll to keep the belt tracking toward the middle of the roller. Sunhill sells a 15-in. machine that utilizes a pneumatic tracking sensor/correction mechanism to oscillate the belt back and forth. This feature (adapted to this small machine from larger, more expensive models) helps to distribute the sanding workload more evenly across the surface of the belt and prevent stripping (see pp. 140-141), which can quickly ruin an expensive belt.

To change belts on a wide-belt sander, you engage a mechanical or pneumatic release mechanism that lowers the idler roller, making the belt loose enough to be removed and replaced. This allows quick changes of grit when taking a board from the rough to near-final smoothness (for this operation, wide-belt sanders are easier to use than drum sanders because changing grits on drum sanders takes substantial time).

It can take a tremendous amount of power to abrade away even a thin layer of wood on a wide surface. A motor draws more power when it is under greater load, so you may find yourself resetting your circuit breakers while trying to thickness-sand wide stock (the same is true for thicknessing with a drum sander, described below). To help prevent this, wide-belt sanders often include an ammeter, which lets you see how much current the tool is drawing from your circuit. By reducing the depth of cut, you can reduce amperage to an amount your circuit can handle, and you will be able to keep working without tripping breakers.

Because of the sheer volume of fine dust generated by wide-belt sanders when taking even a light pass, dust collection is a must. Without adequate collection (see pp. 151-159), dust will quickly clog the belt, and eventually ruin the running gear of the machine itself. Even the smallest (13-in.) wide-belt sanders incorporate a collection hood and provide a port for connection to a portable or central dust-collection system.

Belt changes are easy on a wide-belt sander.

DRUM THICKNESSING SANDERS

Like a wide-belt sander, a drum thicknessing sander has a conveyor belt that feeds the work beneath a spinning abrasive head. But on this machine, the head is a metal drum covered with sandpaper

A drum thicknessing sander does a good job of surfacing and smoothing woods with highly figured grain, which can be a nightmare to handle with conventional bladed planers (note my cat, BouDou, helping me out).

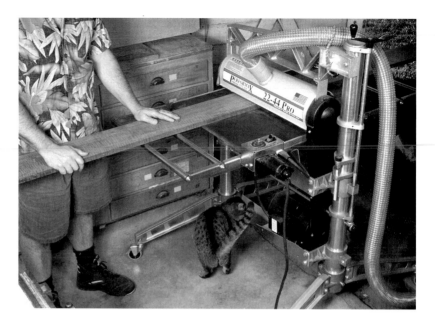

(see the photo above). Unlike a small sanding drum or spindle in an oscillating spindle sander, the drum on a thicknessing sander isn't a single sleeve, but a long strip of sandpaper wound on spirally from end to end. The strip is cut from a roll of cloth-backed abrasive, its ends trimmed to a long taper, so they'll wind up flush with the ends of the drum. Strips are sold precut, or you can buy a long roll of sandpaper (typically 3 in. wide) from whichever grits and types of abrasive you please and cut your own strips.

While the wind-on-strip system provides flexibility, it can also be time-consuming to replace worn-out paper or change abrasive grit—you have to unwind the strip from the drum and wind on another one. You can extend the life of a strip that has stopped cutting aggressively by removing it from the drum and re-installing it backwards.

One problem that early drum sanders had was the sandpaper strip coming loose, due to expansion caused by the heat generated during sanding. Some manufacturers, such as Performax, have solved this problem by installing a special spring-loaded tensioning mechanism to keep the strip taut. The edges of a loose strip can overlap, which will cause grooving on the surface of the work. Therefore, it's important to leave a little space between the edges of the strip as it's installed on the drum, to allow the tensioning mechanism to work properly.

Because of the small amount of stock typically taken in a single pass, depth of cut on a drum thicknessing sander must be set precisely. The method recommended by Warren Weber, product

Holding Small Parts Safely

Most stationary sanders have a work table of some kind to support and align the work during sanding. But occasionally, the workpiece is too small or thin to hold safely. If you are faced with such a situation, don't even consider holding these parts if it means getting your fingers close to the sandpaper. In the words of Nancy Reagan, "Just say no." Sanding off your fingertips is just as painful as it sounds, and can easily be avoided by using a pair of pliers or a shop-made holding device.

One easy way to hold onto most small, irregular parts during sanding is with a pair of locking pliers, such as Vise Grips. You can use them to grab parts that are practically any regular shape. You can avoid scarring the clamped surface of the work by padding the jaws with several turns of masking or duct tape. For holding small work that has parallel faces, you can purchase a ready-made fixture, called the RGT handler (available from Klingspor; see Sources of Supply, which begins on p. 209). This device has adjustable jaws, comfortable handles, and a clear protective shield; it's handy for holding small parts safely during sanding, as well as during routing or cutting operations.

If parts are very thin or delicate, such as sawn fretwork, a carved rosette, or wooden jewelry, you can support the part by temporarily mounting it on a shop-made support—a scrap of plywood that's a little larger than the work with a knob to serve as a handle on the back side. The workpiece is mounted to the face of the plywood with double-stick tape or adhesive transfer tape (a mounting tape that is applied from a special dispenser that lays down a coating of just sticky material—no backing. It's available at any good stationery store or art-supply store that sells picture-framing goods). Carefully press the part against the surface of the belt or disc to sand it, using only light pressure. If you have trouble removing a delicate workpiece after sanding, heat the part with a hair dryer. Then work a putty knife under an edge and carefully lift it off.

If you have a whole stack of delicate parts to sand, you can make a vacuum handle, as shown in the photo below. The handle is a piece of plywood that's mounted with duct tape to the end of a hose from a shop vacuum or dust-collection system. Holes are drilled through the plywood in a pattern that corresponds to the shape of the work, allowing suction to secure it during sanding. A thin strip of wood tacked to the plywood just below the workpiece serves as a ledge to help keep the part from sliding out of place during sanding. To remove the part after sanding, simply turn off the vacuum.

You can support a small, fragile part with suction from a shop-vacuum hose.

manager at Performax, is as follows: First, unplug the sander and set the workpiece under the head of the drum. Then raise the conveyor table to a point at which the drum is making contact with the work, but you can still turn the drum while feeling some resistance. For fast stock removal using a coarse-grit abrasive, follow these instructions, then remove the work and raise the table just a tad more.

Most drum thicknessing sanders I've used have a variable-feed-rate dial, so you can set the exact rate that yields the best result. Setting the feed rate is a bit of a balancing act: The speed should be fast enough so that the surface of the work doesn't burn, but not so fast that chatter marks are left. Generally, hard, dense woods have more of a tendency to burn than others; rock maple and cherry are a couple of the worst in this regard. You can reduce the likelihood of burning by increasing the feed rate and/or taking a shallower cut. Burning is also more likely when the abrasive is worn. If burn marks appear, reverse the direction of the strip on the drum or change to a fresh abrasive. Chatter marks, which look like subtle ripples running across the work, are due to sander vibration or uneven feed rate. These marks can be difficult to see, so it's a good idea to inspect the surface carefully before proceeding with subsequent sanding. To make chatter marks more noticeable, wipe the surface down with a rag that has been dampened with mineral spirits, then hold it up to a strong light.

About the only significant disadvantage of small-shop drum thicknessing sanders is that they are relatively slow. Their maximum feed rates rarely exceed 10 ft. per minute—and that speed is only attainable during very light cuts. Heavier thicknessing passes may slow feed rate to a snail's pace of 2 ft. to 5 ft. per minute.

Arbor-Mounted Sanding Wheels

While most stationary sanding machines are dedicated devices, there are quite a number of sanding tools that can be mounted on a standard grinding arbor. If you have a pedestal-style grinder or other powered arbor in your shop, it's likely that you can simply replace its vitrified-abrasive metal-grinding wheels and buffing wheels with your choice of a variety of different sanding wheels. These wheels, most of which were designed for smoothing contoured or irregularly shaped parts, include flap wheels, mop wheels, brush-back sanding wheels, expanding wheels, and non-woven plastic abrasive wheels.

FLAP WHEELS

If you embedded the ends of dozens of strips of sandpaper into epoxy and mounted the assembly to a central hub, you'd have a sanding flap wheel. These are usually larger-diameter versions of the flap wheels used for sanding with portable power tools, as described on p. 174. Their uses include sanding irregular parts, easing sharp edges, and sanding coves or curved surfaces (convex or concave). Their limitation is that, unless used judiciously, they may reshape the part in an undesirable way, for example, sand one section of a hollow panel deeper than another.

MOP WHEELS

A mop wheel is just like a flap wheel, but instead of dozens of sandpaper strips, there are hundreds of very narrow ($1/16$ in. wide) ribbons of cloth-backed abrasive (see the photo at right). When these little sanding "fingers" contact the surface of a part pressed against the spinning wheel, they conform quite easily to the dips, peaks, twists, and turns of a contoured surface, so mop wheels are ideal for refining and smoothing shapely parts. They can remove hand-tool marks from cabriole legs or oval-section chair stretchers without significantly changing their profile.

The length and narrowness of the sanding fingers allow a mop head to sand deep into crevices, grooves, nooks, and crannies on a deeply shaped or carved surface or molding. Designed primarily for finish sanding, defuzzing, and polishing wood, mop wheels aren't too useful for shaping parts because it's hard to control the profile you'll end up with. And they tend to soften sharp details, say the raised features on a carving, so they are best used judiciously in such applications. Popular-sized 10-in.-dia. mop wheels are designed to run at up to 2,500 rpm, but you can reduce the sanding aggressiveness of the wheel by running it at a slower speed—say, between 1,100 rpm and 1,500 rpm.

BRUSH-BACK SANDING WHEELS

A clever variation of the mop wheel is the brush-back sanding wheel. Also know as a Vonnegut wheel or Wolfhead wheel, these wheels have dozens or hundreds (depending on the size) of narrow sanding fingers, coming through slots around the circumference of the metal wheel's body. There's also a smaller version that can be fitted on to a portable drill or polishing tool (see Sources of Supply, which begins on p. 209).

Strips of abrasive are wound around a pin assembly in the center of the wheel. The end of each roll extends through a slot in the outside edge of the housing and is supported during sanding by a stiff-bristled brush, which keeps it from deflecting. The strips

A mop wheel's hundreds of narrow cloth-backed abrasive strips allow it to conform to complex shapes and contoured parts, sanding down into grooves and hollows. This wheel is mounted on the shaft of a grinding arbor.

A brush-back sanding wheel has a reservoir of slashed (scored) sandpaper strips wound up inside it. As the sandpaper wears out, new material can be released and the worn ends are cut off.

extend between and beyond the brushes anywhere from ½ in. to 1 in. To release new abrasive, the two halves of the wheel body are rotated, to unwind the strips stored in the center of the wheel. As the ends of the sandpaper strips become worn, they are trimmed off, and new material is unrolled (see the photo at left).

Brushes may be replaced after they have worn down. To reach even deeper into recesses, and to lend an even softer touch to delicate sanding operations, a brush-back sanding wheel can be fitted with longer brushes. The cushioning effect of the bristles work the strips of abrasive into corners, hollows, and small openings, and around flutes or reeds. It's best to work with a light touch, not pressing the work too hard against the wheel (this only wears out the strips and brushes quicker). If you're not getting the desired result using light pressure, switch to a coarser abrasive.

EXPANDING WHEELS

Unlike flap, mop, and brush-backed wheels with hundreds of strips of sandpaper, expanding wheels have a single cylindrical abrasive surface. Used in lapidary work (where they are used to rough-grind gemstones), expanding wheels are terrific for accurately shaping and/or smoothing contoured parts. Wheels are typically 6 in. or 8 in. in diameter and 1 in. or 2 in. wide and accept a cloth-backed abrasive belt. The wheel consists of a molded rubber outer rim mounted to a metal inner hub. Angled slots molded into the cross section of the rubber rim add flexibility to allow the sanding belt to conform more easily to the profile of the work, as well as run cool. The slots also help hold the belt on the wheel: Centrifugal force acting on the spinning wheel causes the rim to expand slightly, locking the belt in place. When at rest, the belt can be slipped off the rim with little resistance, making paper changes very easy.

NON-WOVEN PLASTIC ABRASIVE WHEELS

Created from a ribbon of non-woven plastic abrasive wound tightly into a wheel, these arbor-mounted plastic-matrix abrasive wheels come in a huge variety of types, both for metalworking duties, such as surface conditioning or deburring (to remove sharp edges from metal parts) and woodworking jobs, such as smoothing edges and surfaces and polishing finishes. A wheel designed for general woodworking, such as 3M's WW-WL, is great for knocking sharp edges off small parts and for polishing small components for children's toys, jewelry boxes, humidors, wood puzzles, and jewelry. The wheels are easy to use: Simply mount them to spin in the right direction (they're unidirectional), and press parts lightly against them to sand or polish. A wheel's edge can also be shaped to smooth moldings or shaped edges.

Sources of Supply

These source listings, which contain numerous mail-order sources, should make it easier for you to obtain many of the tools and products discussed in this book. First look up the desired item in the list below. Once you have found the item, you can locate the address, phone, and FAX number for its supplier or manufacturer. This listing was compiled in the spring of 1997 and is subject to change.

Items cited in the text

ABC liquid cleaner
Blue Ridge

Automatic electric switch (for dust collection)
Hartville Tool, Trend-lines, Woodworker's Supply

Bronze wool
Jamestown

Brush-back sanding wheel (portable version)
Industrial Abrasive, Woodcraft, Woodworker's Supply

Cork sheets
Meisel

Disc-mount adhesive
Industrial Abrasive, Klingspor

Downdraft sanding tables
Hartville Tool, Penn State, Woodworker's Supply

Dust collectors, air helmets, respirators
Airware, JDS

Flexible shaft tools and sanding drums
Wood Carvers Supply

Graphite-coated canvas
Econ-Abrasives, Klingspor

Graphite sticks
Klingspor

Hook-and-loop conversion discs
Industrial Abrasive

Lathe-sanding products
Craft Supplies, Packard

Metal sanding plates
Products 2000

No. 61 Dull Wax Polish
Industrial Finish Products

PSA-backed sandpaper rolls
Econ-Abrasives, Hartville Tool, Industrial Abrasive, Klingspor, Woodcraft, Woodworker's Supply

Pneumatic sanders and pneumatic-tool supplies
Harbor Freight, Northern

PSA sandpaper discs without holes
Econ-Abrasives, Industrial Abrasive, Klingspor, Woodworker's Supply

RGT Handler
Klingspor

Sanding bows
Klingspor

Sandpaper, sanders, and sanding products
Constantine, Econ-Abrasives, Garrett Wade, Hartsville Tool, Highland Hardware, Industrial Abrasive, Jamestown, Klingspor, Lee Valley, Leichtung, McFeely's Meisel, Mohawk, Norton, Pasco, Penn State, Pyramid, Red Hill, Sandpaper America, Seven Corners, 3M, Tool Crib of the North, Trend-lines, Uneeda, Van Dyke's, Wolfcraft, Woodcraft, Woodworker's Store, Woodworker's Supply

Segmented-drive V-belts
Hartville Tool, Woodcraft, Woodworker's Supply

Steel wool
De-oiled: Woodworker's Store
Long rolls: Klingspor, Mohawk, Van Dyke's

Structured carbide burrs
Wood Carvers Supply

Vibration-reducing gloves
Lab Safety Supply, Woodworker's Supply, Woodcraft

Wol-Wax
Star Chemical

Suppliers and manufacturers

Airware America
Highway 54 South
PO Box 975
Elbow Lake, MN 56531
(800) 328-1792
FAX (218) 685-4458

Blue Ridge Products
1111 E. Currahee St.
Toccoa, GA 30577
(706) 886-1759
FAX (706) 886-1784

Constantine and Son
2050 East Chester Rd.
Bronx, NY 10461
(800) 223-8087

Craft Supplies USA
1287 E 1120 S.
Provo, UT 84606
(800) 551-8876
FAX (801) 377-7742

Econ-Abrasives
PO Box 1628
Frisco, TX 75034
(800) 367-4101
FAX (972) 377-2248

Garrett Wade
161 Avenue of the Americas
New York, NY 10013
(800) 221-2942
(212) 807-1757

Harbor Freight Tools
3491 Mission Oaks Blvd.
Camarillo, CA 93011
(800) 423-2567
FAX (800) 905-5220

Hartville Tool
940 West Maple St.
Hartville, OH 44632
(800) 345-2396 (orders)
FAX (216) 877-4682

Highland Hardware
1045 N. Highland Ave., NE
Atlanta, Ga 30306
(800) 241-6748 (orders)
(404) 872-4466
(information)
FAX (404) 876-1941

Industrial Abrasive Co.
642 N. 8th St.
Box 149955
Reading, PA 19612
(800) 428-2222
FAX 610-378-4868

Industrial Finish Products
465 Logan St.
Brooklyn, NY 11208
(718) 277-3333

Jamestown Distributors
28 Narragansett Ave.
PO Box 348
Jamestown, RI 02835
(800) 423-0030 (orders)
(401) 423-2520
FAX (800) 423-0542

JDS Co.
800 Dutch Square Blvd.
Suite 200
Columbia, SC 29210
(800) 382-2637

Klingspor
PO Box 3737
Hickory, NC 28603
(800) 228-0000 (orders)
FAX (800) 872-2005

Lab Safety Supply
PO Box 1368
Janesville, WI 53547
(800) 356-0783
(800) 356-2501 (safety
and technical information)
FAX (800) 543-9910

Lee Valley Tools
1080 Morrison Dr.
Ottawa, Ontario
Canada K2H 8K7
(800) 267-8767

Leichtung Workshops
4944 Commerce Pkwy.
Cleveland, OH 44128
(800) 321-6840 (orders)
(800) 542-4467
(information)
FAX (216) 464-6764

McFeely's
712 12th Street
PO Box 3
Lynchburg, VA 24505
(800) 443-7937
FAX (804) 847-7136

**Meisel Hardware
Specialties**
PO Box 70
Mound, MN 55364
(800) 441-9870
FAX (612) 471-8579

**Mohawk Finishing
Products**
4715 State Hwy. 30
Amsterdam, NY 12010
(800) 545-0047 (orders)
(518) 843-1380
FAX (518) 842-3551

Northern
PO Box 1499
Burnsville, MN 55337
(800) 533-5545
FAX (612) 894-0083

**Norton Co., Coated
Abrasive Division**
Troy, NY 12181
(518) 273-0100
FAX (518) 273-0100, Ext.
725

Packard Woodworks
PO Box 718
101 Miller Rd.
Tryon, NC 28782
(704) 859-6762
FAX (704) 859-5551

**PASCO (Pacific Abrasive
Supply Co.)**
7050-D Village Dr.
Buena Park, CA 90621
(800) 755-2042
FAX (714) 994-4723

Penn State Industries
2850 Comly Rd.
Philadelphia, PA 19154
(800) 377-7297
FAX (215) 676-7603

Products 2000
17839 Chappel
Lansing, Il 60438
(708) 418-5042
FAX (708) 418-3034

Pyramid Products
7440 E. 12th St.
Kansas City, MO 64126
(800) 747-3600

Red Hill Corporation
PO Box 4234
Gettysburg, PA 17325
(717) 337-3038

Sandpaper America
816 N. Dorman Ave.
Indianapolis, IN 46202
(800) 860-7263
FAX (317) 631-7266

Seven Corners
216 West 7th St.
St. Paul, MN 55102
(800) 328-0457
FAX (612) 224-8263

Star Chemical Company
360 Shore Dr.
Hinsdale, IL 60521
(312) 654-8650

3M (manufacturer)
St. Paul, Minn 55144
(800) 364-3577 (consumer
product info)

Tool Crib of the North
PO Box 14040
Grand Forks, ND 58208
(800) 358-3096

Trend-lines
375 Beacham St.
Chelsea, MA 02150
(800) 767-9999 (orders)
(800) 877-3338 (automated
ordering)
FAX (617) 889-2072

Uneeda Enterprises
PO Box 209
Spring Valley, NY 10977
(800) 431-2494
(914) 426-2800
FAX (914) 426-2810

Van Dyke's Restorers
PO Box 278
Woonsocket, SD 57385
(800) 843-3320 (orders)
(605) 796-4425
FAX (605) 796-4085

Wolfcraft
1222 W. Ardmore Ave.
Itasca, IL 60143
(708) 773-4777
FAX (708) 773-4805

Wood Carvers Supply
PO Box 7500
Englewood, FL 34295
(800) 284-6229
FAX (941) 698-0329

Woodcraft
7845 Emerson Ave.
Parkersburg, WV 26101
(800) 535-4482 (customer
service)
(800) 225-1153 (orders)
FAX (304) 428-8271 (orders)

Woodworker's Store
21801 Industrial Blvd.
Rogers, MN 55374-9514
(612) 428-2199
(612) 428-2899 (technical
service)
FAX (612) 428-8668

Woodworker's Supply
1108 North Glenn Rd.
Casper, WY 82601
(800) 645-9292 (orders)
FAX (505) 821-7331

Index

A

Abrasives:
auto-body, for use on wood, 94-95
cleaning, 96-97
useful life of, 102-103
See also specific materials.
Air cleaners, 155
Air helmets, 150
Air hoses:
for portable-sander dust collection, 150
tether for, 146, 151
Aluminum oxide (ALO):
as grit material, 12
for power sanding, 141
ANSI grading, 16-17, 18-19
Aught grading, 17, 18-19

B

Backing pads:
for detail sanders, 164
graphite, 144-45
hard vs. soft, 144, 163
Backings:
cloth, weights of, 25
film, weights of, 26
hook-and-loop, 32
information on, 8-9
paper,
fiber reinforced, 24
weights of, 23
wet-dry 24
PSA, 31
Bandsaws, for narrow-belt sanding, 191-92
Belt sanders:
portable,
belts for, 157
and belt tension, 159
and belt tracking, 158
described, 157-58
edge-sanding jig for, 189-90
as face-frame sanding tool, 105

graphite backing pad for, 144-45
as leveling tool, 46-47
and platen truing, 159
and roller cleaning, 158
sanding frame for, 158-59
as shaping tool, 41
work stand for, 160
stationary,
ball-sanding jig for, 196
See also specific machines.
Belts:
anti-static, 155
butt-spliced, 33-34
hangers for, 100-101
lap-spliced, 35
tension adjustments for, 159
tracking adjustments for, 158
zigzag-spliced, 34-35
Bond systems:
hide-glue, 28-29
resin, 29
Bronze wool, 38-39
Brush-back sanding wheels, 207-208
Burning (of workpiece):
causes of, 109, 139
with drum thicknessing sanders, 206
remedies for, 109-10
Burnishing, 103

C

Carpal-tunnel syndrome, 64
Cartridge rolls, 180
Ceramic minerals:
friability of, 142
as grit materials, 14-15
for power sanding, 141
Chamfering, jig for, 187
Chatter marks, 138-39, 206
Circles, sanding jig for, 193

Cleaning (foam sanding blocks), 73
Cleaning (sanded wood):
with compressed air, 69
after scuff sanding, 73
with shop vacuum, 69
with tack cloth, 69-70
Cleaning (sandpaper), 96-97
Clinkers:
defined, 21
and swirl marks, 109
Coatings:
anti-loading, 30
anti-static, 32
closed vs. open, 27
Combination belt/disc sanders, 195
Composition boards, abrasives for, 142
Compounding:
compounds for, 82, 95
lubricants for, 82
for satin finish, 81-83
Corners, sanding at, 165
Crocus, as grit material, 7
Cylinders, sanding, 130-31

D

Defects:
inspecting for, 59-61
localized, sanding technique for, 44
Dents, removing, 63
Detail sanders, 164-65
Dewhiskering, 65-68
Die grinders:
abrasives for, 171
dust hood for, 153
flap wheels for, 174
pneumatic, 181
sanding rolls for, 180
snap-locking discs for, 175-76
speed-reduction strategies for, 171
Discs, foam-backed, 178
Disc sanders, 192-94

Dremel tools:
accessories for, 172-73
flap wheels for, 174
uses for, 172
Drills:
backing pads for, 170
flap wheels for, 174
sanding rolls for, 180
as sanding tools, 170
snap-locking discs for, 175-76
Drum sanders:
described, 197
dust hoods for, 154-55
Drum thicknessing sanders, 203-206
Dust:
health hazards of, 148
masks against, 148-50
Dust collection:
for portable sanders, 151
for wide-belt sanders, 203
Dust hoods:
for portable sanders, 153-54
for stationary sanders, 154-55
Dust table, shop-made, 152-53

E

Edge sanders:
described, 185-86
dowel-pointing jig for, 187
platens for, 186
for profile sanding, 188-89
starting pin for, 147
tables for, 186
tilting, 186-87
Edge sanding:
on portable belt sander, 189-90
techniques for, 186-87
Emery boards, as sanding tools, 127
Emery, as grit material, 7, 9
End grain, sanding technique for, 57

Evenness:
    defined, 60
    test for, 61
Expanding wheels, 208

F

Face frames, sanding
        sequence for, 105
Feed rate:
    and burn marks, 139
    and depth of cut, 138
    for portable power
        sanders, 139
    and smoothness of
        surface, 138
FEPA grading, 16-17,
    18-19
Finishes:
    cure times of, 77-78
    gloss vs. matte, 76
    matte,
        grits for, 78-79
        leveling techniques for,
        78
    oil, and sanding schedule,
        54
    removing, 87
    for rubbing out, 76
    solvent-based, and
        sanding schedule, 53
    stains, and sanding
        schedule, 54-55
    water-based, and sanding
        schedule, 53
Flap discs, 173
Flap wheels:
    arbor-mounted, 207
    described, 172, 174
    maximum speed of, 138
    safe use of, 147
Flexible-shaft sanding
        tools, 173
Flint, as grit material, 10
Flush trimming, 47
Flutter-sheet wheels, shop-
        made, 174-75
Foam-backed abrasives,
    37-38
Fretwork, sanding
        technique for, 58

G

Garnet:
    as grit material, 10-11
    worn, for burnishing, 103
Generic grading, 17, 18-19
Glazing:
    of lumber, 48-49
    of sanding belts, 111
Gloves, anti-vibration, 48
Glue:
    removing, 63-64
    test for, 64
Gouges, filling vs. sanding,
    63
Grading systems, 16-17,
    18-19
    See also specific systems.
Grading tolerance, 21
Grain:
    raised, 65
    and sanding schedule, 52
    woolly, 107
Grits:
    for hand-sanding on
        lathe, 131-32
    natural mineral, 9, 10-11
    sizing, 17-20
    synthetic, 11-16
    See also Sanding
        schedules. specific
        materials.

H

Hook-and-loop backings,
    32

I

In-line sanders. See
        Straight-line sanders.

J

JIS grading, 16-17, 18-19

L

Lathes:
    foot-operated clutch for,
        133
    hand-sanding on,
        131-33
    non-powered sanding on,
        178
    power sanding on, 177

Leveling:
    at angle to grain, 45
    defined, 40
    grits for, 45, 48-50
    with portable belt sander,
        46
    techniques for, 44, 45
    tool speed for, 137
Louvers, sanding, 165

M

Make coat, defined, 28
Metal-backed abrasive
        plates, 39
Micro-mesh, 39
Micron grading, 16-17,
    18-19
    tolerance in, 22
Moldings:
    dewhiskering, 68
    sanding technique for, 58
Mop wheels, 207

N

Narrow-belt sanders:
    benchtop, 190-91
    pneumatic, 161, 181
    uses for, 41, 160-61
Narrow-belt sanding:
    with bandsaw, 191-92
    with narrow-belt sander,
        190-91
Non-woven plastic
        abrasives, 35-37, 208

O

Orbital sanders, 162-64
Oscillating spindle sanders,
    198-201

P

Pad sanders. See Orbital
        sanders.
Paper changing, frequency
        of, 143-44
Plastic laminate, abrasives
        for, 142
Platens:
    for sanding profiles,
        188-89
    for stationary edge
        sanders, 186
    truing, 159
    for wide-belt sanders, 202

Pointing, jig for, 187
Polishing, 83-84, 95
Portable sanders:
    dust collection for,
        151-52
    starting and stopping,
        146-47
    uses for, 156
    See also specific machines.
Power buffers, 82, 84-85
Power cords, tether for, 146
Powered body files. See
        Straight-line sanders.
Power files. See Narrow-
        belt sanders.
Power sanders:
    variable-speed control
        for, 110, 137
    See also specific tools.
Power sanding:
    abrasives for, 141
    backing weights for, 143
    belt splices for, 143
    grits for, 142-43
Pressure-sensitive adhesive
        (PSA), 31
    See also PSA discs.
Pressure:
    and burning of
        workpiece, 139
    and swirl marks, 139
    and veneer sand-through,
        139
Profile sanders, 169
Profile sanding, on edge
        sander, 188-89
PSA discs:
    removing, 102-103
    storing, 99, 101
Pumice, 75

R

Random-orbit sanders:
    backing pads for, 144
    backings for, 167
    discs for, 167
    dust collection for,
        167-68
    grips for, 166-67
    limitations of, 168
    pneumatic, 181
    vs. orbital sanders, 162
Resin (in wood):
    removing, 99
    and sanding schedule, 52

Respirators:
cartridge, 150
See also Air helmets. Dust.
Right-angle grinders:
abrasives for, 171
for abrasive shaping, 42, 171
backing pads for, 171
dust hood for, 153-55
flap discs for, 173
pneumatic, 181
structured carbide discs for, 174
Rims, leveling, 123
Ripple, 48-49
Rottenstone, 75
Rubbing out:
compounds for, 95
film thickness and, 76-77
hand-sanding technique for, 80
lubricants for, 79
power-sanding technique for, 80
purpose of, 74
three-pass method for, 80-81
as three-step process, 74-75
wet vs. dry, 79
See also Compounding. Polishing.

S

Sanders:
pneumatic, 181-83
portable, 156
stationary, 184-85
See also specific machines.
Sanding, pre-assembly, 58
Sanding blocks:
convex, 118
cove-cut, 119-20
curved, 117-20
of expanding foam, 123-26
kerf-cut, 118-19
profiled, 123
for PSA paper, 115
shop-made, 114-15
store-bought, 114
Sanding bows:
shop-made, 122
store-bought, 121
Sanding cords, 39, 133

Sanding drums:
abrasives for, 178-79
butt-spliced, 33-34
described, 178
lap-spliced, 35
for pattern sanding, 197
pneumatic, 179, 197-98
uses for, 178
zigzag-spliced, 34-35
Sanding frames, 158-59
Sanding pads:
of folded sandpaper, 134-35
for PSA discs, 135
Sanding planes:
for non-PSA paper, 117
for PSA paper, 117
shop-made, 115-17
Sanding rolls, shop-made, 180
Sanding schedules:
guidelines for, 55-56
for leveling, 48-50
for pigmented stains, 54-55
for smoothing wood, 52-54
Sanding screens, 26
Sanding spindles, shop-made, 179-80
Sanding sticks, 126-27
Sanding strips:
as sanding tools, 127-28
for softening sharp edges, 128-29
using, 128
Sanding tapes, 39
Sanding wheels:
arbor-mounted, 206-208
See also Brush-back sanding wheels. Flap wheels. Mop wheels.
Sandpaper:
changing, on orbital sanders, 163
as clamping aid, 93
cutting methods for, 89-90
and effects of humidity, 100
flexing, 91
folding, 134-35
gluing down, 92

manufacturing process for, 6-7
PSA, sources for, 92
for sharpening tools, 93
storing, 100-102
wear-extending tips for, 98
working qualities of, 8
See also specific grit materials.
Scraping, as alternative to sanding, 51
Scratches:
cross-grain, 103-104, 106
and grain patterns, 57
inspecting for, 59-61
from orbital sanders, 108
Scrollwork, sanding technique for, 58
Scuff sanding, 70-73
Shaping:
with belt sanders, 41
of curves, 42-43
defined, 40
grits for, 42
resin-on-resin sandpaper for, 42
with right-angle grinder, 41
speeds for, 42
Silicon carbide (SIC):
as grit material, 13
for power sanding, 141
uses for, 142
Silicones, disadvised, 64-65
Size coat, defined, 28
Small parts:
holding, 205
sanding method for, 129
Smoothing, 40, 50, 52-54, 56-57
Snap-locking discs:
described, 175
drill extension for, 176
Splices:
butt, 33-34
lap, 35
for power sanding, 143
zigzag, 34-35
Steel wool:
for dewhiskering, 68
grades of, 38
Sticker stain, 49

Straight-line sanders:
abrasives for, 168
described, 168
as finish leveling tool, 80
leveling with, 169
pneumatic, 168-69, 181
uses for, 168
Streaking, causes of, 110
Stripping, 140
Structured abrasive:
discs from, 174
as grit material, 15-16
Swirl marks:
avoiding, 144
causes of, 108, 139
remedies for, 109
removing, 86
and rotary sanding tools, 170

T

Table saws, as disc sanders, 194
Tack cloths, 69-70
Thicknessing sanders, 201-202
Top skiving, 34
Trueness:
defined, 60
test for, 61

V

Veneer sand-through:
causes of, 111, 139
metal shield against, 112
prevention of, 111-12
Vonnegut wheels. *See* Brush-back sanding wheels.

W

Washboarding, 106-107
Wax, removing, 64-65
Wide-belt sanders, 202-203
Wolfhead wheels. *See* Brush-back sanding wheels.
Wood species, and sanding schedules, 52, 55-56

Publisher: JAMES P. CHIAVELLI

Acquisitions Editor: RICK PETERS

Publishing Coordinator: JOANNE RENNA

Editor: RUTH DOBSEVAGE

Layout Artist: SUZANNA M. YANNES

Illustrator: VINCE BABAK

Photographer: SANDOR NAGYSZALANCZY

Typeface: PLANTIN

Paper: WARREN PATINA MATTE, 70 lb., NEUTRAL pH

Printer: QUEBECOR PRINTING/HAWKINS, CHURCH HILL, TENNESSEE